Contemporary Sociological Theory

WARREN H. HANDEL

Southern Illinois University at Edwardsville

Prentice Hall, Englewood Cliffs, New Jersey 07632

Library of Congress Cataloging-in-Publication Data

Handel, Warren H.
    Contemporary sociological theory / Warren H. Handel.
       p.   cm.
    Includes index.
    ISBN 0–13–175423–8
    1. Sociology. I. Title.
HM24.H364 1993
301'.01—dc20   92–33160
                                         CIP

Acquisitions editor: Nancy Roberts/Charlyce Jones-Owen
Editorial/production supervision: Bridget Mooney
Interior design: Mary McDonald
Copy editor: Linda Pawelchak
Cover design: Joe DiDomenico
Prepress buyer: Kelly Behr
Manufacturing buyer: Mary Ann Gloriande

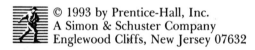

Printed in the United States of America
10 9 8 7 6 5 4 3 2 1

ISBN 0-13-175423-8

Prentice-Hall International (UK) Limited, *London*
Prentice-Hall of Australia Pty. Limited, *Sydney*
Prentice-Hall Canada Inc., *Toronto*
Prentice-Hall Hispanoamericana, S.A., *Mexico*
Prentice-Hall of India Private Limited, *New Delhi*
Prentice-Hall of Japan, Inc., *Tokyo*
Simon & Schuster Asia Pte. Ltd., *Singapore*
Editora Prentice-Hall do Brasil, Ltda., *Rio de Janeiro*

For Ethan and Reuben

Contents

Preface

The contemporary period in sociological theory began approximately 30 years ago as the domination of sociological theory by the structural functionalists collapsed. Several schools of thought have emerged in sociology during this period—conflict theory, role theory, symbolic interaction, social exchange, and ethnomethodology. All are negatively grounded in critiques and rejection of structural functionalism, especially as formulated in the work of Talcott Parsons. But each emerging school has distinctive philosophical and methodological commitments and substantive interests and each retains a distinctive identity. There are many, including myself, who see common interests among the current theories and grounds for their integration in an encompassing theory. However, although many attempts have been made to develop an integrated sociological approach, none has been widely accepted. As a result, although it is important to emphasize common interests and convergent ideas among them, the boundaries and integrity of the schools of thought must also be respected.

The general outline of this book reflects these characteristics of sociological theory. Parsons's approach is reviewed, less because it has continuing significance than because it has been the common focus of criticism by contemporary theorists. I look forward to the time when this negative integrative focus—contemporary sociology as not-functionalism —can be replaced by a generally accepted positive integrative focus. Each of the contemporary approaches to sociological theory is presented as a coherent approach to its own selected topics. The intellectual and historical background of each is summarized along with important developments over the past three decades. Each theory is presented as a developing set of ideas, responsive to accumulated evidence in the context of evolving intellectual commitments, not as a static, given position.

My presentation of contemporary theory is distinctive in two important respects. The first concerns the strategy of presenting and explicating theoretical arguments. Explicit theoretical arguments have two relatively distinct contexts—the intellectual commitments of the theorist and the empirical research the theory organizes and explains. Most theory texts emphasize the intellectual context of theory, often to the almost complete exclusion of its empirical basis. In this book, for several reasons, considerable attention is given to the empirical application of these theories. First, the content of the theories cannot be clearly understood without instances of what the terms and propositions mean. This information lies in operational definitions and studies. Second, the diversity of sociological theory makes it especially important to provide students with illustrations so that they can evaluate how convincing the various types of explanations are. Finally, the empirical applications of the theories reveal common interests that are often concealed by terminological and stylistic differences.

The second distinctive characteristic of this book is substantive. Robert Merton developed an approach to social roles based on the resolution of normative conflict by the distribution of resources among positions. Although his image of social roles and the explanation based on it are fundamentally different from those proposed by Parsons, Merton's work on this topic is often mischaracterized as compatible with Parsons's. This correction is important for two reasons. First, aspects of Merton's theory are being tested using some of the statistical techniques called *network analysis*. As a result, the details of his theory are regaining significance in their own right, despite having been neglected for many years. Second, Merton's role set/role conflict imagery was adopted as context by theorists of interaction processes and provides an essential link between those theories and the large-scale structural concerns of sociology.

I should like to take this opportunity to acknowledge the contributions of several reviewers of this text: James T. Duke, Brigham Young University; Ronald Glassman, William Paterson College; Frank Hearn, SUNY–Cortland; and Seymour Levertman, Boston College. They made many worthwhile suggestions toward improved clarity, coverage of important topics, and order of presentation. Larry Riley, Southern Illinois University at Edwardsville provided bibliographic help.

Warren H. Handel

1

Introduction

The origins of society, how society works, the nature of a just society, the tension between social obligation and individual autonomy, unequal distribution of goods, and other concerns of modern sociology have all been issues in the Western intellectual tradition beginning with the earliest surviving records. Both sociology and society have come a long way since Xenophanes (approximately 575 B.C.) complained in his philosophical poems of the excessive honors awarded to athletes, relative to poets and philosophers of course. Athletes, he claimed, do not contribute to the good government or to the material prosperity of the city. Politically, this sentiment represented an early antiaristocratic, potentially revolutionary beginning of humanistic philosophy or, at least, a humanistic emphasis on the social and moral responsibility of the highly placed (Guthrie, 1962:360ff). Scholars can trace many of our modern theoretical ideas back through the work of successive generations of philosophers, social thinkers, and, recently, sociologists to their roots, which are surprisingly often in the quite ancient works of Plato and Aristotle.

The most important contributors to this tradition, the philosophers and social thinkers in the Western tradition, have a compounded influence on later developments, reflected directly in the work of their imme-

1

diate successors and then indirectly in the work of their successors' successors. But the original work is also read and reinterpreted by each new generation of scholars, so that Plato, for example, has a direct influence on social thought to this day, in addition to the cumulative effect of the historical response to his work. It is interesting that the summary of historically important ideas filtered through generations of commentary is often quite different from the preserved original work. In effect, when an important work is reconsidered by a new generation of scholars, later work influences the earlier. Often, it is less important to know whether ideas are accurately attributed to a historical figure than to understand what the ideas are and why they are important and/ or flawed, whatever their origin.

It is always somewhat arbitrary to isolate a fragment of this complex history of ideas—to begin anywhere but the beginning and to end anywhere but the end. In isolating contemporary sociological theory, I have followed a venerable strategy. I have included a fairly detailed presentation of the most important representative of the period just prior to our main concern, Talcott Parsons, but not of his background. Contemporary work is then summarized in its own right and also characterized, as it developed, as a critical response to Parsons and the period he represents. In this way, although we do not trace the ideas to their origins, we at least get a sense of how contemporary figures develop their ideas in critical response to others.

PARSONS AS WATERSHED

The contemporary period in sociological theory began in an extraordinary time of theoretical creativity, lasting from approximately the middle of the 1950s until the middle of the 1960s. During this relatively brief period, seminal statements defining the several dominant contemporary schools of sociological thought appeared in rapid succession. *Conflict* theories were proposed by C. Wright Mills, Lewis Coser, Robert Merton, Ralf Dahrendorf, and others. George Homans and Peter Blau set the foundations of *social exchange* theory. Herbert Blumer and Erving Goffman made crucial statements in the *symbolic interaction* tradition. Harold Garfinkel made his initial statements of *ethnomethodology*. William Goode recharacterized the coordination of individual decisions in the context of a conflict approach to social roles.

As we will see later, these diverse statements founded somewhat divergent schools of sociological thought. There are methodological differences among them, differences in selection of topics, and differences in primary philosophical commitments. Nonetheless, these early statements, and to an extent the schools of thought that developed from them, share an important theme: criticism of the work of Talcott Parsons. Thus, Parsons is not merely a convenient representative of work preceding the contemporary period. Rather, the contemporary period is defined, at least negatively, by its grounding of theoretical arguments in criticism of structural functional thought, especially that of Parsons.

Although his impact on American sociology, beginning with his first major book, *The Structure of Social Action* (1937), has been singular, Parsons's theories are representative of a school of thought called *structural functionalism*. Structural functional theories dominated sociology and anthropology from the early part of this century until the theoretical transitions that began during the 1950s. The ideas of this school are developed in more detail later, but a very cursory introduction will be helpful now.

Structural functionalists drew an analogy between a society and an organism. Much of their approach can be expressed as implications of that analogy. A biological organism is a functioning whole, but it can be conceived as consisting of several organs or subsystems, each with specialized functions. Thus, the heart, lungs, and blood vessels comprise the circulatory system, which has distinctive functions from the muscles and skeleton. The functions of an organ or subsystem are its normal contribution to the health and survival of the organism as a whole. Although blood vessels accumulate cholesterol and fatty deposits, that is not their function. By analogy, a society is conceived to be a functioning whole made up of subsystems called *institutions*. The task of sociology was conceived to be the identification of subsystems (comparable to organs) and the determination of their function or contribution to societal survival. Stability and harmony in a society are regarded as analogous to health in an organism. Societies were conceived to have internal mechanisms to maintain stability and harmony analogous to the organism's mechanisms to sustain health. Societal change occurred in an evolutionary fashion—slow, adaptive, and occasioned primarily by external events. Existing social subsystems were seen as evolutionary survivors and, to a large extent, as necessary to survival.

Parsons held a distinctive intellectual place among structural functionalists, which accounts, in part, for his work's being singled out when dissatisfaction is expressed with the entire approach. First, Parsons codified the contributions of the structural functionalists in a single coherent framework that was also the most general expression of that approach. With acceptable qualifications, Parsons's work was uniquely suited to represent the point of view of the group as a whole. Second, Parsons grounded his work in a synthesis of selected major historical theorists and philosophers, attempting to show that logical difficulties in their approaches were resolved by his own, and that each contributed arguments that converged on the structural functional position. He characterized his own approach, somewhat immodestly, as encompassing modern sociology (e.g., 1968). Since Parsons's work was simply too important to ignore, substantive theoretical disagreements were necessarily cast as responses to it and as redefinitions of the nature and boundaries of sociology.

Alexander (1987) characterizes the 1950s as a period of revolt against the Parsonian synthesis and shows how each emergent school of thought begins in that revolt. He links the revaluation of Parsons's work to changes in global political and economic realities. Racial and other conflicts persisted in the United States, undermining the credibility of Parsons's emphasis on the integrative capacity of society to maintain stability and harmony. The then-increasing power of the Soviet Union and Communist parties in Western Europe increased the credibility of Karl Marx's theories, which were relatively ignored by Parsons. Failure of third world countries to develop economically and to adopt Western values also tended to emphasize the importance of division and conflict rather than integrative values. The multiplication of sociology departments in the United States, feuled in large part by Parsons's success, ironically provided his critics with independent institutional bases. These institutional bases (jobs and access to grants and scholarly journals) gave necessary material support to intellectual innovation when substantive differences were regarded as breaching the legitimate boundaries of sociology.

In Alexander's view, the criticism of Parsons constituted a self-conscious revolt against his influence. Academically, the revolt was part of the self-defining process of new schools of thought. But Alexander observes that the self-consciously thorough rejection of Parsons guaranteed his continuing influence and the perpetuation of his errors. Parsons's work served as a negative defining pole for his critics. And by defining themselves consistently as negations of Parsons, his critics, in effect, allowed Parsons to define their own views dialectically as well as his own.[1] (If Parsons said yes, his critics were bound to say no.)

Although contemporary theorists share opposition to Parsons, they are in some other respects divergent. Each contemporary school of thought is grounded in a different critique of Parsons or structural functionalism. There are common themes, of course, which will be apparent as we review each school of thought. However, each school incorporates different evidence and philosophical considerations that encourage development along separate paths. *Conflict theory* originated primarily in considerations raised by Karl Marx, a theorist of enormous importance who was slighted by Parsons. *Symbolic interaction* developed from the American pragmatic school of philosophy, virtually ignored in Parsons's early work. *Social exchange* theory is grounded in behaviorism and microeconomics. *Ethnomethodology* is grounded in phenomenology. In addition, the preferred research methodologies in the various theory groups differ.

Because the differences among these schools of thought are in areas usually considered to be fundamental—underlying philosophy and methodology—there is a tendency to regard them as incompatible, and hence as competitive or antagonistic. Emphasis on Fundamental differences among them, there is a tendency for adherents of each school to regard that school as the proper basis for redefining the entire field of sociology.

I assume that you have read an introductory text in sociology. This sense that sociology is composed of competitive, incompatible approaches was probably reflected in the presentation of several separate perspectives and their separate application to many, if not all, substantive topics. The field of sociology may appear to be a mere container for these fragmented and relatively discrete schools of thought and an arena for disputes among them.

But the divergences among contemporary theories have been exaggerated and the contemporary period can be characterized positively as well as by its negative self-definition as "not Parsons." There are no serious challenges to the conflict theories regarding questions of structure and process at a societal level. There are differences among the conflict theorists, but they are not fundamental differences. The other major schools of thought are primarily concerned with microsocial processes and structure, especially social interaction. And although these schools have different historical origins, they have come to overlap considerably as they developed. The problem of integrating sociological theory is not necessarily an ill-defined, abstract problem to be solved by the presentation of another new and better theory. Rather, it can be conceived, relatively concretely, as coordinating the existing theories of microprocesses with one another within a conflict framework.

This approach requires the view that the differences among the philosophical commitments of the various theory schools can be set aside. Theories are only loosely linked to their historical and philosophical origins. When theorists are inspired by philosophical ideas, they do not necessarily derive their own position by rigorous logical argument. There are gaps and intuitions in the chain of thought. Further gaps and intuitions generally occur when a theoretical idea is applied to empirical cases, especially in the development of operational definitions. In addition, once a theoretical statement is made, its development is responsive to many influences besides the original philosophical base—especially, the compilation of new evidence and other contemporary ideas from many sources. In short, it is never rigorously shown and should not be assumed that theories are logically compatible with their own inspirational sources nor that they are incompatible with other philosophical systems. As a result, it is logically possible for theories that originated within different philosophical systems to be compatible with one another, even when those philosophical systems are not compatible with one another. More important, this convergence actually occurs.

In summary, then, this book defines the contemporary period chronologically as beginning during the 1950s and conceptually as characterized by a rejection of and self-conscious revolt against the then-dominant structural functional school and, especially, the work of Talcott Parsons. Four somewhat divergent schools of thought have emerged during this period—conflict theory, symbolic interaction, social exchange theory, and ethnomethodology. Each school defined itself from a particular philosophical point of view in its criticisms of Parsons. Self-conscious definition of theory in terms of its distinctive philosophical origins has contributed to a tendency to regard the theories themselves as fundamentally different. In my view, this conclusion is neither logically valid nor empirically accurate. In this book, the theories are addressed in terms of their contribution to an overall understanding of social life in the context of the uncontested view that at least at the societal level, social structure and process are characterized by internal conflicts.

ORGANIZATION OF THE BOOK

We begin with a summary of Parsons's theory as the crucial representative of structural functional theorizing in sociology (Chapter 2). The summary is as straightforward as possible and is based on a variety of Parsons's work, but not on secondary characterizations or critiques of it. Next we review the transformation of structural functionalism from a grand theory to a research methodology in the work of Merton and others (Chapter 3). This group, called functional analysts, retained interest in the consequences or functions of social structural arrangements but rejected Parsons's theory. Their method is part of the core of contemporary sociology, although their terminology and rationale have been largely abandoned. Merton's discussion of middle-range theorizing is included as an important statement of the relationships among existing theories.

Chapters 4, 5, and 6 present the basic themes and specific examples of conflict theory. Initially, these were developed to supplement Parsons by providing theories of change and conflict to be combined with his theory of integration and stability. Later, however, attempts began to develop a conflict theory of integration and stability as well. They imply process of integration based on conventional arrangements, rather than normative consensus. These conflict theories of integration incorporate ideas and concerns developed by various microtheorists. Chapter 7 presents Merton's conflict theory of social roles. It provides a potential link between conflict theories of societal scale processes and social interaction.

Chapters 8, 9, and 10 present contemporary theories of microsocial processes, especially social interaction. Each is summarized as an important theory in its own right. The distinctive origins and development of each are summarized, but each is presented in a way that emphasizes relevance to a conflict theory of roles and, in turn, a conflict theory of societal process in which it is grounded.

Chapter 11 presents the integrative theme of the book more explicitly.

FORMS OF THEORETICAL EXPLANATION

A theory is an exceptionally precise and public form of explanation. In the natural sciences, the normative ideal of theory is a system of propositions, with all terms clearly defined, both conceptually and operationally, and following agreed upon rules of logic. The statements generated by such a theory can be understood by any properly trained person and any research described in its terms should contain instructions that allow replication of the study and its results. To the extent that the phenomenon being explained is subject to cause and effect analysis, such theories allow prediction. Rules of logic are applied to the theoretical concepts and statements to deduce some result that has not yet been observed, but must happen if the theory is correct. Then, by creating or finding appropriate conditions, the theory can be tested by comparing the actual results to those predicted.

In the natural sciences, testing theories in this manner is the standard for argumentation and research and for revising theory. There are many topics in the social sciences as well that are addressed in this way. However, in the social sciences substantive complications arise that may reflect fundamental characteristics of human conduct that are unsuited to expression as the relationship among variables. Humans act on the basis of their own perceptions, including the meaning of events as they perceive them. This seriously compromises operational definitions. The same observable events can mean different things to different people at different times and in different situations and, therefore, have different effects on conduct. How can we stabilize our operational definitions? Do we expose subjects to different stimuli, so selected, that the meaning is the same to all subjects, even though the stimuli are different? Do we expose subjects to the same stimuli, knowing that their perceptions of them are different? Which approach is more standardized? This issue is the core of the very practical controversy over cultural bias in standardized achievement tests. Second, there is considerable evidence that the terms in ordinary language are not defined precisely nor are they used in accordance with logic.[2] Third, there is the phenomenon of free will or voluntarism. To the extent that this exists, the form of theorizing appropriate to deterministic, cause and effect reasoning cannot apply.

In the social sciences, then, exclusive commitment to a form of theorizing prejudges a variety of important and unresolved substantive issues. The substantive commitments entailed in the apparently methodological preference for deductive theorizing has been noted since the beginnings of American sociology (cf., Thomas, 1927). Some theory in the social sciences is in the deductive form, and the proportion of such theory is certain to grow as appropriate topics are addressed more precisely. But other topics in sociology may never yield to that kind of theorizing for substantive reasons. It is simply not appropriate. Insofar as the study of different topics is specialized, we can expect different specialties in the discipline to continue to organize their theoretical explanations in different forms. We can also expect that within all the specialties, the number of topics deductively organized as relationships among variables will increase. When topics amenable to variable analysis are theoretically organized in other forms, some precision is lost. When topics not amenable to variable analysis are forced into that format, some of their essential substantive aspects are lost.

Theory is what theorists write.

NOTES

1. Alexander (1987) saw these challenges as establishing a one-sided antagonism against Parsons from which his critics could not escape. I believe this oversimplifies the process by which the new schools of thought emerged in sociology. Initially, at least in the cases of conflict theories, symbolic interaction, and some exchange theorists, the explicit goal was to supplement Parsons's work, not replace it. The fundamental opposition to doctrines espoused by Parsons was seen as a device to identify topics excluded in Parsons's approach. Theories developed in this way were to be combined with Parsons's own in a broader framework. Our discussion of conflict theory develops this interpretation more fully, and Dahrendorf's detailed argument along these lines is summarized. The idea of excluding Parsons from an emergent synthesis seems to have developed later and is consistent

with treating Parsons as representing an earlier period of thought, rather than as a contemporary competitor.

2. Chapter 10 reviews the ethnomethodological approach to this evidence. There is a great deal of related evidence that cognition does not observe rules of logic. A discussion of many of the important issues and review of evidence is found in work by Tversky and Kahneman (1974, 1981).

REFERENCES

Alexander, Jeffrey. 1987. Twenty Lectures: Sociological Theory Since World War II. New York: Columbia University Press.

Guthrie, W. K. C. 1962. A History of Greek Philosophy. Cambridge: Cambridge University Press.

Parsons, Talcott. 1937. The Structure of Social Action. New York: Free Press.

Parsons, Talcott. 1968. Social Class and Class Conflict in the Light of Recent Sociological Theory. Pp. 323–335 in Essays in Sociological Theory. New York: Free Press.

Thomas, W. I. 1927. The Behavior Pattern and the Situation. *American Sociological Association Publications* 22:1–13.

Tversky, Amos and Daniel Kahneman. 1974. Judgement Under Uncertainty. *Science* 185 (27 September):1124–1131.

Tversky, Amos and Daniel Kahneman. 1981. The Framing of Decisions and the Psychology of Choice. *Science* 211 (30 January):453–458.

2

Talcott Parsons: Social Systems in an Analytic Action Frame of Reference

Talcott Parsons's substantive theoretical contribution to sociology had two essential foci. The first was the development of an analytic theory of social action, within which social structure emerged as a consequence of the actors' mutual orientation toward and dependence upon one another in the course of their own action. Second, he developed a theory of social structure as a component of systems of action. These two interrelated theories provided a systematic statement of the structural functional school of thought that dominated sociology during the 1940s and 1950s and, later, a focus for criticism of it. The criticism of Parsons extends beyond the substance of his theories to include his theoretical approach—what could be called his philosophy of science. And so, to understand the special way in which Parsons uses important terms and concepts and to understand the criticisms of him, we will ground our discussion in his commitment to general analytic theorizing.

GENERAL ANALYTIC THEORY

Theory as a Conceptual System

Parsons (1945) observes that the term *theory* is used in a variety of ways, with few overlapping meanings. He uses the term to mean a system "of logically interdependent generalized concepts of empirical reference" (1945:43). The theoretical system, which is composed of concepts and relationships among them, is differentiated from empirical systems. Empirical systems are phenomena in the observable world that can be described and ordered by the theoretical system (Parsons, 1968b).

A system, whether theoretical or empirical, exists when regularities of relationships can be discerned among a set of parts and processes (Parsons, 1968b). The parts of a system may be systems themselves. Any system that is not all-inclusive will have regular external relationships with its environment. The environment of one system will also be a system if it has orderly internal relationships among its parts. Thus, any system may be composed of smaller systems simultaneously acting as environments to one another and as component parts of the larger system. Any system that is not all-inclusive and its environment could, in principle, be considered components of a still larger system.

Illustrations may help. The discernible regularity in the relative positions of the Earth, sun, moon, and other planets, empirically observed, constitutes an empirical system. The rotations of the planets around their axes and their revolution around the sun, the revolution of moons around planets, the occasional and predictable occurrence of eclipses and the appearance of comets can be ordered by applying theoretical systems of astronomy and physics. Of course, other theories could be applied to the same observations and were, prior to the development of our current theories.[1] As another example, the education system, the family, and the government are all systems in their own rights. All are subsystems of our society. Each is environment to the others.

Theoretical adequacy, treated as a programmatic goal, requires extending the dynamic analysis of relationships between conditions and their consequent effects (Parsons, 1945:44ff.). This is done by adding theoretical concepts that could serve as newly discernible conditions or consequences and by specifying additional relationships among the concepts in the theory. The laws or explicit regularities of a fully developed theory would form a system linking all the concepts to one another simultaneously. The model adopted by Parsons is the set of simultaneous equations that link all the concepts in Newton's physics.

The substantive theoretical importance of simultaneously consider-ing all factors is indicated by Parsons's (1954) criticism of Marx's theory of the inevitability of class conflict. Parsons acknowledges six important tendencies toward class conflict within social structures. Most important, perhaps, in the hindsight provided by later developments, are (1) the tendency of those with power to utilize their advantageous positions to exploit and dominate the less fortunate, (2) the development of separate cultures based on position within the society, and (3) the tendency of family structure in the lower classes to promote attitudes that perpetuate disadvantage. But Parsons argues that Marx did not demonstrate that these tendencies actually produce deep-seated and chronic conflict. Other factors in the social structure may counteract them, and in Parson's view, Marx simply picked a few tendencies and ignored the possible contrary and stronger effects of others.

Parsons provides no evidence on this point. He addresses only this flaw in the *theoretical* system and does not provide evidence concerning the actual empirical state of affairs. That is, he places paramount impor-tance in the theoretical argument, in which he detects a flaw. The conclu-sion may have been correct. The emphasis on argument is consistent with Parsons's view that "the most important single index of the state of maturity of a science is the state of its systematic theory" (1945:42).

Parsons (1945) is clear that a theory need not include every empiri-cally observed relationship, but only the important ones. The importance of a regularity is determined by the conceptual content of the theory. For him, regularities are important insofar as they have functional sig-nificance for the system as a whole. By looking at function, the empirical system can be addressed theoretically as a "going concern." *Function* refers minimally to the regular interrelationship of the part of the system being considered and the rest of the system. Usually, an additional con-notation of appropriateness, analogous to health in biology, is also in-tended. In social systems, this appropriateness is defined by values.

For example, in the minimal, mathematical sense, it is a function of gambling to provide cash flow to loan sharks so that they can finance drug deals and other business ventures that the banks neglect. However, such interrelationships are generally considered to be a disturbance of the proper operation of the system, rather than a part of the system to be explained along with the rest. Which system does this arrangement disturb? It does not disturb the empirical system, which simply is what-ever it is. Whether it upsets the theoretical system is dependent on the theory applied. It is clearly consonant with market theories and regularly predicted and understood as a consequence of entreprenurial decision making. However, it does disturb the normative or preferred system that logically follows from certain values. That is, people who hold certain values do not like the arrangement. Many so-called deviant activities and their consequences are similarly related to empirical, theoretical, and value systems. When the concept of *function* is used to evaluate as well as describe empirical relationships, the theoretical system and all the descriptions generated by its application become fundamentally linked to a particular set of values.

All relationships among parts of the theory can be considered in terms of whether they promote or impede the stability or orderly development of the system as a whole. When less inclusive issues are considered, only some of the relationships are relevant. For example, the defense industry or military-industrial complex can be identified as an empirical system and a theoretical system can be constructed to define and explain its internal relationships. Empirical identification of the system to be studied allows the study of theoretically relevant relationships with other empirically identified systems and their internal workings to be addressed separately. Thus, for example, while the educational system and the defense industry are crucial environments for one another, the internal workings of each system and their relationship to one another can be addressed as three relatively separate topics. By concentrating on the system as a whole, all the particular regularities must be explicitly linked to one another to determine their collective effect. The consideration of function in the evaluative sense is a discrete substantive commitment, not following necessarily from the systems view of theory. But once function is addressed in this type of theory, functional significance for the entire system becomes equivalent to system preservation. It must be noted that if one disagrees with some values incorporated in the system, or perceives some injustice in the system, it follows that functionality, contributing to the preservation of the system, is undesirable.

Theory as General

Put simply, a theory becomes increasingly general as it encompasses more aspects of the empirical systems to which it is applied and as it can be successfully applied to more instances of the same type of empirical system. Ideally, a theory could be applied to all instances of its appropriate type of empirical system and could include all the discernible interrelationships among variables. Even so, it would not necessarily encompass every detail of the empirical systems, because some details may not be interrelated with the others in the system. The relevant factors are abstracted from the totality of empirical detail. For example, the classical physical laws governing the motions of objects do not mention the color of the objects. Objects have color, but color is not related to motion through space. A general theory of some portion of human conduct, which at this time must be considered hypothetically, would not need to include every discernible aspect of the conduct, but only those systematically related to other aspects.

When applied to systems of action and social systems, the attempt to develop general theory has profound implications. Both social systems and the action systems of which they are part exist in a great range of sizes from routinized interpersonal relationships to our global economy. In addition to differences of size, social and action systems differ with respect to which and how many of their members' needs they meet and how they are met. Parsons, et al (1951) recognizes, for example, that humans have biological needs. These needs vary with respect to how much flexibility the person is allowed in meeting them. Although the need for oxygen is very specific, the need for food can be met by a wide variety of biologically adequate diets. Social and action systems on the societal scale must include arrangements to meet these needs and also to define the appropriate ways to meet them. But different societies meet these needs in different ways. Smaller, less inclusive systems, the subsystems of a society, need not include arrangements to meet these biological needs at all. And, of course, the specific behavior patterns will vary from system to system, even when the same needs are being met.

In order for a theory of action or of social systems to be general, it would have to apply to all the diverse instances. To do that, the theory would be confined to relationships among abstract factors or variables common to them all. It could not include specific features of any society or group of societies that were not common to them all. Those specifics would have to be linked to the theories by operational definitions as instances of the more abstract factors. Social systems are made up of roles as their basic units in Parson's approach. But no characteristics of specific roles are included, only characteristics of all roles. In effect, a type of abstraction is required that allows the theorist to include all empirical instances by removing reference to the specifics of any of them.

Theory as Analytic

How are we to identify and define the abstract concepts and relationships among them that constitute a systematic theory? One approach, which Parsons rejects, is *induction*, abstracting principles from empirical generalizations developed by observing empirical systems. Induction, often proposed as a crucial part of scientific theorizing, involves reasoning to a conclusion about all members of a class by examination of a few specific cases. In practice, this means that empirical cases are compiled and principles are created to account for the observations.

But Parsons (1945:50) argues that empirical generalization only becomes possible when a generalized theory exists. The theory is to be developed by *analysis*. Analysis refers to breaking a complex whole into its component parts. Parts identified as components must be meaningful as objects in their own right (Parsons, 1936:30ff.). To be a meaningful part of the system is to have functional relationships with the other parts and with the system as a whole. Thus, for example, removing the piston from an engine is analysis—literally and physically if the part is actually removed, conceptually if the part is identified as such cognitively. On the other hand, breaking a window into shards of glass is not analysis. The pieces of glass generated are not parts of the glass in the sense required. Parts of a window included in an analysis would be the frame, the glass pane, and the stick to hold the window up when it is open.

Organic systems, Parsons argues, can be conceptually analyzed but not physically taken apart without destruction or permanent disintegration of the system. Thus, analytic theorizing involves conceptually breaking complex systems into component parts and identifying the relationship of each part to the others and to the whole, in terms of the operation or functioning of the whole. The parts, to be general, must be conceptualized sufficiently abstractly to apply to all appropriate systems. How one perceives parts and their relationships to wholes is unclear both philosophically and psychologically. We are however, able to do it: We can perceive a family as a unit, for example, and still perceive its members as separable in our thoughts.

Parsons (1936) argues that the analytic elements or components are the variables in scientific theory and the laws of the theory are the relationships among them. The analytic elements are conceptually derived from the specification of the topic of study. Parsons is concerned with action systems. Once the concept of action is defined, the implications of the definition are developed through analysis. Thus, for example, action is by definition (to be developed more fully in a later section purposive and involves choice. Thus, one general component of systems of action must be some mechanism or process for evaluating alternatives. That is, choice *must* be a general component *to remain consistent with initial definitions* of the topic of study.

Parsons's discussions omit a crucial caveat: This sense of the term *must* assumes no important errors or omissions in analysis. This is especially important when the conceptual analysis precedes substantially beyond empirical observation, which is the ultimate test of a theory. Criticisms of Parsons's approach, many suggesting errors of analysis, will be encountered throughout this book. For now, it is important to indicate the significance of a chronic weakness of the analytic approach—the cultural specificity of important substantive assumptions.

When comparing ourselves to other sciences and scientists, we in the social sciences are inclined to emphasize astounding successes, the very few who have altered the world by developing new ideas rather than commanding power. Isaac Newton, by most accounts an absolutely singular success, is a special favorite. However, we ought not to forget Georg Ernst Stahl and his phlogistin theory of fire.[2] Before the chemical elements had been conceived and partially specified, the phenomena we now recognize as chemical transformations were very difficult to understand. Fire was an important and well-recognized case. For approximately one hundred years, Stahl's phlogistin theory dominated chemistry before it was replaced by our modern conception of chemical reactions among elements—one hundred years.

Stahl reasoned that in order to burn, substances *must* have a component part that made them combustible. This substance, named phlogistin, was mixed with the other components and released by combustion, including both fire and the corrosion of metals in the air (rust). The combustible material was conceived to be made up of phlogistin plus the residue of combustion. Wood was made up of wood ash and phlogistin, iron of rust and phlogistin, and so on. It was observed that the end products of combustion weighed more than the original fuel, but this observation was regarded as insignificant until oxygen was discovered and combustion was reconceived as the combination of oxygen with fuel rather than the removal of an element from it. Analytically, the phlogistin theory, with roots in ancient Greek philosophy, had a premise that if somethings were combustible and others not, the combustible items *must* have an ingredient in them to account for this. An analytic *must* is vulnerable to basic, implicit assumptions and limitations of knowledge of its time. Stahl's theory codified a great deal of information and survived for a long time. He was an important historical figure. He was also wrong in a very fundamental way due to assumptions in his analysis that no longer seem sound, and his work is not part of our current approach to chemistry.

ACTION AND ACTION SYSTEMS

Action

Parsons (1936) specifies the "act" as the basic unit of action systems and the basic analytic components of the act, upon which his theories are built. By specifying the act as his basic component, Parsons excludes other forms of human conduct from his systems. Habitual behavior and behavior resulting from conditioning or instinct fall outside Parsons's theory, and appropriate theories to account for them must be coordinated with Parsons's own. If, empirically, other forms of conduct seem more prevalent, or if it seems more fruitful to apply other theoretical systems to the empirical system of human conduct, the analysis, even if internally sound, may be applicable to very little. We can define concepts any way we choose. We cannot, however, force nature to provide examples.

Parsons (1936:44) identifies four general analytic components of the unit act. An act implies an *agent* or actor who is able to exert a degree of voluntaristic (free will) control over events. The conduct of the agent is not fully determined by circumstances. Second, an act implies an *end* or goal, a state of affairs toward which the action is oriented. The agent is capable of estimating what will occur if he or she exerts no control as well as differences among outcomes of various actions he or she might take. An act is an effort to bring about a chosen outcome. Third, acts occur in a *situation*. The situation includes *conditions* of action—trends and circumstances the actor cannot control—and *means* of action—trends and circumstances the actor can control. Acts occur when ongoing trends in the situation will not result in a desirable end and when means are available to achieve a more desirable end than will result from inaction. Finally, action implies a *normative* component. The preferences among outcomes and among means to achieve them ultimately involve basic values, preferences that are valued in themselves and not instrumentally as a means to another end (Parsons, 1936:75). Action must be understood in part from the actor's point of view because his or her knowledge of both means and choice of ends is essential.

Action, as a type of human conduct, implies acceptance of philosophical doctrines that (1) there is an element of voluntary control or free will in conduct that is purposive and guided by estimates of future outcomes and (2) the preferences among outcomes are partially normative as opposed to instrumental and instinctual. But if we put the philosophical phrasing aside, the unit act can be understood this way: A person sees that if he lets things slide, they will not work out for him. He uses what he's got to get what he wants. Action is taking care of business.

Interaction and Interdependence

Action becomes sociologically interesting when the success of each actor's plans is contingent upon the decisions of other actors as means or conditions. I can decide to stop off at the grocery store for milk. However, this simple plan will not work if someone else has decided to close the store at that time, or if someone else has not yet repaired the refrigerators, or if someone else has not delivered the milk to the store, or if someone else has failed to process my paycheck on time, or if someone else has a traffic accident so that I cannot get to the bank to cash my paycheck, and so on, and so on, and so on. Because my planning involves the contributions of others, my conduct becomes interactive with theirs, rather than being just an individual action.

Action, as opposed to interaction, requires isolation from and independence of others. The limiting case, mentioned by Parsons, is the Robinson Crusoe situation—a socialized human, with the knowledge and values necessary for agency, becomes isolated for a while from others so that many of his activities neither depend upon nor influence the conduct of others. Even in this case, the isolation is not complete because his survival depends on salvaging tools and supplies from his wrecked ship, because the plantation he builds and the island he claims are held with others in partnership, and because those to whom he entrusted his business affairs when he went to sea have acted on his behalf throughout his absence. Parsons (1968b) and Parsons et al. (1951) refer to the dependence of success upon both our own conduct and the conduct of others as *double contingency.*

Because other actors are capable of voluntaristic choices, their conduct is harder to predict than the conduct of inanimate objects. We can be relatively precise in our expectations of what machines and inanimate objects will do, and so our plans involving them can be made with confidence. To understand this point, one need only think about how thoroughly car trouble—a type of unpredictability from an important machine—can interfere with plans. How can we achieve a reasonable degree of confidence in our predictions of what other people will do, knowing that they can freely make up and change their minds?

Parsons calls the coordination of an individual's line of action with those of other individuals the *integration* of systems of interaction. He argues (1968b:43) that "the most important single condition of the integration of an action system is a *shared basis of normative order.*" The basis of order, he argues, "*must* be normative. It must guide action by establishing some distinctions between desirable and undesirable lines of action." We can understand his reasoning if we remember that the conditions and means of action are given in a situation. Everyone can do certain things and not others. The distinction between which things can be done and which cannot be done is not up to the individual, although the individual may be unaware of available means. But, within the available alternatives, normative choices will be made on the basis of values. So to coordinate these choices (rather than having a basically random and unpredictable assortment of choices from among the possibilities), the values must be shared and known in common.[3] (This is an analytic *must*. An alternative, based on conventions, is discussed in Chapter 5.)

Role

The normative coordination of choices and actions in action systems is achieved by dividing the tasks of the action system into specialized units called *roles* or *status roles* (Parsons, 1936, 1951, 1961; Parsons et al., 1951). An action system is made up of those necessary actions by a plurality of actors that enables all of them to achieve their specific goals. The action system in which I involve myself when I stop at the store to pick up milk involves *shared* values at a highly abstract level. For example, our societal understanding of property is implicated: I am expected to pay for the milk. More concretely, each participant has goals of her own that are met by participation in the system. I get milk, many people earn wages, the community gets sales taxes, the store owner makes a profit, and so on. Each does her part in the overall system and each gets specific benefits from participation.

Different people can and do perform essentially similar parts in the system—there are many customers, many clerks, many farmers. We can think of people as entering and leaving these specialties and of the system as being made up of the specialties or people acting them out. Each specialty—customer, clerk, and so on—is called a *status*, and the set of activities that are proper for the status is a *role*. Although they are not necessarily written down and not necessarily explicit, a status is a job title and a role is a job description.

We know that when a person takes a job, he or she does not necessarily follow the job description in every detail. That is true of all types of roles as well. Parsons defines the role in normative terms—in terms of the actions that should be performed if the action system is to be as efficient and smooth running as possible, relative to some specific set of values. In a perfectly efficient system, complete scientific knowledge would allow the selection of the most effective means for every task relative to all the values of the system simultaneously. The role is defined in terms of the expectations the actors have for one another rather than their actual conduct, which is the result of other factors as well as the role. The role is specified as a series of *norms* or verbal expressions of the rights and obligations of the actor. In addition, *sanctions*, rewards and punishments administered by the other actors, are specified.

For several reasons, we do not conceive of the individual as participating in a system of acts, but only the individual in a role. First, the system is defined ideally, so only some of the individual's conduct will be part of the action system, even while he is performing the role. For example, when the counter workers in a fast food restaurant talk with their friends who are customers while they are serving them and other customers, they are enacting two specialties (friend, counterperson) at the same time. Parts of their conduct are related to each role, but not the other. Also, even if they are not enacted simultaneously, each person holds multiple roles and is not completely involved in any one. The person is, in part, a collection of roles which he or she will have to organize into a life, just as each action system organizes the roles of various participants.

The counterpart to smooth functioning or efficiency of an action system at the individual level is rationality. At both levels, the standard is *maximizing utilities*, that is, achieving as many of the task-defining objectives as possible with as little waste or cost as possible. Waste or cost is defined in terms of other values in the action system. For example, suppose I can grab a drive-through burger at two locations. However, one location requires a longer drive in more traffic and costs a little more. Plans to go to either place will be *effective* in terms of getting the burger, but the more *efficient* plan would be to avoid traffic, keep the drive short, and keep the price down. These things are more efficient because I value them too, although my plan only mentions burgers as a goal.[4] Parsons is clear that rationality and efficiency can only be defined in terms of prior value commitments. Whether the choice of means and their application are rational cannot be determined without reference to goals. The values or goals come first and rationality is applied as a resource or means for calculating costs and advantages in the service of those goals or values. The individual will be interested in calculating rationally in the service of both the particular role in which she is engaged and her other roles and commitments. For example, there will be normative expectation and sanction applied by the supervisor to encourage counterworkers to participate in the restaurant action system in a way that serves that system best. Talking and joking with friends may be discouraged. On the other hand, the friends may have more to offer for honoring their expectations. Even in the presence of more general values favoring, for example, work over play, at least during work hours, there will be conflicts between the rational advantages of honoring friends' wishes and the normative pressure to be businesslike.

Three Foci of Action Systems

Parsons (e.g., 1936, 1951, 1961, 1968c, 1968b) and Parsons et al. (1951) analyze three distinct aspects or foci of action systems from this complex web of considerations: the *cultural* system, the *personality* system, and the *social* system. Roles coordinate actions and choices by linking these three systems.

The cultural system is a shared set of values and knowledge and is the basis of normative order. It includes the norms and roles of the societal action system. It is a system because changes in some ideas or values in the culture will result in changes in other ideas or values within the system. That is, knowledge and values act like components in a system. The personality system integrates the various roles of the individual and his biologically given needs. The social system is the system of actual interactions among a plurality of actors.

For Parsons, the smooth or efficient operation of a social system rests on shared norms. The process will be specified in more detail when the social system is discussed in the next section, but the general process can be described here. The norms and more general values of an action system enter the process twice. They are part of the culture and also part of the personality system. As part of the culture, through their influence on the other actors, the norms and values of the society are a condition of an individual's conduct. As part of her own personality, they are part of her normative preferences and influence her choices.

There are a variety of integrating forces and mechanisms, but in Parsons's view, the primary and necessary mechanism is the internalization of cultural standards and values in individual personalities. Without this, self-interested rationality would be greatly influenced in the direction of values enforced by others' sanctions, but one's own values would influence choice in other directions. Sanctions would become unpredictable to the degree that the values they protect are not shared and, therefore, less effective in maintaining mutual predictability. Parsons (1945:62) argues that "*both* the motives associated with 'ideals' and 'conscience' and those associated with self-interest must be mobilized in the interest of the *same* directions of behavior." (This is another analytic *must*. The same criticism that Parsons made of Marx—emphasizing one factor without considering the possibility of compensating ones—seems to apply here.)

Parsons recognizes that the cultural values are never perfectly internalized and shared and that they are never fully consistent and integrated as a system. For these and other reasons, the internalized cultural values are never perfectly reflected in conduct. *Institutionalization*, the expression of cultural values in interaction, is variable. To the extent that action systems are institutionalized, they will operate smoothly and efficiently because action will conform to norms, making it predictable and coordinating it in the service of the same goals.

SOCIAL SYSTEM

Social interaction is, most generally, the mutual influence of members of the same species. But not all mutual influence is systematic. Influence is systematic only if there is a regular or orderly relationship among the units influencing one another. In the action framework, regularity and order of influence are the result of interaction in a status-role that is institutionalized. Thus, for Parsons, the person is not the unit of the social system, even in the most comprehensive systems societies. Rather, the unit is the acting person in a role. This analytic distinction excludes idiosyncratic conduct that is not part of a role and is either irrelevant to the system or disturbs it. These idiosyncratic behaviors may be orderly at the level of personality.

A *collectivity* is a social system made up of human individuals in roles and governed by specifically relevant normative expectations, expectations that apply to some but not all status-roles, as opposed to the most general values that are common to all (Parsons, 1968c). For example, all participants in a restaurants system are expected to meet standards of cleanliness, but only some are expected to carry food to others. Technically, an entire society can be considered a collectivity if its most general values are specifically relevant only to members of that society but not to members of other societies. However, the most common use of the concept is to refer to subsystems within a society that are organized around specific tasks or goals within the broader framework. A university is a collectivity. A factory is a collectivity. A family is a collectivity.

Different collectivities of the same type (or different sets of people holding the same interrelated roles—different families, different universities, etc.) will not be identical in their conduct. In some families, children are beaten; in others, they are not. In some families, both parents work; in others, only one or neither work. These differences represent, in part, different degrees of conformity to the culturally prescribed norms applicable to that type of collectivity. For Parsons, the primary focus of sociological analysis is the articulation between normative systems and collectivities (1968c). The extent to which the collectivities of a given type are articulated to the normative structure is the degree to which the norms applicable to that type of collectivity are institutionalized.

Collectivities are organized around specifically relevant normative expectations. To the extent that the most general of these specific expectations are met, the collectivity can be seen as an actor. For example, the most general expectations applicable to a university might be to educate students and provide each student with credentials that reflect performance. That task is not accomplished by any one person or role, but rather collectively by the university. The products of a collectivity are its outputs as a system and are inputs to other collectivities. In the case of the university, credentialed students are inputs to employers. When the collectivities are well articulated to the normative structure, each receives its appropriate and expected input from the others and provides appropriate and expected output to them.

Structure, Function, and Integration

In the action frame of reference, the "structure of social systems consists of institutionalized normative culture" (Parsons, 1961:37). For Parsons (1961:36), the structure of the system is its slow changing features that can be treated as constant relative to the small, rapid, and continuous fluctuations that characterize the empirical system. Because the normative expectations that make up culture provide regularity by being internalized in personalities and then expressed or institutionalized in behavior, a statement of the regularities in the system will be primarily a statement of the shared normative expectations governing conduct. The rules making up the structure of a social system are institutionalized because they enter the rational and moral considerations of the actors in the system in such a way that the consequences of actions based on those rules will tend to reconfirm them.

Only the institutionalized normative expectations make up the structure of social systems. The culture of a society contains all of its shared values, but for a variety of reasons, only some of these are institutionalized. This is a primary difference between the normative expectations considered analytically as a cultural system and normative expectations considered analytically as a social system.

The structure of a social system may include features that create chronic imbalances in the input–output relationships among collectivities. A system is well integrated to the extent that the input–output relationships among the subsystems or collectivities comprising the system are balanced. Another way of saying this is that each system receives as input what it expects and needs for its own internal functioning and provides other systems with what they need. Integration is a matter of degree. A system is well integrated when it is stable or when there is an orderly process of change that does not affect its most basic and general values. In various places, Parsons emphasizes that system integration is the major concern of sociology. He argues that the concern for integration includes failures of integration and forces impeding integration as well. Similarly, the concern for smooth functioning includes concern for failure to function smoothly (1968c). That is to say, if some values of a set of variables promote integration or smooth function, other values promote dysfunction and poor integration.

Compensatory mechanisms and arrangements develop within systems to overcome input–output imbalances without necessarily affecting the core structure of the system—its basic values. For example, if universities (collectivities) give exaggerated credentials, employers may compensate by increasing their on-the-job training programs or internship programs. The specific goal of adequately trained employees is met, but the increased costs to the employers may result in reduced and imbalanced outputs to other collectivities. These collectivities may adjust, in turn, to the imbalances. All of this can occur without the institution of the university—the complex patterns of normative expectations applicable to all the specific universities—being altered. The still more basic values are even more insulated from change by compensatory arrangements.

Functional requirements.   To understand Parsons's emphasis on the integration of systems and his approach to functional requirements, we must remind ourselves of his approach to theorizing. Functional requirements must be general. That is, they must apply to every social system regardless of size or complexity or other functional differences among systems. Societies are made up of more or less institutionalized collectivities, each having specific input–output arrangements with other collectivities that are stabilized by specifically applicable normative expectations (institutions). These input–output relationships define the functions of the collectivity. The social system is the institutionalized portion of these input–output relations, the portion with stability and order.

Any expectations that are specifically applicable to some, but not all, collectivities and their consequences for input–output relationships cannot be functionally required. If only some collectivities produce food as an output, for example, the specific function of producing food as an output cannot be general, and norms that regulate how food is to be produced cannot be generally necessary to all social systems. What can be general is the need to preserve any social system as a systemic whole. Every system must do that to remain a system. Integration is the term for the stability of systemic arrangements. And so, general theory within sociology must focus on the integration of social systems. In the action frame of reference, it must study institutionalized arrangements of integration. Specific theories may be required in addition to account for the achievement of specific functions.

Parsons (e.g., 1961) identifies four general functional requirements, four functions that must be accomplished for a system to survive as a system—*adaptation, goal attainment, integration,* and *pattern maintenance. Adaptation* refers to obtaining disposable goods and facilities from the environment to be allocated among tasks. *Goal attainment* refers to allocating goods and facilities among competing goals within a system so that specific goals can be achieved. *Integration* refers to coordinating inputs and outputs among various subsystems, each with its own specific goals. *Pattern maintenance* refers to maintaining the structural patterns of the institutionalized culture of the system, especially its basic values.

Pattern variables or value dilemmas. These specific functions can be met by a great number of different specific institutionalized patterns, as is evident by the variety of human society. For example, obtaining food, an instance of adaptation, can be done by hunting and gathering, or by agriculture and domestication of animals using diverse technologies, or by trade. The specific norms can also be characterized in terms of the underlying value orientations they reflect. These value orientations are organized by Parsons (e.g., 1951) as five variables, defined by their polar extreme alternative styles or patterns in value choices. They are generally called *pattern variables.*

Parsons (e.g., 1951) identified these five general value alternatives that must be resolved by societal institutions: (1) Actors must orient themselves toward a societally defined proper balance between immediate gratification and disciplined, delayed gratification. This dilemma or value alternative is called *affectivity vs. affective neutrality.* (2) Actors must orient themselves toward a societally defined proper balance between collective and personal interests. This dilemma is called *self-orientation vs. collectivity orientation.* (3) Normative expectations must reflect a societally defined proper balance between specific applicability to certain types of actors and specific situations and universally applicable principles. This dilemma is called *universalism vs. particularism.* (4) Treatment of other actors in roles must be linked to a societally defined proper balance between their performance and their characteristics independent of performance. Such characteristics include gender, race, and religion, which can serve as the basis for differential treatment of people separate from any performance or competence they exhibit. This dilemma is called *achievement vs. ascription.* (5) Orientation to other actors must display a societally defined proper balance between limitation of interest in the actor to instrumental considerations related to the specific situation and diffuse consideration of the actor in a variety of situations. This dilemma is called *specificity vs. diffuseness.*

Conditions of integration and stability.   The coordination of the actions of multiple actors across time and space, integration, is achieved and sustained by a variety of means. The first, which bears repeating here, is the institutionalization of shared cultural expectations. Parsons emphasized repeatedly that institutionalization is necessary for integration and is the most important means of achieving it. Integration is enhanced by consistency among the norms. Sometimes inconsistency in the norms applicable to a single person occurs because of involvement in multiple roles. Students with jobs and friends will have to strike a balance among the time and effort demands of those three roles. Other times, a single role may include unresolved consistencies. For example, in work situations, expectations for productivity and quality often conflict in practice. The balance between "make it fast" and "make it good" will be struck personally if it is not set by cultural standards. If set individually, quality and speed expectations will be unreliably met due to personal differences.

Integration is enhanced when normative content can be changed at lower levels without major structural change. For example, students at the university level may now be expected to be computer literate, a new specific expectation that becomes applicable without changing the more fundamental expectations and values of the student role. Similarly, shifts can occur in the balance between ascriptive and achievement orientations with respect to certain roles—for example, by opening them to groups of people who had been excluded. Again, although this change may fundamentally affect the ascriptive roles, such as gender or race, the roles opened to achievement may not be otherwise affected. Even admission into many new roles on the basis of achievement may not require or precipitate a fundamental change in the ascriptive roles.

Specialized roles and subsystems of roles for integration emerge from system complexity. Legal systems, for example, integrate systems by resolving competing claims to rights. Political systems distribute the right to invoke binding obligations. Religious institutions provide a ritual base for reaffirming solidarity with group values. Different levels of prestige are achieved in different roles. When these are grounded in shared values, they can enhance integration.

In addition, three generalized media of exchange facilitate input–output relations among various subsystems and actors. *Money* is the most obvious generalized medium of exchange. Many tasks and goods can be assigned a monetary value and the money used to transform output, for which money is received, into inputs for which money is paid. *Power* is the generalized medium for the exercise of authority and is distributed by the political system. Parsons (1961) defines power as the generalized ability to influence the allocation of resources in the service of legitimate goals and the use of legitimate sanctions.[5] The third generalized medium of exchange is *commitment* or *loyalty* to the values of the society. Expression of that commitment, especially in rituals, can be exchanged for a variety of other goods.

Parsons identifies four mechanisms through which integration is enhanced. First is *integrative communication*—the sharing of information. Second is *ritual*, which is a mechanism for expressing commitment or loyalty to the group and its values. Third is *permissiveness*—allowing limited amounts of diversity enhances integration. Among other things, it allows individuals to resolve problems generated by their unique combinations of roles and allows differences to be expressed without conflict that might implicate more fundamental values. Fourth, there is *mutual support*.

Conditions of conflict and change.   Parsons (1961) recognizes both exogenous and endogenous sources of structural change. Exogenous or external sources are changes in the environmental systems with which the social system interacts. As the environment changes, the system itself must change, especially with respect to adaptation. Strains or imbalances of input–output relations among subsystems are the endogenous or internal sources of change. Strains result from imperfect integration of various parts of the social system.

Parsons et al. (1951) suggest that no social system is ever completely integrated. In poorly integrated sectors of a social system, expectations cannot be fulfilled in institutionalized roles, and people's need dispositions are frustrated by expectations held for them. Strains will be countered by the integrative mechanisms and resources of the system. Thus, the tendency will be for the system to resolve the strain, returning to stability, or for mechanisms to develop to confine the strain to a sector of the system. However, when these mechanisms for preserving the system against strain fail, structural change occurs. The strain-producing normative relations are redefined. Notice that sometimes deviance has the effect of preserving the system when the norms produce strain.

Parsons (1968c) identifies several common foci of structural conflict. These are common problems in societal normative systems. The first is stratification. Stratification has an integrative effect when the underlying values are shared. However, as previously noted, there are aspects of stratification that tend to promote conflict, especially class conflict, if unchecked by safety-valve measures. Regional, ethnic, and religious differences tend to produce strains within a society. Some societies, of course, are more uniform with respect to religion and ethnicity than others, and the number of identifiable regions varies as well. A pluralistic society that incorporates variety must develop mechanisms to reduce the internal strains caused by the value differences. Finally, the presence of discrete interest groups pursuing their own interests introduces strain.

Parsons (1951) distinguishes between change *in* a system and change *of* a system. Change *in* a system is produced by attempts to maintain equilibrium in response to strain. Sometimes there are even specific institutions to generate strain and change, such as science, which produces many technological changes. This sort of change is a natural part of social systems and usually does not involve changes in the most important values and may not affect normative structure at all. Change *of* a system refers to large changes in the normative structure. Parsons argues that there is insufficient knowledge for an analysis of this type of change. His framework, although it recognizes fluctuations in ongoing social systems, does not encompass the occasional transformation of societies on an historical scale.

ANALYTIC RESEARCH

Parsons's strategy for developing general theory was analytical, grounding theory in the logical implications of its defining concepts rather than in inductive generalization from empirical observations. In addition, more specific theories and empirical research in Parsons's structural functional tradition also employed analysis. One of the most controversial and important of these studies was Davis and Moore's (1945) discussion of the functional necessity of social stratification. Many of the criticisms of Parsons, and the structural functional school of thought, apply primarily to the extension of analytic technique and its relative demotion of empirical observation.

Davis and Moore (1945) argue that a society must distribute its members in social positions and motivate them to perform the associated roles. This is a specific application of Parsons's functional requirements. However, Davis and Moore also take as necessary that (1) roles differ in pleasantness, (2) roles differ in their importance for societal survival, and (3) roles differ in the amount of training or ability they require. *Inevitably*, they argue, a society *must* have rewards to induce performance and *must* distribute them differentially. Societal rewards can contribute to (1) sustenance or comfort, (2) diversion, or (3) self-respect. Societies *must* distribute all three types of rewards differentially. Every society *must* differentiate people in terms of prestige and esteem in order to ensure that the most important positions are filled by the most qualified people. Positions with the greatest importance for society and those that require the most ability or training receive the most rewards and therefore have the highest rank.

Why are rewards necessary? Is it analytically possible, even if no empirical cases exist, for a society to motivate members to serve the collective good rather than their personal interests? In such a society, would people need extrinsic rewards to perform important tasks or might they perform them willingly for the intrinsic rewards of contribution? In such a society, might people need to be extrinsically rewarded to perform the less important, less vital tasks as a compensation for their failure to be assigned to the desired ones? Putting aside the difficulty of determining which tasks are most important, Davis and Moore's analysis of functional necessity at the societal level also makes substantive assumptions about what kinds of reward can work and which interests (collective or personal) will always be pursued.

The introduction of still more assumptions in the transition from general to more concrete and specific theorizing rather than employing empirical data has been very troubling to sociologists. It is, of course, a methodological problem, and one that is chronic to analytic techniques. It is also a substantive problem in that each new assumption adds to the risk that the theoretical result will be based on premises that are simply wrong.

We must return to the issue of how we might determine which roles are most functionally important for societal survival. If we accept the Davis and Moore analytical argument of the necessity of stratification, we must conclude on the basis of financial and entertainment rewards, and sometimes prestige, too, that the role of providing illegal drugs is among the most important in the society. As an industry, the pay scale is very high. Apprenticeship and rites of initiation are extensive. And in some circles, prestige is also very high. In fact, during some periods, the prestige levels in this industry were high among a large segment of society. On the other hand, perhaps differential reward is not *necessarily* based on the importance and difficulty of the role.

OVERVIEW

Humans are purposeful and exercise a degree of agency. That is, they choose a course of action among alternatives based on a rational appraisal of the consequences of the various alternatives in terms of their own goals. The various actions of an individual are organized and ordered by personality.

When individuals become mutually dependent, their actions must be ordered and organized socially as well as personally. The primary mechanism for socially coordinating the action of mutually dependent individuals is a shared culture. By internalizing the values and knowledge of the culture, each person orients his activity to the same culturally defined goals. Internalized values are morally salient and others' internalizations, expressed in their reactions, make the same values rationally salient. The structure of social systems consists of shared values routinized or institutionalized in conduct. Unless the environmental conditions change, shared values will produce behavior that tends to preserve their own salience. Individuals who express the values in their action will have their expectations met and will have favorable social responses from others.

Social systems must meet general functional requirements to survive as systems. The norms (structure) providing for the achievement of functional requirements can vary substantively from society to society. In addition, the norms express societal resolution of value dilemmas that affect the style with which they are met.

The functional requirements and the importance of institutionalization of shared culture are established analytically, rather than inductively. Their applicability to empirical systems depends upon, among other things, the balance between integrative forces and those forces that produce strain, conflict, and change. In general, analytic theories do not provide good explanations of empirical systems unless they are combined with separate theories of those matters excluded analytically. An explanation of social life constructed around an analytic theory of action would require additional theories of at least habit, instinct, coercive power,[6] and change of systems.

NOTES

1. Until the time of Copernicus in the mid-sixteenth century, for example, the Earth was *assumed* to be the center of the universe and the sun and planets were believed to revolve around it. Although this view is in accord with the experience of Earth's stability and solidity, detailed astronomical observations could only be accommodated to the assumption of a stationary, central Earth by theoretically attributing paths of motion to the sun and planets that are bizarre by our current standards. Among the movements were figure eights, reversals of direction, loops, and a variety of curlicues (see Kuhn, 1959). In historical examples such as this one, it is clear that applying a theoretical system to organize and explain empirical cases is not neutral. We can also see how empirical observations test the theoretical system in this case, by suggesting organizing principles that are not credible in important respects. Finally, we can see the influence of a priori theoretical assumptions.

2. The Micropedia portion of the Encyclopedia Britannica has excellent entries on Georg Stahl and phlogistin.

3. Decisions are also coordinated by shared cognitive knowledge of means. However, since our participation in action systems is specialized, knowledge of means is not generally shared, even though it is part of the culture. The refrigerator has mechanic knowledge of means for refrigerator repair that are unknown to the supermarket customer. Abuse of specialized knowledge is controlled by shared values.

4. A distinction is often made between effectiveness (achieving goals) and efficiency (avoiding costs). This distinction, though, reflects only the degree of completeness in stating goals. If a few goals are stated, other goals affected by the action will appear as costs and are evaluated in terms of efficiency. If all the relevant goals are stated as such, effectiveness and efficiency are the same. If the goal is to get a burger, drive time, social opportunities at the drive-through, and price are encountered as costs. If the goal is to get a burger and get it quickly, at a low price, and to flirt with the person at the drive-through and if these are our only concerns, there is only effectiveness. Price is incorporated into the goals instead of being made explicit later.

5. This definition of power is quite different from most definitions. Most sociological interest in power is focused not on its connection to legitimate goals and expectations but to the element of force by which people are constrained to act against their will. Parsons refers to this aspect of power as "coercive power," which does not have an important place in his analytic scheme.

6. As we will see in our discussion of Giddens's analytic theory (Chapter 5), control by coercive power is not compatible analytically with action. To the extent that coercive power is implicated in conduct, action does not occur as a pure type and an action theory has explanatory usefulness only in concert with a theory of power.

REFERENCES

Davis, Kingsley and Wilbert Moore. 1945. Some Principles of Stratification. *American Sociological Review* 10:242–249.

Kuhn, Thomas. 1959. The Copernican Revolution. New York: Vintage.

Parsons, Talcott. 1936. The Structure of Social Action. New York: Free Press.

Parsons, Talcott. 1945. The Present Position and Prospects of Systematic Theory in Sociology. Pp. 42–69 in Georges Gurvitch and Wilbert Moore (eds.), Twentieth Century Sociology. New York: Philosophical Library.

Parsons, Talcott. 1951. The Social System. New York: Free Press.

Parsons, Talcott and Edward Shils. 1951. The Social System. Pp. 190–233 in Talcott Parsons and Edward Shils (eds.), Toward a General Theory of Action. New York: Harper and Row.

Parsons, Talcott, et al. 1951. Some Fundamental Categories of the Theory of Action: A General Statement. Pp. 3–29 in Talcott Parsons and Edward Shils (eds.) Toward a General Theory of Action. New York. Harper and Row.

Parsons, Talcott. 1954. Social Class and Class Conflict in the Light of Present Sociological Theory. Pp. 323–335 in Essays in Sociological Theory. New York: Free Press.

Parsons, Talcott. 1961. An Outline of the Social System. Pp. 30–79 in Talcott Parsons, Edward Shils, Kaspar Naegele, and Jesse Pitts (eds.), Theories of Society, Vol. I. Glencoe: Free Press.

Parsons, Talcott. 1968a. Social Interaction. Pp. 429–441 in David Sills (ed.), International Encyclopedia of the Social Sciences, Vol. 7. New York: Crowell, Collier, and Macmillan.

Parsons, Talcott. 1968b. Social Systems. Pp. 458–473 in David Sills (ed.), International Encyclopedia of the Social Sciences, Vol. 15. New York: Crowell, Collier, and Macmillan.

Parsons, Talcott. 1968c. An Overview. Pp. 319–335 in Talcott Parsons (ed.), *American Sociology*. New York: Basic Books.

3

Functional Analysis

By the late 1950s functionalism or structural functionalism had ceased making important new contributions to sociological thought. Several new positions, new schools of thought, were emerging and beginning to make important contributions to sociology. All of them defined their own positions in critical contrast to functionalism. The practice of presenting new ideas by contrasting them with those of functionalism remained widespread through the 1960s. It is still occasionally done. However, new functionalist contributions or defenses to answer these criticisms were scarce or nonexistent. Although still under attack, functionalism was an undefended, empty castle (Goode, 1973).

On the surface, an important group of theorists appeared to maintain continuity with the structural functional view. They continued to address the systematic relationship between social structure and its functions or consequences. They modified, but did not discard, the terminology of structural functional theory. They continued to address the question of how social systems remained stable. In addition, they did not introduce new general assumptions about society, opting instead for a strategy called *middle-range theorizing*, which introduced more modest theoretical analyses of specific topics. However, they did reject the basic assumptions of structural functionalism, opening them to empirical scrutiny, which made all the arguments based on those assumptions invalid. In addition, they rejected the methodology of the structural functionalists as inadequate.

In some senses, this way of rejecting structural functionalism was quite successful. The discipline as we know it today is still characterized by middle-range analyses of specific topics, although attempts to construct grand unifying theories are becoming more common again. The sociology curriculum reflects this middle-range strategy by dividing the discipline into substantive courses, each concerned with specific institutions or processes—deviance, the family, bureaucracy, and so on. In addition, the research methodology developed within this strategy has become the discipline's standard for comparison.

On the other hand, no unified school of thought has emerged in this group. For one thing, the middle-range theoretical strategy implies that far from embracing one theory, middle-range theorists do not even develop theories of the same subject. Rather, a variety of specific theories have developed that are not clearly related to one another. In addition, by rejecting the assumptions of structural functionalism without replacing them, and grounding its criticisms in methodological issues, this group suggests that scientific methodology is the core of the discipline, rather than a specific theory. As we will see, the application of this methodology requires theoretical assumptions. However, contrasting assumptions can also be made, and therefore this approach cannot resolve theoretical issues unless the empirical evidence is compelling, a situation that does not exist for most issues in sociology. In general, theoretical commitments rather than underlying methodological ones define the group boundaries within sociology.

The methodology proposed within this group is called *functional analysis*. Its adherents could be called functional analysts, although few identify themselves in this way whether they adhere to the methodology or not. In reviewing this critique of structural functionalism and the methodological alternative to it, we will see that the methodology is not substantively neutral. Addressing the assumptions of structural functionalism as empirical questions implies turning away from the questions raised by those assumptions. The image of society and social process is transformed as well. The methodological approach leads to radical revision of our view of society. It lacks, however, prior commitment to the nature of a new theory, except that it will be scientifically sound. Whether this characteristic is a strength or weakness of the approach is debatable. Many substantive disputes in the discipline hinge on this valuation.

PROBLEMS WITH THE TERM *FUNCTION*

Although the substance of functional theorizing had been abandoned, the method of functional analysis remained in widespread use. To understand how functional analysts, who were often severe critics of the substance of functionalism, distinguished between their method and functional theory, we will have to review some terminological problems surrounding the use of the term *function*. Many of the criticisms of functionalism, some argued, were based on confusion about what functionalists were really saying. Davis (1959), for example, argued that the method of functional analysis was sound and used even by the critics of functionalism. Functional analysis does not have the faults attributed to functionalism, he suggests, and clarifying the term *function* should show that many of the criticisms addressed to functionalism do not apply. (They would be good criticisms if they did, though.)

In one sense of the word, derived from mathematics, function refers to causality, especially when it can be expressed in a numerical relationship. The unemployment rate in the United States is higher for some racial groups than others. This can be stated as follows: The unemployment rate is a function of race (and other factors). Sometimes it is put this way: Race has the function (or consequence) of contributing to differences in the unemployment rates of racially different groups. Neither approval nor the necessity of the connection is implied. In this sense, as Davis (1959) argued, functional analysis merely makes causal arguments about systematic relationships between variables. It is what all sociologists do, however they phrase their arguments. It is what all scientists do. This sense of the word *function* is the one that is defended by Davis and others. Davis also argued that this is the sense of the term that functionalists had intended all along.

But the term derives some of its meaning from biology as well. A biological observation such as "the function of the heart is to circulate the blood" has additional connotations. Two of them are important in this context. First, this function of the heart is selected from among the many things the heart does because of its contribution to the survival of the organism. The heart makes a pleasant thumping sound, too, but that is not identified as its function. Often, when functionalists identified a social function, they seemed to mean a contribution to the survival of the institutions of the society, even if they did not say that explicitly. This implication was strengthened by a tendency not to identify other kinds of contributions. Second, the heart has *evolved* as a device for circulation. The characteristics of the heart may have appeared initially as a result of a genetic accident, but they are selected and spread through the population because they increase fitness. In this sense, *function* is close in meaning to *purpose*. Biologically, the heart is essential for our survival. In the context of our overall system of organs, it cannot be replaced except by another means of circulation. Even our artificial substitutes are pumps. Sometimes, functional arguments seem to imply that all parts of our society are indispensable in this way.

Finally, the term *function* has important connotations in everyday language. The most confusing of these has been the connotation of propriety or approval or obligation of the observed connection. For example, when we identify teaching arithmetic as a function (job, responsibility) of the public schools in nontechnical discussions, we are not so much asserting that they actually do teach arithmetic as we are asserting that the schools have developed for that purpose and ought to teach arithmetic. In addition to introducing implicit approval, this connotation makes it difficult to tell whether one is saying what consequences really occur or what consequences ought to occur.

When these three senses of the term are used without careful specification, it is difficult to tell whether the sociologist is merely describing a causal connection or whether she also intends that the connection has evolved and is maintained because it is essential to the survival of the society in its current form. It is also not clear whether she finds the connection appropriate and approves of the survival of the institutions of a society in their current form. This last issue does not arise often in biological contexts because approving of biological survival is taken for granted. But many of our social arrangements—racism, illiteracy, poverty, for example—are quite controversial.

FUNCTIONAL ANALYSIS OF JEALOUSY

To appraise Davis's (1959) evaluation and criticisms of functionalism, it will help to consider his (1936) own analysis of the social function of jealousy to see what confusions might arise about it even though it is a relatively thorough and explicit analysis. First, Davis points out that jealousy implies a relationship between people as a property relationship—ownership by one person of another. Davis distinguishes love property from strictly economic property. Although he recognizes that humans feel possessive about one another as means to other ends (e.g., to satisfy vanity), he considers those cases in which the love of the person and the sense of property are ends in themselves. Jealousy is seen as a "fear reaction in the initial stages of rivalry." It is a "fear and rage reaction fitted to protect, maintain, and prolong the intimate association of love." That is, jealousy protects intimate relationships by warding off intruders early in rivalry. Davis observes that jealousy can be counterproductive because it is so emotional and may harm the relationship.

Second, Davis argues that jealousy involves the entire community as well as the rivals and their common object of affection. The occasions for jealousy are defined in the institutions of society and vary from society to society. Davis recognizes the inherited, biological component in emotion but specifically rejects the idea that jealousy is instinctual. Rather, he argues that each society defines the sorts of situations that will stimulate the emotional reaction. The presence of jealousy as a right, as an obligation for people in certain circumstances, and as an expression to which the loved one is entitled in situations of rivalry defends the social institutions surrounding property and the legitimacy of personal relationships. Thus jealousy, although it may disrupt individual relationships, has the function of preserving the institutions of the society that regulate them. He also explicitly recognizes that the analysis assumes a stable culture and must be expanded to include the complications caused by anomie (normlessness).

Davis's (1936) analysis of jealousy does not include many of the major faults attributed to functionalism. It recognizes negative as well as positive consequences of jealousy. It recognizes that the argument is specific to stable institutions and must be completed by consideration of anomic societies. It implies that the institutions that legitimize jealousy are not necessary because they vary from society to society and are disturbed within a society by anomie. To a large extent, then, Davis's own work can be read as merely stating causal connections in functional terms. Still, some confusion survives even this careful treatment.

First, the recognition that social institutions legitimate and stimulate the expression of biologically inherited physiological changes that we call emotion still leaves the question of selection and inherent purpose in the biological sense open. Must every society impose some set of rules governing jealousy, even though each may impose its own? Why do we have such emotional reactions? Were they evolved to help regulate property or did they evolve for some other reason and become connected to existing institutions governing property? If the latter, what were those purposes, how did the connection with property occur, can it be broken, and should it be? I am not suggesting here that Davis is remiss in not providing answers to these questions. They are empirical ones and some go far beyond the bounds of sociology, let alone this particular analysis. Rather, the term *function*, especially when biological inheritance is involved, has confusing connotations. The raising of empirical questions is not the problem. The problem occurs when the term leads us to *presume* the answers to those questions in our studies and theories. Functionalists are accused of assuming too freely that every society must have a variety of arrangements such as jealousy, that they have evolved either biologically or through social evolution to do what they are doing, and that they cannot be eliminated without undermining the institutions of the society.

They are also accused, and that is our next area of confusion, of placing a positive value on the existing institutions of society without reflection. Davis (1936) criticizes the "hasty readiness to praise or condemn" jealousy before careful analysis. Some, he argues, assume jealousy is instinctive and condemn it as an animal urge to be mastered without recognizing its connection to institutional structure. Others focus on subcultural variations in deciding when jealousy is appropriate. These variations produce patterns of jealous responses that can be extreme relative to the dominant institutions, which interpreted in the context of their own romanticism and individualism lead the intelligentsia to give jealousy a negative value. Davis does not argue explicitly that jealousy is a "good." However, he does recommend that these other positions are wrong in condemning it. However, the only counterargument he offers is that jealousy is defined in and defends existing institutions surrounding love property. This argument can be taken to mean, in a merely causal way, that jealousy has consequences and involves processes that we do not understand. Therefore, we should suspend judgment until we study further. However, usually, this argument is taken another way: Jealousy has the favorable consequence of preserving existing institutions. This counterbalances its negative consequences and justifies accepting it as a net good or necessary evil.

The final issue is the empirical status of Davis's functional analysis. Is it intended as a hypothesis to be tested empirically, or is it intended to be a fact? Davis identifies an interesting connection between the expression of emotion and social institutions concerning love property. If we accept that connection, we still find no evidence that the function of *preserving* those property institutions is served by jealousy. Consider this alternative: Expression of jealousy, by disrupting personal relationships governed by the institutions, especially when there are disagreements about whether and how much jealousy is warranted, tends to discredit those institutions. In other words, jealousy may be a force promoting change. Certainly the institutions regulating love property in our society have changed greatly in the more than 55 years since Davis analyzed them. Did jealousy moderate the change or promote it?

Davis's intentions, of course, are not the crucial matter. Rather, we must be concerned with the standards of proof applied to functional arguments. Functionalists have been accused of *assuming* that observed relationships contribute to the stability of social institutions. Their critics link this to the analogy drawn between social and biological evolution and to seeing the implication of fitness in social institutions as biologists do in physical organs. The lack of follow-up studies that provide supporting evidence suggests that functional arguments are meant as complete without them.

The attacks on functionalism were well underway by the time of Davis's defense, although the systematic theoretical alternatives were just emerging. Davis (1959) identifies a method of causal analysis as the worthwhile core of functionalism. In the process of this defense, though, he denies that functionalists ever intended the theoretical assumptions that were under attack. The facts weigh against this. Functional arguments taken as a group seem to assume, rather than empirically demonstrate, functional connections and assume that existing social arrangements make positive contributions to the fitness and stability of institutions rather than promoting change. Even Davis's own analysis can be read this way. As we consider Robert Merton's discussion of the method of functional analysis, it is critical to remember that the substantive theories and the assumptions of the functionalists were rejected by functional analysts.

MERTON'S CODIFICATION OF FUNCTIONAL ANALYSIS

Resolving Terminological Problems

Robert Merton (1968/1949), unlike Davis, found fundamental errors in the substance of structural functional thought as well as in its terminology. He combined these criticisms with a detailed statement of how functional analysis should be conducted as a research strategy. The criticisms and the research strategy are inseparable because the strategy is designed specifically to eliminate the substantive assumptions of the structural functionalists and to substitute more rigorous empirical studies of functional connections. To express the empirical complexities omitted by the structural functional assumptions, new terminology was introduced.

The first terminological change was required because the possibility of consequences that tended to change or destroy existing institutions was recognized. The term *function* retained its existing meaning: an objective consequence that contributes to the adaptation or adjustment of a given system. Merton used a new term, *dysfunction*, to refer to objective consequences that lessen the adaptation or adjustment of the system. The seldom-used term *nonfunctional* was suggested for social arrangements with no adaptive implications.

By reserving the term *function* for objective consequences, Merton tried to eliminate the confusion concerning whether intention or purpose is implied. To indicate whether intention was implied in specific cases, Merton distinguished between *manifest* and *latent* functions. Manifest functions are recognized and intended by participants in the system. Latent functions are neither intended nor recognized.

To apply these terms, two separate empirical questions must be answered: (1) What are the adaptive consequences of the social arrangement? and (2) Are these consequences known and intended by participants? For example, one function of lotteries run and regulated by the government is to raise revenues. One dysfunction may be to increase jury awards in liability cases by providing a new standard of comparison for "getting lucky." The former is clearly manifest. The latter, if it occurs, is probably latent. Whether it is latent, however, depends on the knowledge of the public, as well as the reality of the consequence. Because different groups in society have different knowledge, whether a consequence is manifest or latent must be a matter of degree rather than a simple binary choice. Consequences may be manifest in some groups but latent in others.

Finally, in recognition that adaptive functions might be served by various social arrangements, Merton used the term *functional equivalents* or *alternatives*. These are alternative means or arrangements that could have some equivalent consequences within a given system. Equivalence is a matter of degree. The utility of this concept is not to identify various arrangements with identical consequences, but rather to identify arrangements with identical or similar functions (effectiveness) but reduced dysfunctions (increased efficiency). For example, it might be possible to alter the social arrangements related to evaluating and screening job applicants in a way that continues to discriminate on the basis of competence but not on the basis of race, ethnicity, or gender. In technical terms, the new screening procedure would be functionally equivalent to the old with respect to selection by competence but would have fewer latent dysfunctions due to reduced discrimination by race or gender.

Rejecting the Postulates of Structural Functionalism

Merton (1968/1949) argues that functionalists in sociology and anthropology adopt three interconnected postulates. These postulates, he argues, are debatable and unnecessary. What is a postulate and what does it mean to say that one is debatable? A *postulate* is a fundamental principle assumed without proof as the basis of further arguments and used as a given in order to prove other statements. To say that a statement or argument is debatable, then, is to deny its use as a postulate and to deny the validity of all of the theoretical arguments built on it. Particular empirical functional analyses might be sound, but structural functional theory is rejected when its basic statements are rejected as postulates and reduced to simple empirical questions. Only the method and the concern for social stability and change remain.

The postulate of the *functional unity* of society is the assumption that the *standardized features of the society are functional for the society as a whole*. Even the apparently negative institutions of our society, such as racial discrimination, are assumed to make some contribution to the survival of the society's institutions. Merton (1968/1949) denies two aspects of this assumption. First, he argues that not all societies are well integrated. As a result, some of their institutions may be dysfunctional for the overall institutional structure and may promote their change. Second, he argues that the effects of a standardized arrangement must be considered in terms of various interest groups as well as the society as a whole. Thus a functional analysis should identify which groups in society are hurt by its institutions as well as which groups are helped. Whether the society as a whole is made more or less stable as a result of institutions is considered as an empirical question.

The postulate of *universal functionalism* is the assumption that *every standardized social or cultural form is functional*. In contrast, Merton (1968/1949) argues that some arrangements may have developed to fill some function but have survived with no current functions. In addition, he suggests that if the subgroups in the society that benefit from an arrangement are powerful enough, they may be able to be preserve the arrangement even if it is harmful to other groups and dysfunctional for the society as a whole.

The postulate of *indispensability* is the dual assumption that *there are certain functions that must be accomplished if a society is to survive and that the institutions that fulfill these functions are therefore indispensable*. Merton (1968/1949) accepts the idea that certain functions must be met for a society to survive, but he rejects the idea that the institutions that meet them are indispensable. Instead, he argues that there are alternative means for accomplishing necessary functions. In addition, he rejects the position that the necessary functions are known.

Functional Analysis as a Method

The concerns of functional analysis. Merton (1968/1949) and the functional analysts did not substitute a new set of theoretical premises for the abandoned assumptions of the structural functionalists. Rather, a set of methodological commitments was to unify the discipline of sociology, instead of a grand unifying theory. The reason for this new approach to defining the core of sociology was the extreme separation of structural functional theorizing from an empirical base. As we review the criticisms of structural functionalism, it is apparent that the difficulties were more fundamental than overgeneralizing from limited facts or using terms with confusing connotations. Those are correctable problems. Rather, by adopting a set of *assumptions* about society as the core of theory and utilizing those assumptions to interpret specific cases rather than studying the cases in an effort to test and refine the assumptions, the structural functional school had departed from basic principles of science.

In science, theory and empirical research have a complex relationship. On the one hand, existing theory suggests the topics and appropriate methods for empirical research. On the other hand, the results of empirical study have priority over existing theory in the sense that the theory must be modified to accommodate the empirical findings. In many versions of how science ought to be conducted, the topics of research are most appropriate when they are selected intentionally to test a theory. To test a theory, one derives an empirical statement (hypothesis) that has not been studied empirically and will show some part of the theory to be false if the empirical results are unexpected. By utilizing assumptions without subjecting them or deductions from them to empirical tests, the structural functional school departed from most versions of proper scientific procedure on this crucial point.

Although the attempt to establish a firmer scientific basis for sociology explains the placement of method at the core of the discipline, the failure to suggest new theoretical assumptions to accompany it reflects an additional judgment. Is the state of our empirical knowledge of society adequate for us to adopt a sociological theory at this time? Apparently, Merton concluded it was not. Instead, his position is that we must begin with modest theoretical arguments and develop a grand core theory later after we have developed detailed empirical knowledge. Merton called the modest theories he thought appropriate *Middle-range theories.* These are theories of delimited topics, such as a theory of reference groups, or crime, or the family.

As we review Merton's (1968/1949) proposed core for sociology, it will be helpful to remember that it is not a theory but a method and research program. It does not organize facts or principles of social life. Instead it specifies what information we need to gather in order to develop a sound theory. The resulting specification is not theoretically neutral or "wide open," of course. If followed, a methodological strategy dictates what topics the resulting theory will cover by making some information available while excluding other information. It constrains the form of the theory as well. It functions as a sort of outline to be filled in with empirical details whose relevance is defined in advance by the outline itself.

In Merton's formulation, functions or dysfunctions can be imputed only to standardized items such as social roles, institutional patterns, and social structure. By *standardized*, Merton means patterned and repetitive. Considered negatively, this means that single events cannot be made the subject of functional analysis. Thus, for example, neither the attempted assassination of President Reagan nor the successful assassination of President Kennedy considered as singular events had functions or dysfunctions, although each had consequences. The pattern of violence in American politics, however, is subject to functional analysis. Such isolated events and their consequences have sociological significance only as instances of the pattern. Considered positively, this position affirms Durkheim's (1966) argument that social facts consist of rates of occurrence.

Functional analysis should specify the mechanisms or processes by which consequences occur and alternative arrangements by which functions can be achieved. Functional alternatives are limited by structural constraints. A process or mechanism that has consequences in one structural context may not have the same consequences in another. For example, in many civilian situations, tension is regularly reduced by joking among participants who have different degrees of status (cf., Coser, 1980; Goffman, 1961), but this might not work in the military if respect for rank is more rigidly enforced. This topic requires comparison of different systems to determine the degree to which mechanisms and institutional arrangements can be transplanted.

Functional analysts recognize that the concept of function suggests consideration of which functions must be achieved for a system to survive—that is, functional requisites. However, the lists of functional necessities suggested by structural functional theorists are rejected as conceptually vague and empirically unfounded. Merton argues that standards for establishing functional necessity must be established before the issue can be seriously addressed.

At the same time, the significance of individual motivation and knowledge is recognized. Individuals are conceived to have motives, knowledge, and intentions that organize their conduct. But the knowledge is not necessarily accurate relative to the standards set by scientific research. As a result, the intended and recognized (manifest) consequences of patterns of action must be distinguished from the unintended and unrecognized (latent) but nonetheless real consequences. These consequences may be functional or dysfunctional. In addition to identifying and distinguishing between manifest and latent functions, a functional analysis should account for the distribution of intentions and knowledge as a function of other social patterns.

The recognition that arrangements can be functional for some groups within a society but dysfunctional for others requires a substantial shift in the focus of research. Instead of concentrating exclusively on the effects of particular social arrangements on the society as a whole, functional analysis should identify the diverse groups within the society that are affected by the arrangement and assess its impact on each of them as well as the impact on the society as a whole. Manifestly, this modification adds a dimension to structural functional research—the consideration of diverse interest groups. But it has a less obvious effect as well—the diversion of attention from the consideration of the effects of arrangements on society as a whole. To understand this consequence of functional analysis as a methodology, we will need to consider the strategy of middle-range theorizing.

Deferring analysis of society as a whole.   Merton's (1968/1949) endorsement of the development of middle-range theories followed from his assessment of structural functional theory, which, especially in Parsons's hands, was an attempt to provide a general explanation for all social phenomena in a single, integrated, comprehensive theory. Such efforts are called *grand theory*. Merton argued that grand theory is so abstract and remote from social behavior that it cannot account for the observed regularities. He proposed that the appropriate course was to define limited aspects of social behavior and to generate theories that accounted for them. For example, we should generate separate theories of reference group behavior, of deviance, of organizational change, of the family, of criminology, of suicide, and so on. These theories would organize bodies of information but remain relatively concrete and close to their empirical bases. The possibility of more general and more abstract theory is not denied, neither is its value. However, such general theories would be constructed by synthesizing well-supported middle-range theories as they became available. For example, theoretically organized knowledge about families; about the school system; about the opportunities available to children of different races; about subcultural differences among racial, ethnic, and religious groups; about the differences in opportunities available to males and females could be pooled for a more general theory about adolescent behavior. In turn, that theory could be combined with others to form a still more general theory.

Suppose that you were committed to begin with middle-range theorizing and to utilize functional analysis as a methodological strategy. How could you answer a question about the contribution of some particular social arrangement to the society as a whole? To begin, you would have to identify the variety of groups within the society that are affected by that arrangement. You could not stop with the groups most obviously affected because that would tend to underestimate the latent functions of the arrangement. To complicate matters, the information about the diverse interest groups would be organized in different middle-range theories. Thus, to the task of gathering information would be added the task of articulating the various theories to one another. We expect that a functional analysis will reveal that any given arrangement is functional for some groups but dysfunctional for others. Will the change and instability within particular segments of the society be sufficient to destabilize the overall society? Will the means for controlling and isolating the dysfunctional consequences on some groups have additional adverse effects? For example, the AIDS epidemic is catastrophic to the communities of gay men and intravenous drug users. If it does not spread beyond these groups, will it still be destabilizing for the society as a whole? If we attempt to confine the epidemic by imposing a quarantine of some type, will we be forced to undermine our civil liberties so that the solution to the AIDS problem is itself a destabilizing force? These sorts of questions are, of course, empirical. In principle, then, we could answer them and proceed to conclusions about the society as a whole. However, in practice, that is not possible because there are so many questions to answer. In the absence of an integrative theory, there is no real justification for deciding which questions are important and which are trivial—that is, for knowing when the latent consequences to be discovered by further research will be too small to affect overall judgments. In effect, answering any questions about functionality within the society, even if they related only to a specific segment, requires virtually complete empirical knowledge of the society as a whole.

This problem has not paralyzed the application of functional analysis or the formulation of middle-range theories. Rather, in practice, the questions of overall social stability and change are deferred. Although they are part of the program, actual research and theoretical statements are not sufficiently developed to include such issues. Thus, in practice, functional analysis addresses the relationships among groups within the society with respect to particular issues and arrangements. It does not often extend to consider the relationships among interest groups across multiple issues or the overall consequences of issues and social arrangements for the society as a whole.

Contention among interest groups. Functional analysis is an attempt to establish causal connections between standardized, repetitive patterns of social life and their consequences. It is expected that these consequences will be different for different groups within the society. As a result, groups must be identified and differentiated from one another on the basis of how the patterns of their society affect them. They may be identified and differentiated in various ways—by social role, social status, demographic characteristics, religious affiliation, subcultural affiliation, and so on. They are not necessarily, then, groups of people with similar occupations or social class standing or of the same race, gender, or religion. They are groups of people with similar *interests*. Insofar as latent functions exist, however, members of the group may not recognize their own interests or with whom they are shared. A functional analysis, then, begins by identifying interests groups created by social structure.

The expectation that structural arrangements have dysfunctional aspects and may be, on balance, dysfunctional for specific interest groups is the most fundamental departure from structural functional theorizing. This expectation is more extreme than the recognition that some groups will benefit more than others from social structural arrangements. In conjunction with the distinction between manifest and latent consequences, it directs research to some distinctively sociological questions. Why do groups or their members cooperate in social arrangements that are against their interest? Are they aware of the disadvantages? Can they be made aware of them? Are they dissatisfied? How is the dissatisfaction expressed? How are the disruptive consequences of the dissatisfaction ameliorated? How do some groups and individuals come to have their interests served at the expense of others? Are they aware of that process and do they control it?

When we consider these questions as a group, an image of society and social relations emerges. We approach society in terms of how and how well groups within it pursue and protect their interests and how groups with different interests relate to one another. Groups within a society share common interests as well, which promote cooperation rather than conflict. Thus, sociological research is directed to the balance of cooperation and conflict among interest groups.

An illustrative study: The political boss.   Merton's (1968/1949) own study of the functions of the urban political machines illustrates these characteristics of functional analyses. In Merton's analysis, the key function of the political boss is to maintain central control over the power dispersed throughout our formal political organization and to utilize that power to satisfy the groups needs that are not satisfied by the legitimate structures. Merton identifies three such groups.

The first constituency group of the political boss is the needy, many of whom find that applying for aid through official channels is too impersonal and robs them of dignity. The political machine can provide aid without explicit scrutiny of eligibility or formal inquiry into private lives. From the perspective of the recipients of informal aid, the political machine performs the positive functions of the formal welfare system with reduced dysfunctions. To an extent, this is an example of functional equivalence. But we should not overestimate the degree of equivalence. The needy do not receive their aid from the political machine for free.

Rather, they pay for it with personal political loyalty to the boss and party instead of by filling out forms and establishing their formal right to the aid. In this way, the use of an informal system for distributing aid transforms the political realities. In effect, the incumbents utilize their offices to buy votes, not by direct bribery at election time, but by doing personal favors. A possible dysfunction of this arrangement for those who need and receive these favors is to entrench the political machine and stabilize the disadvantaged condition, which is then ameliorated by favors.

The second constituency group of the political boss is the business community. The political boss provides a good business climate by informal manipulation of the diverse agencies with which business must deal. This involves coordinating the paperwork involved in the variety of permits and licenses required of business and regulating competition by helping some businesses but not others. This service is provided for money in the form of bribery and political contributions. Merton explicitly argues that identifying the services provided for the business community in exchange for bribery does not justify them. Rather, it identifies the structural context that generates these informal practices and, in so doing, identifies the needs that must be served by other means if a reform is attempted. Removing personnel will not eliminate the problems if the new personnel find the same problems and opportunities facing them.

The third constituency group discussed by Merton are those who are unable to advance within respectable career channels because of their group membership. Disadvantaged ethnic and racial groups share the desire to succeed but are excluded from many opportunities. They are not excluded from participation in vice-providing organizations, however. Providing goods such as drugs and pornographic items and services such as gambling, prostitution, and loans is big business. The political machines provide a favorable climate for vice by setting predictable informal standards within which these businesses can operate. This involves selective failure to enforce the vice laws in favor of illegal enterprises in ways that are similar to the selective failure to enforce zoning, building, and sanitation codes in favor of legal ones. Naturally, bribery is involved.

This illustrative example is incomplete, of course, but it does make many of the strengths and weaknesses of this form of analysis apparent. The major strength is the attention to previously unobserved consequences of social arrangements. Descriptively, they are an important topic. More important, they are essential knowledge for any attempt to alter or protect these arrangements. By identifying interest groups that are served by political machines, we identify loci of resistance to change and the resources that they bring to bear to protect their interests. The needy provide a bloc of votes and the legal and illegal business communities provide money. An attempt to alter this style of government must either meet the needs of these constituencies in other ways so that they withdraw their support from the machine or it must mobilize greater resources, presumably from other constituencies, in opposition. Similarly, the influence of legal and illegal businesses must be redirected or countered.

It is the implication that there are many other constituencies that is most troublesome in this form of analysis. For example, if businesses are allowed to violate sanitation codes, do their customers suffer? If buildings are constructed with irregular wiring, are they more likely to burn? Are fire fighters, tenants, and customers likely to be injured? Do these irregularities drive up insurance rates? At whose expense? Do families who try to raise children in areas in which vice is allowed to flourish constitute a constituency? Are they helped by the available jobs, money, and mobility more than they are hurt by their illegitimacy? Are businesses that cannot or will not pay bribes a constituency? How many constituencies or interest groups are there?

Equity and reform.   It is clear that both descriptively and strategically, many factual questions remain to be answered. But whereas a thoroughly detached science could answer them at leisure, developing a complete description at its own pace, an engaged or applied science, a social engineering enterprise, needs to have a greater sense of urgency. The distribution of many goods is always at stake in social structural arrangements. There is, therefore, always a question of distributive justice or equity.

But even if we agree on the nature of justice, evaluations of equity face the same methodological difficulties as evaluations of functionality. Absent theory, identifying crucial interest groups can only be done by studying so many of them that we become certain that the remaining ones are not involved in pivotal latent ways. Thus, theory becomes important not only to guide research, but also to indicate when enough has been done to make judgments of scientific completeness and equity. Theoretical positions, then, define not only one's substantive interpretation of data, a much observed relationship, but also one's sense of professional responsibility to respond to inequities in society. Approached in this way, the question is not so much whose side we are on, but whether we are ready to take sides, and if so, whether we know enough to take sides effectively.

The presence and exploitation of poverty is a structural arrangement that is blatantly dysfunctional for the poor. It is conceivable that there are no functional alternatives to poverty—that the elimination of poverty would undermine the social system to the extent that even the poor would be worse off. However, that is so unlikely that we can dismiss the possibility for purposes of discussion. So in poverty we have an institution that is dysfunctional for some within the society and could be eliminated. I think we can agree that such an institution is unfair and ought to be eliminated. By agreeing on these problematic judgments in the case of poverty, we can look at how functional analysis contributes to the strategy of reform. We have the luxury in this case of knowing our knowledge is inadequate. In cases in which we see a need for action and in which action has been attempted, we can infer from our lack of success that we do not know how to fix the problem.

Designing a strategy requires the same sort of information as assessing functionality or equity. We need to know whose interests poverty does serve—specifically, how it serves their interests—and what alternatives are possible. Such information would possibly allow those interests to be served by means other than the maintenance of poverty. We need to know what resources are mobilized to preserve those interests, what additional resources are available to preserve them, and what resources are available to counter them. Such information would allow us to evaluate the feasability of removing poverty against the interests and possible resistance of those who are served by it.

Gans's (1972) functional analysis of poverty identifies a variety of interests served by the institution of poverty and suggests functionally alternative arrangements. Two points become clear in his analysis. First, when the diverse specific interests served by poverty and the alternatives to them are considered as a unit, we see that poverty is deeply embedded in our society and that its removal would require extensive changes in our institutions. In a great variety of ways, poverty is exploited by those who are already advantaged to increase their advantage at the expense of the poor. Second, when we address specific sets of interests, it becomes concretely clear that removing a disadvantage from one interest group (in this case the poor) requires the reduction or removal of an advantage from another interest group. The unanswered question is thus brought into focus: Specifically, how can advantaged groups be persuaded or coerced into reducing or surrendering their advantages? Functional analysis leads us to define the challenge of institutional change in that way; but without theory and more detailed knowledge, problems can be defined but not solved.

Gans (1972) divides the positive functions served by poverty into four categories: economic, social, cultural, and political. By looking at examples of each, we can begin to understand the diversity of ways in which interest groups are formed and served. In addition, Gans's analysis illustrates the difficulty of making judgments of functionality and the importance of theory in guiding and compiling empirical observations.

1. Poverty coerces the poor into accepting work at lower wages than would be otherwise required to attract a labor force. The poor generally lack the skills to compete for highly skilled employment. In addition, they lack the accumulated resources necessary to reject unattractive offers and endure unemployment while waiting for better ones. As a result, the poor must take physically dirty or dangerous, menial, dead-end, profane, or undignified work at low salaries. Without the needy labor force provided by the institution of poverty, higher wages would have to be paid to attract a labor force to these jobs. By accepting these low wages, the poor subsidize those who purchase the goods and services to which their labor contributes. In addition, the industries producing those goods and services are made profitable in their present form by substandard wages. Among the industries involved are the restaurant industry (fast-food workers, busboys, etc.), agriculture (migrant farm labor), and the garment industry. In addition, as our discussion of the political machine indicated, illegal enterprises are staffed by the poor (prostitutes, numbers runners and other gambling personnel, low-level drug dealers, etc.). An alternative to this aspect of poverty is to raise wages, which would raise the prices of many goods and services and threaten some industries in their present form.

2. Poverty creates jobs in professions that serve the poor and shield the more affluent from them. The former include illegal gamblers, illegal drug dealers, operators of pawn shops and inexpensive liquor stores, prostitutes, and pentecostal ministers. The latter include the police and the penal system. Social workers, workers in medical clinics, and related service providers perform both functions. They protect the affluent from the poor by serving the poor.

3. The poor buy less desirable goods at reduced prices, such as day-old bread, overripe fruits and vegetables, used clothing and cars, and deteriorating buildings. New clothes that are imperfectly manufactured or left over from the previous season are also sold at discount. By extending the economic life of these items, the price of the more desirable items is reduced. For example, the price of new cars is reduced by the amount received for used ones. The cost of producing clothes is reduced by the amount received for imperfect or leftover items. This is reflected in reduced cost of the new, perfect items. Through their purchases, the poor subsidize the more affluent.

4. The poor subsidize the more affluent in a number of other ways. Local property and sales taxes and some state income taxes are not graduated. As a result the poor pay a higher proportion of their income in taxes than do the more affluent. This subsidizes state and local programs that serve the more affluent. A final form of subsidy illustrates the difficulty of judging functionality. The poor serve disproportionately

as "guinea pigs" in medical experimentation. Of course, only the more affluent can afford the innovative treatment after it has been perfected. Therefore, Gans argues, the poor are subsidizing the more affluent by submitting to untried medical techniques—that is, by absorbing risks.

Descriptively, this may well be accurate. But is there a subsidy with respect to risk? This is a complex judgment depending on the risk of trying untested medical techniques relative to the risk of not trying them. Suppose that the untested medical techniques is for a fatal disease. There is nothing to lose by trying the technique if someone else (e.g., researchers) pays for the treatment; there is a chance of cure. For a great many serious diseases, then, access to untried medical techniques is an *advantage*. If there is a subsidy in this area, it is financial only and involves the funding of research. Is this farfetched? Not to AIDS patients who are lobbying to change the entire structure of medical testing. They see denying any treatment to an AIDS patient as putting the gathering of scientific knowledge about treatments ahead of their own survival. This is a case, then, in which evaluation of functionality requires more evidence than description of consequences and/or causal argument. Evaluations of equity in specific exchanges require still more. As we make evaluations, we must add knowledge of alternatives to knowledge of the instance at hand.

5. The poor can be punished disproportionately to uphold the legitimacy of norms and to demonstrate the competence of social control agents. An alternative is to remove financial status as a consideration in the legal process. The relatively affluent would have to pay more for the defense of the indigent through their taxes, but the overall cost would depend upon whether fairness were achieved by punishing fewer of the poor or more of the affluent. In either case, though, the proportion of the punished who are relatively affluent would increase.

6. The poor provide diverse emotional satisfactions for the more affluent, such as the opportunity to express compassion and charity. Stereotypes about the life-styles of the poor provide vicarious pleasure. The poor provide a standard against which others can feel satisfied with their success and status.

7. Denying opportunity to the poor reduces competition and helps maintain the advantaged and increases upward mobility among the more affluent.

8. The poor are an identifiable group that serves as a symbolic constituency and opponent for politicians.

9. The poor can be forced to absorb a disproportional share of the costs of change and development. For example, construction of roads, stadia, and urban renewal projects can be done in poor neighborhoods.

10. Although they serve as a symbolic constituency, the poor do

not participate in party politics or vote as much as others. They can, therefore, be ignored. Because their interests include fundamental changes, their lack of participation stabilizes the political situation, including the distribution of advantages.

SUMMARY

Structural functional theory was criticized for making too many and incorrect assumptions about society. As summarized by Merton, these assumptions arise from an evolutionary view of society. Society was assumed to be so well integrated that functions should be assessed only with respect to the whole. The constituent parts were assumed, that is, to have common interests. The evolved social structures were all assumed to have been selected on the basis of their contributions to the survival of the system. Additionally, they were assumed to contribute vitally and, therefore, to be indispensable. These assumptions served as postulates in structural functional theorizing and analyses. Therefore, when they were denied as assumptions and regarded as empirical questions by functional analysts, structural functional theory was effectively abandoned.

Although functional analysis is a methodological rather than theoretical position, it has profound theoretical implications. The research task it defines is unmanageable without theory to direct attention to significant groups, routines, and consequences. For example, the partial functional analysis of poverty is compelling, in part, because we have prior knowledge of social classes. Our knowledge of the class structure makes it possible to see these few functions as examples of extensive common interest among the poor and among the affluent. It also justifies not demanding a catalog of conflicting interests within each class and interests held in common by different classes to determine the overall balance of these multiple and diverse exchanges between the classes. And because additional latent consequences may always exist, the question of when the existing information is adequate for various purposes must always be answered theoretically, in part. Finally, although the postulates of structural functional theory are not rejected as false, but rather regarded as empirical questions, the conception of society implied by the research program is radically different from that of structural functionalism.

The structural functionalists regarded society as a well-integrated whole whose constituent units contributed vitally to its survival and each of whose interests was served by the survival of the whole in its existing form. Testing this as an empirical hypothesis, however, requires us to consider the separate interests of various groups and the effects of societal arrangements on them individually. That is, we are led to look at society as composed of interest groups rather than as system components.

The production and distribution of goods and services are intimately related. A society cannot distribute what it does not produce and cannot produce without distributing. In addition, the capacity to produce is greatly influenced by the pattern of distribution that motivates the members of society, distributes skills and opportunities, and so on. Nonetheless, the shift of emphasis from seeing society as a system of production to seeing society as a system of distribution is a conceptually radical one. One important difference between production and distribution is the role of rationality. In principle, production can be rationalized, at least for tangible goods and services.[1] For any desired level of production, the means are defined by technology and even the recruitment and motivation of labor can be treated as a technical problem. The interesting questions about production are those that boil down to how to produce. But many of the interesting questions about distribution do not concern the technology of distributing goods and services, but rather the policy defining which goods and services will be available and who will receive them. This policy intrinsically requires consideration of values and equity.

NOTE

1. The production of symbolic goods, such as prestige, reputations, and credibility, may not be rational in the same sense.

REFERENCES

Coser, Rose. 1980. Some Social Functions of Laughter. Pp. 81–97 in L. Coser (ed.), The Pleasures of Sociology. New York: Signet.

Davis, Kingsley. 1936. Jealousy and Sexual Property. *Social Forces* 14:395–405.

Davis, Kingsley. 1959. The Myth of Functional Analysis as a Special Method in Sociology and Anthropology. *American Sociological Review* 24:757–772.

Durkheim, Emile. 1966. The Rules of the Sociological Method. New York: Free Press.

Gans, Herbert. 1972. The Positive Functions of Poverty. *American Journal of Sociology* 78:275–289.

Goffman, Erving. 1961. Role Distance in Encounters. New York: Bobbs-Merrill.

Goode, William. 1973. Functionalism: The Empty Castle. Pp. 64–94 in Explorations in Social Theory. New York: Oxford University Press.

Merton, Robert. 1968/1949. Social Theory and Social Structure, enlarged ed. New York: Free Press.

4 _____

Conflict Theories:
Basic Themes

_____

Conflict theories have replaced structural functional theories as the dominant approach to sociological analysis of the large-scale structure of society. The basic assumptions of structural functional analyses of social structure had been systematically challenged, and alternatives had been proposed, even during their dominance over sociological thought. We have already seen that some sociologists argued that functionalist theory had given way to a theoretically neutral research methodology (functional analysis) by the 1950s and that by the early 1960s there were no defenders of the theoretical assumptions of functionalism. Although it is hard to fix a precise date, the discontent with functionalist approaches had certainly been followed by widespread acceptance of a new approach to the study of large-scale social structures, the conflict approach, by the middle or late 1960s.

SUBSTANTIVE CONCERNS

Most generally, the term *conflict* refers to any form of social malintegration, but the conflicting interests of different groups in the outcome of social arrangements is its most common application. In discussing functional analysis, we saw that different groups within the society are affected differently by social arrangements. On the assumption that each person would prefer not only material rewards, but also to be rewarded fairly, these differences in consequences define different interests as well. The conditions influencing how conflicting interests are expressed in social life and the complex relationship between conflict and social change are central topics of conflict theory. Interest in social change, of course, requires a historical dimension in the analysis of society. Recognition that groups participate in social arrangements in which they are disadvantaged suggests the importance of the domination of some groups by others. Domination suggests, in turn, the importance of power, and because power is often not explicitly used, the importance of the manipulation of disadvantaged groups, especially by promoting their ignorance of their own best interests. These concerns reflect attention to specific topics not well addressed in structural functional theory, but they also reflect a different underlying image of society—an image based on conflict among more or less malintegrated parts, rather than a well-integrated system of positions in a smoothly functioning division of labor.

Conflict theory will be addressed in three chapters. This chapter develops the basic themes of conflict theory. The next reviews several theories, some concerned primarily with structure and others primarily with the role of voluntary action. The third chapter (Chapter 6) discusses the development of a conflict theory of roles, especially that of Robert Merton. It is separated from the other chapters because the mainstream of conflict theorizing has not been concerned with the division of labor for reasons partly discussed later. This disinterest in the systems aspect of society has been so complete among conflict theorists that Merton is typically misclassified as a functional theorist.

Basic Image

The conflict theories were developed in systematic and explicit argument with structural functional theories. As a result, the basic tenets of the conflict theories have been explicitly stated in contrast to those of structural functionalism. Dahrendorf (1974) saw four major assumptions as a starting point for structural functionalism and stated contrasting assumptions as the foundations of conflict theory. The structural functionalists characterize society as (1) a relatively persisting, (2) well-integrated configuration of elements, (3) each of which contributes to societal functioning, with (4) each society based on a consensus of its members. In opposition, Dahrendorf suggested that conflict theory postulates (1) ubiquitous social change and (2) conflict among elements of society (3) to which each societal element contributes, with (4) every society resting on the constraint of some members by others.

The explicit statement of these different images of society allows us to illustrate the truism that theory not only addresses attention toward specific topics, but also directs attention away from others. The functionalist assumption of persistence directs attention to the internal systemic structure of a society and away from historical developments. Perhaps more important, the assumption of consensus not only directs attention away from power and other forms of domination, but as Dahrendorf (1974) and Mills (1959) observe, it makes them difficult to express in functional language, even if one were interested in doing so. In contrast, the conflict theorists' assumption of constraint makes the apparent presence of social norms difficult to explain and accommodate. Our discussions of various conflict theorists will include four quite different approaches to that issue.[1] Similarly, structural functional emphasis on consensus and voluntary compliance makes the enforcement of norms by sanctions problematic. Gibbs reports that 19 conceptually distinct types of norms are discussed in the literature (1965) and that 32 types of sanctions are implied conceptually by various theoretical discussions (1966). Frequent reworking of an issue within a framework often indicates a lack of closure, an unresolved intellectual difficulty of continuing interest.

THE LAW OF VAGRANCY—AN ILLUSTRATIVE STUDY

First Vagrancy Laws

In 1349 the first vagrancy statute was passed in England. Giving alms to the able-bodied was made a criminal offense "so that thereby they may be compelled to labour for their necessary living." Any able-bodied person, not already employed or practicing a trade or craft, was compelled to work for whoever required his service. If the person refused to work, he could be sent to jail until he agreed to work. Any person who left employment before the end of the agreed upon term could also be sent to prison. A standard wage for laborers was established. In 1351, the provision was added that a laborer could not leave the place in which he spent the winter to work elsewhere, during the summer if work was available in his winter residence. Prison terms were established as punishment for this offense as well.

William Chambliss (1964, 1973), whose studies summarize the history of vagrancy law, relates these provisions to the need to control the movement of laborers following the Black Death, a plague that struck England in approximately 1348 and killed about one-half of the population. The sudden loss of population, combined with the growth and industrialization of the towns, severely reduced the number of inexpensive workers available for farm work. Former serfs, both men and women, had been to purchase their freedom from the nobility who needed money to pay for the Crusades, and were able to move from place to place to receive the best wages for farm labor or work in growing industries. Serfs, still legally bound to the land, were able to move illegally, find better employment, and evade punishment.

In this context, wealthy landowners, the most powerful group in England's still basically agricultural economy, used their influence to introduce vagrancy laws as a means to guarantee a stable supply of relatively cheap agricultural labor. The standard wage served to enforce solidarity among *employers* by making it a crime to compete with one another for workers by raising wages. Giving alms was treated as aiding a fugitive, which is still a crime in England today. This prevented employers from concealing higher wages and also discouraged solidarity among the laborers. Confining the laborers to their winter residence stabilized the supply of farm labor and reduced competition for their services.

Conflict Theory and Functional Analysis

Before continuing our discussion of the vagrancy laws, we should take the opportunity to consider how the conflict theory approach relates to the method of functional analysis and its difficulties in this context. With respect to the effects of the plague, an uncontrolled event, and the development of industry in the towns, a historical development driven by technological change, conflict theory utilizes straightforward functional analysis. Interest groups are identified and the consequences for those groups are explicated. As in Gans's discussion of poverty (see Chapter 3), a supply of cheap labor with few options is shown to subsidize other segments of the society. The historical dimension, here represented by the rapid, drastic reduction of the labor supply, gives credence to that asserted function by documenting the results of changes in the size of that supply and the alternatives available to it. The utility of functional analyses is illustrated here by the setting of a standard wage to reduce the cost of labor. In our time, supporters of a minimum wage argue that the same structural arrangement, standardized wages, increases the wages of the disadvantaged. Particular structural arrangements are variable in their consequences.

However, the discussion of the law introduces a new element, suggested by the conflict approach. A powerful group, the agricultural land-owners, collectively and with awareness of its own interests, utilized its influence to preserve its advantage by controlling another group in the society. The coercive power of the law is used in the interests of a segment of society to the disadvantage of other segments, labor and industrialists, for example. And so the historical development of society reflects a mixture of uncontrolled events and their consequences, events that some powerful group initiates and attempts to control.

Finally, also relative to Gans's study of poverty, the adoption of the conflict perspective allows a diminution of detail in systems analysis. The differences among the landowners that required the enforcement of solidarity through the standard wage are not explicated. The important thing is that the landowners acted in their common interests and not, in this case, that there are some divergent interests as well. Similarly, the consequences for different occupational categories, for serfs and free men and women, for apprentices, and so on, need not be documented in detail. The crucial issue is their common interests, and not the differences among them.

Changes in the Vagrancy Law

Over the next two hundred years, although never repealed, the vagrancy laws diminished in importance. They were not enforced or significantly altered, and their original purpose disappeared with changes in English society. Feudalism decayed and disappeared and agriculture ceased to be the center of the English economy.

In the 1530s new provisions were added to the vagrancy law. It became an offense for the able-bodied to beg, to have no visible means of support, to engage in crafty and unlawful games (gambling) and plays (minstrels), to practice crafty sciences (e.g., fortune telling) or counterfeiting of licenses and passports, or to provide vice services (pimping). The penalties for these offenses included being whipped until bloody (scourged), being held in the pillory (wooden blocks holding the head and hands like a collar while the individual stands), and having an ear cut off. Five years later, the death penalty was added for second offenders.

Chambliss (1965; 1973) argues that the nature of the offenses and the seriousness of the penalties reflect a new purpose for the vagrancy laws. By the sixteenth century, England was increasingly dependent upon trade and industry. Thousands of merchants were engaged in foreign trade, much of it with Italians, who were disliked by the English populace. The merchants traveled with valuable goods, which were often stolen and sold. Once stolen, and especially once converted to cash, the legal ownership of goods was hard to establish and so theft was difficult to prove. The vagrancy laws were used as a means to control theft. No longer valued as potential labor but rather as fugitive labor, vagrants were treated as felons when no other felony could be proven. The fact that an able-bodied person was unemployed was presumed to be evidence that he or she was supported by the proceeds of felony or was capable of becoming a felon.

Once again, we observe the law as an instrument to serve the interests of a powerful group within society, in this case merchants and industrialists. When the consequences of a type of behavior, such as able-bodied unemployment, threaten no powerful interests, the law is neglected. No new legislation is passed and enforcement of existing legislation is weak. However, when powerful interests are threatened, the law is revised and mobilized in an attempt to protect those interests.

Retaining unused laws on the books has consequences as well. The statute, whatever its original purpose, can be reapplied after periods of disuse if a new purpose is found for it. Some of the provisions of the vagrancy law have been reactivated in the United States in recent years. For example, the "war on drugs" includes the seizing of property for "continuing criminal enterprise" from people who have never been convicted of any felony, but who have extensive assets and no legitimate account of their origin and who are suspected of unproven felonies. Similarly, property can be seized as being involved in drug trafficking on the basis of any drug seizure, even if the property's owner is not involved. For example, a yacht can be seized (and some have been) if crew members bring small amounts of marijuana aboard in the absence of the owner and without his or her knowledge. Conflict theory leads us to expect such revivals and focuses our consideration of whose interests are being served.

Administrative Convenience and Vagrancy

In the 1740s the concept of vagrancy was enlarged again, bringing the English law to essentially its modern form, and to the form incorporated in American law. Confidence games, such as collecting for bogus charities, seeking alms under false pretense (e.g., feigned injury), sleeping in barns or outdoors, and deserting one's family all became offenses. People who committed these offenses were neither felons nor avoiding work. Their offense is one against public order or decency. Professional law enforcement found this ability to use the law against nuisances administratively convenient. Thus, this alteration of the vagrancy laws is an example of professionals' gaining the power to establish policy and standards in their area of expertise. Doctors' exclusive power of prescription is another example. In this case, the power to influence the law does not arise from wealth or economic importance but from administrative control and expertise.

POWER ELITES

A major theme of Chambliss's (1964; 1973) study of the vagrancy law is the influence of powerful groups, elites, over the creation and administration of law in their own interests. In his analysis, the state is, at least in part, a coercive force that can be used as a tool of control or domination of one group by another. To utilize the state in this way, the group must have enough power to influence the activities of the state to achieve its interests to the detriment of others. The group members must share awareness of their common interests and be willing to put aside their divergent personal interests sufficiently to pursue the common ones. They must, finally, share a sense of how those interests might be served—of means and strategies. Otherwise, these separately powerful individuals would cancel each other out, with each attempting to influence the state in different ways. C. Wright Mills's (1959) discussion of power elites provides the theoretical context for Chambliss's historical case study.

Elites and Ordinary Men

Mills describes elites in contrast to ordinary people. Ordinary people, he reminds us (1959), have lives bounded by the commitments and concerns of everyday life—work, family, and neighborhood. Within these boundaries, they make decisions, but the decisions of any ordinary person are constrained by the imposition of poorly understood forces and do not ordinarily influence the lives of many others, let alone make history.

There are exceptions, of course. Sometimes a person of limited resources and ordinary origins such as Mahatma Gandhi or Martin Luther King Jr. is able to make history through personal charisma—an ability to command loyalty from others that has been named but not understood, or through unanticipated consequences of an almost ordinary act (e.g., videotaping the police beating of an arrested suspect), or through some technological invention (the cotton gin). But for the most part, ordinary people influence events only collectively, by the summed effects of their small decisions.

These exceptions are crucially important, however, because they show that ordinary people can take control of their lives and even make history despite their initial lack of position and resources. Mills (1961) identifies the essential element in this process as the quality of mind necessary to see one's own life and its problems in historical context. Each society forms the nature of the people within it, people who are aware in some ways, repressed and ignorant in others. Even when information is plentiful and reasoning ability is present, the ordinary person cannot be liberated or take control without the specific awareness of how the ideas that come to seem natural in her own society compare with the broader human potential revealed in historical variety.

Members of the power elite, Mills (1959) argues, are different from the ordinary people in their societies. First, they hold positions in society in which they make decisions with major consequences on a historical scale. Second, they transcend the everyday environments of ordinary people by having the quality of mind necessary to control events. There are psychological and social bases for the development of these qualities of mind. The elite tend to have similar origins within the society—similar educations, careers, and life-styles. Socially, they are in contact with one another in overlapping "crowds" or "cliques." The interests of the institutions in which they hold key positions overlap, creating unity and cohesion. There is both formal and informal coordination of decisions among leaders in powerful positions. These contacts, recognitions of common interest, and coordination both produce and result from an awareness of society that is different from that of ordinary people.

Institutional Basis of Elites

The major institutions of a society provide the means and context through which elites exercise power and make history. As Chambliss's articles indicate, different institutions are powerful in different historical epochs, providing different bases of power and elites with different characteristics. No one can be truly powerful, however, except through control of major social institutions.

In modern America, Mills (1959) argues, the means of centralized control have expanded greatly and command posts or centers of power are found in three centralized institutions—the government, large corporations, and the military. These three have in common, besides their overlapping interests, extraordinary centralizations of power allowing control over many people and resources. As a result, the actions of these institutions and the decisions of their leaders have extensive consequences. By contrast, religious, family, and educational institutions are not centralized and are not autonomous centers of power on a national scale. Instead, these institutions are shaped in the exercise of their own power by the overriding influence of the three truly national ones. Although leaders in these decentralized institutions are more powerful than ordinary people, they are not, in Mill's view, as powerful as the leaders in the more centralized institutions. Mills's recognition of gradations of power based in various institutions contrasts with the views that (1) power is held absolutely and unilaterally by a small group or (2) our lives are not controlled by the more powerful.

Fate

Not all events of historical scale and importance are shaped by elites. Neither are all societies nor all epochs equal in the extent to which they are controlled by purposeful decisions of an elite. To some extent, historical events occur as the summed unanticipated consequences of many small decisions made by ordinary people. This process can be considered *fate*—history made without purposeful human control. Different societies and different epochs in the history of each society differ in the degree to which history is controlled by fate in this sense.

A modern example illustrates this concept. There is an epidemic of a disease—AIDS—for which there is no cure. Also, there is enough time before a person becomes symptomatic to pass the virus along to others. The disease is transmitted through two of the least centralized activities in our society—sharing hypodermic needles and sexual intercourse. The eventual social, economic, political, and demographic impact of this disease will be shaped by decentralized decisions about sex and needles and only secondarily by the reactive institutional attempts to control the epidemic. If the effects are large, they will constitute a fateful historical event, as the Black Death did in Chambliss's discussions of vagrancy laws.

Although less heralded than his discussion of the influence of power elites, Mills's recognition of the importance of the summed consequences of relatively independent decisions by ordinary people is a crucial contribution to our understanding of social processes. When the summed effect of these decisions is to adhere to custom or follow powerful leaders, these effects are seldom attributed to the decisions of ordinary people at all. Our discussions of leadership and custom seldom emphasize that "going along" is the result of choice. Instead, the qualities and dynamics of leadership and the force of custom are emphasized. The true importance of the summed consequences of uncoordinated decisions becomes apparent, however, when their effect is to undermine custom or leadership, such as the ruinous inefficiencies that contributed to the disintegration of the Soviet Union. In Mills's approach, the decision process and the processes of partial and informal coordination are critical aspects of social life. These issues will be addressed in detail in our discussions of micro theories.

Public and Mass

We should note, here, that if the correct qualities of mind could be developed in the population, the patterns of decisions could become more rational. We could direct our fate, so to speak, in areas not centrally controlled and perhaps influence or decentralize the decisions governing our lives. That is the role of a public in the political theory of democracy. A public shares common interests. There is rational discussion among its members resulting in an understanding of what should be done in accordance with conscience. The public would then influence its representatives to enact its will.

But the conception of a public is not closely matched to the empirical realities of society. Interests within the society are not common, but rather in conflict. Reasoned discussion is compromised by the irrational element in human thought, by the domination of the policy-making process by experts, as in the case of law enforcement administrators adjusting the vagrancy law to their own interests, and by the socially limited nature of thought. As a result, Mills (1959) argues that our society has developed away from having a variety of publics shaping and controlling its institutions and increasingly toward a mass society.

Publics and masses can be contrasted by considering four dimensions: (1) In a public, expression of opinion is widespread relative to receiving opinions. In a mass, very few people express the opinions that are received by a relatively large number of people, especially through the mass media. (2) In a public, communication channels allow quick response to expressed opinion. In a mass, it is virtually impossible for the individual to respond quickly or effectively. (3) In a public, opinion is readily expressed in action. In a mass, the expression of opinion in action is controlled by authorities. (4) The public is autonomous in its action. The mass is effectively controlled by authorities. In the jargon of political discourse, the leaders of institutions in a community of publics is accountable to public sentiment. In a mass society, those leaders are not accountable in their actions and, in fact, exercise control over the development of opinion and its expression in action.

Elite and Class

The term *class* is used variously and loosely in sociology, sometimes referring to no more than relative income and education levels. But in the work of Karl Marx, the original investigation of social class, the term had a specific meaning and theoretical context. Although each of the conflict theories can be understood in its own terms, the thematic similarities among them cannot be appreciated without considering the technical sense of social class as it appears in Marx's work. Marx's image of society is characterized by conflict between groups with different resources and different interests and members with different levels of awareness of themselves as a group with common interests. The conflict theorists accept this image but modify the details of Marx's specific theory in various ways. Despite the different terminologies they employ and the differences among them, they include variations on a theme. The theme is not to correct or defend or update Marx's work in a simple way, but to develop a sound theory within the conflict imagery and, of course, with due respect to Marx's specific theory as well as his broader vision, and to other historically important theorists.

To Marx,[2] the core of social organization was the means of production of the material necessities of human life—food, clothing, and shelter. Each society has its own technology for meeting these needs, and this technology defines the essential core of social relationships and participation in the society. Marx is not centrally concerned with the tasks defined by the division of labor. Except for the details of how they are divided among people, these are determined by the technology. Marx's concern was with the relationships generated among people by the manner in which the basic means of production are owned and controlled in a society. For example, the use of irrigation, chemical fertilizers, and motor-driven plows in farming implies a great many tasks that must be done regardless of the social arrangements in which they are embedded. It does not imply whether the ownership of the farms and factories will be private or collective, nor does it imply who will decide the exact division of tasks, the setting of policies concerning what will be grown, what safety measures to take, or the distribution of the products. In short, it does not imply whose interests are to be served by the use of the technology. Sociological interest in this approach is focused on those relational matters that are not technologically determined, vary among societies, and appear to be alterable within any given technological levels.[3]

Specifically, Marx addressed the relationship of ownership and control of the basic means of production and its implications. He divided society into two main conflicting classes—those who owned and controlled the basic means of production and those who were employed in other's service. Other groups in society were present primarily as surviving forms of previous epochs (such as agricultural landowners in industrial society) and as transitional forms. When enough members of the owning class, capitalists in our era, become aware of their class membership and its interests, the class is able to coordinate its activities to preserve and enlarge its advantage. The members of the working, employed class are unaware of their common situation and interests. Their focus is more on local concerns than on the societal scale and more on the differences among tasks and rewards than on their common interests. Among these interests is their common alienation from the means and products of their own work and the expropriation of some of those products as profits.

Control by the owner class is made more efficient by the discrepancy of awareness. For example, when market situations provide incentives for members of the dominant class to bid competitively for labor, the class can act in concert to favor collective interests over competitive individual ones. Landowners in an agricultural society can establish a standard wage for farm labor, or owners of NBA basketball franchises can establish a maximum total salary for the players on each team. In effect, then, each member of the unaware class bargains with the entire aware class, not with its individual members. This advantage is more crucial to control than the material advantages that can only be maintained efficiently if the employed class is compliant. Forced labor is not efficient, nor is it clear that a society can sustain itself with forced labor for an extended period.[4]

Marx proposed a predictive theory of history. A subordinate class would not accept its position willingly. Thus, the development of class consciousness in that class would be expressed in revolutionary redistribution of ownership and control. Marx anticipated a series of revolutionary episodes that could not stabilize unless the basic means of production were collectively administered and owned by no one. If that occurred, differences in task (and perhaps reward) would remain, but there would be no classes as defined, and no alienation because the controllers and laborers would be one. All would participate in the setting of policy in the interests of all. The development of consciousness of one's place in history and society becomes a crucial issue, even though many aspects of social life are regarded as determined by technological and class structure.

The similarities of Marx's position to Mills's discussion of power elites are apparent, even in this rudimentary version. The centrality of the distinction between dominant and subordinate groups and the crucial importance of consciousness of one's place in history and society remain. But Mills does not restrict domination to ownership of the means of production by definition. The heads of large corporations sometimes meet that criterion, but leaders in the government and military seldom do. Mills leaves it as an empirical question whether these three institutional centers of power and control are further combined into a true class in the case of this country. But Mills makes it clear that power elites are not necessarily a true class in every case. In the history of vagrancy law, the agricultural landowners seem to meet this criterion of a true class, but it is not clear that influential merchants did, and it is still less likely that law enforcement professionals met it. That is, the image of domination of one group by another remains, but the basis of domination is not necessarily restricted to ownership of the means of production.

Mills further complicates the issue of domination by recognizing a variety of bases of varying degrees of power, simultaneously operating more or less independently. In addition to the power elites in the three major institutions of our society, there are community power bases and other decentralized sources of power, including other institutions. The relatively simple view that two groups are in conflict gives way to a view that a number of powerful groups may be present. The degree to which they approximate a two-group conflict varies and is an empirical question, not a matter of definition.

Finally, Mills retains the interest in consciousness but, again, does not assume that class consciousness is the form that the necessary "quality of mind" must take. The structure of the society is not expressed necessarily as a conflict between two classes; therefore, knowledge of place in history and society cannot be assumed to be class consciousness. It might, rather, take the form of awareness of membership in a differently defined interest group. For example, the development of awareness among law enforcement officials that the law could be tailored to meet their own interests is not class consciousness.

THREE THEMES IN CONFLICT THEORY

In the discussion of conflict theories, we will emphasize three themes, already indicated in the context of Mills's theory of power elites and common in the other theories we will summarize.

Social Structure

To Marx, the basic social structure of society and its future development were already specified. Society would take the form of two classes that would be redefined in episodically violent conflict until class structure was eliminated. The direction and outcome of change was specified in all but detail. However, when the basis of power and domination is opened to empirical investigation and the course of change no longer predicted, questions about the structure of society, the means of domination, the distribution of power, and the consequences of various structures are raised.

Regularities of Conflict

In Marx's formulation, this theme is virtually the same as the first. But once a variety of power bases and a variety of groups holding gradations of power are recognized, the question is raised whether there are regularities in the exercise of power, whether specific advantaged groups are mobilized in their own interests, whether the consequences of attempting to mobilize power in various ways differ, and so on.

Studies by Pampel and Williamson (1988) and Pampel, Williamson, and Stryke (1990) demonstrate the interaction among demographic factors, societal means of resolving political disputes, and mobilization of specific groups within a single type of social structure—advanced industrial democracies. Pampel and Williamson (1988) argue that welfare spending is increased in modern democracies by demographic factors affecting the number eligible, by the interests and resources of groups competing for available funds, and by political interest group activity and voting. Within the structural environment of private ownership and democratic forms of government, the activity of interest groups creates a sufficient basis of power to influence the policies governing distribution of welfare funds. Given an elastic, but real, limit on overall spending linked to the political realities, the diverse groups seeking aid are in competition with one another. Perhaps in a more thorough study of the political process, we would find that the conflict and its outcome are manipulated by more powerful elites. But the virtue of analysis in terms of interest groups, differently aware and differently active, is to reveal the importance of the interaction among several factors and the effects of success by one group on the lives of others. In effect, this competition sets disadvantaged groups against one another, results in their exploitation of one another, and whether this is orchestrated or not, prevents the sort of broader awareness that could result in a more equitable arrangement.

Pampel and Williamson (1988) found that as the percentage of elderly people in the population increases, spending on pensions rises. Partly this is a demographic effect. If a benefit is provided for everyone over 65, for example, as the proportion of people in that age category rises, the overall spending will rise. However, the rise in spending was greater than would be predicted simply from the increasing number of people eligible. Pampel and Williamson took this as evidence that political activity and voting resulted in additional increases. The administrative procedures or policies governing the funds must have been altered to the benefit of the elderly due to this activity.

Hurd (1989) reports that for the first time in our history, the elderly are not worse off financially than the rest of the population and may be better off. Hurd links this change in status to increases in social security, Medicare, and Medicaid benefits. In fact, current recipients are receiving much more in benefits than they put in under earlier rules. Of course, unless the rules are altered again, the discrepancy will be reduced for later recipients who will put in payments and take out benefits under the same rules. In the meantime, in the process of redressing a historical problem, the politically active group has achieved a windfall of sorts in the transition.

Pampel, Williamson, and Stryker (1990) found that the nature of the political institutional arrangements to set policy gives advantages to some groups over others. Some of the advanced industrial democracies have societal-level policy negotiations by officially sanctioned organizational representatives of business and labor. This sort of arrangement tends to reinforce the class structure by giving an official role in setting policy to representatives who differ along class lines. Where this arrangement exists, influence of the aged, as an interest group, is diminished, as is pension spending. We should hypothesize that nonorganized labor would also be disadvantaged in such arrangements, because the representatives of that class will be chosen from labor organizations. If racism, ethnic biases, or sexism exist in a country, this way of setting policy should disadvantage the subordinate race, gender, or ethnic group.

This brief case study of social programs for the elderly incorporates a great many aspects of the workings of power and conflict. First, the study recognizes broad structural conditions that are parametric to the political conflicts and processes being studied. These technological, political, and economic parameters, the institutions of advanced industrial democracies, we believe, are greatly influenced by the operation of very powerful elites, perhaps even a class in the technical sense. But within this framework we observe bases of power, other than class membership, and patterns of relative advantage. We see that sufficient power can be mobilized to redress relative disadvantage, in this case the historical pattern of poverty among the elderly. Perhaps, the short-term windfall to the elderly who paid premiums under older rules and receive benefits under newer ones indicates a small domination achieved through that power. We see on a societal scale that differential access to institutionalized policy-making procedures results in patterns of advantage and disadvantage. Further study would indicate whether powerful elites orchestrate and manipulate these political conflicts as well as maintain broad structural parameters. Perhaps, too, the mere fact that power bases are turned against one another rather than against the institutional parameters themselves is sufficient, and the outcome of these struggles may be irrelevant to the maintenance of those parameters. Regularities in conflict or the exercise of power within the structural parameters of societies is a crucial topic as well as the conflict on a historical scale that results in the development, change, and stability of those structural parameters. The processes involved in the two types of conflict may be the same, except for scale.

Mind or Agency

The scope and importance of the issue of mind or agency has expanded enormously. Originally, the issue was raised as a matter of class consciousness—awareness of one's class and its collective interest. Later, in formulations such as Mills's "quality of mind," the concept was expanded to a general appreciation of one's historical place, corresponding to the expanded idea of bases of power. In both versions, ways of thinking were conceived in terms of the characteristics common to members of a group. The dominant group was conceived to think in a different way, one that was superior with respect to mobilizing its resources.

Kohn et al. (1990) provide evidence that patterns of dominance in a society are reflected in cognitive functioning, whether the domination is based on ownership or not. They used the term *class* but broadened it to include control over the labor of others and control in the sense of directing one's own work rather than being directed by others. Three societies were studied—the United States, a Western capitalist country; Japan, a non Western capitalist country; and Poland, a socialist state. Kohn et al. were interested in whether the sort of domination defined would have similar consequences in diverse structural environments and whether they could be differentiated from the consequences of stratification. Stratification is indexed by education, occupational status, and income and has consistent consequences in all industrial countries.

Within each country, job classifications were evaluated in terms of ownership and control over means of production and the labor of others. A typology of "class" was then constructed for each country in its own terms. Class position was found to be highly correlated with, but distinct from, position defined by stratification indices. Advantage in society increases the value placed on self-direction for children, intellectual flexibility, and self-direction in psychological orientation whether defined by stratification or class membership. However, when class position was controlled, the effect of stratification was much reduced. That is, material advantage has an effect, but most of the effects on cognitive functioning come from class or dominance differences. People who direct themselves and control others, elites, think differently than those they control, regardless of the basis of their power.

The manner of thinking about interests was embedded in a still broader concern with the culture of each group—in modern terms, its subcultural variation relative to other groups in the society. The subculture was implicated in the maintenance of the groups' positions in society, for good or ill. Thus, for example, Oscar Lewis (1965) reports on the culture of poverty, which transcends regional, urban–rural, and national differences. The culture of poverty includes family structure, nature of kinship ties, familial relations, time orientation, value systems, spending patterns, and sense of community. Decisions made within this culture tend to preserve the culture and membership in it, just as the decisions made by elites preserve advantage and the elite culture. We see then, that even though the outcome of conflict is dominance of some groups by others, the coercion is limited. The culture of the dominated groups leads their members to make choices that voluntarily contribute to their domination.

In the most general formulations, the issue is expanded still further to the nature agency or the ability to make choices and the relationship between agency and the social structure. In Mills's terms, we are looking for regularities in the operation of fate, the cumulative impact of many small decisions, even when those regularities are not coordinated or intentional. The assumption that social structure determines or even strongly constrains choice and interaction has also been questioned. In some cases, the structure is seen to depend upon the pattern of choices as well to constrain it.

NOTES

1. Mills (1959) treats norms as a part of the structurally encouraged ignorance of subordinate groups in a mass society. They are a problem, among others, to be resolved by increased consciousness of one's place in history. Giddens (1984) treats norms as the product of ongoing social microprocesses. The body of norms does not exist in his approach, except as constructed in particular interactions, and the constructed norms have a very different causal role than in Parsons's approach. Collins (1975, 1981) substitutes consensus on ameliorative interaction rituals for normative consensus. Merton (1957) denies consensus on values and interests. He argues that the distribution of structural resources stabilizes conduct without consensus. We will return to these approaches to this theoretical problem at length later. There are others, as well, but they will not be considered systematically.

2. An excellent summary of Marx's position and of the theoretical and empirical issues involved in social class is found in Lipset (1968).

3. As we will see in the discussion of role theories, conflict extends to the definition of tasks and to the degree that they will be done as technologically required. Thus, although technology and social relations appear in various combinations, it is not clear that the combinations work equally well. Human nature is quite malleable, but we never have the luxury of starting from scratch in molding one another and there may be evolutionary parameters as well.

4. The ruinous inefficiencies within the Soviet bloc may be a case in point. The failed attempt of the Nazis to extract forced labor from various groups prior to their extermination is another.

REFERENCES

Chambliss, William. 1965. A Sociological Analysis of the Law of Vagrancy. *Social Problems* 12:67–77.

Chambliss, William. 1973. Elites and the Creation of Criminal Law. Pp. 430–444 in William Chambliss (ed.), Sociological Readings in the Conflict Perspective. Reading, MA: Addison-Wesley.

Collins, Randall. 1975. Conflict Sociology. New York: Academic Press.

Collins, Randall. 1981. The Microfoundations of Macrosociology. *American Journal of Sociology* 86:984–1014.

Dahrendorf, Ralf. 1974. Toward a Theory of Social Conflict. Pp. 324–341 in R. Denisoff, Orel Callahan, and Mark Levine (eds.), Theories and Paradigms in Contemporary Sociology. Itasca, IL: Peacock.

Gibbs, Jack. 1965. Norms: The Problem of Definition and Classification. *American Journal of Sociology* 70:586–594.

Gibbs, Jack. 1966. Sanctions. *Social Problems* 14:147–159.

Giddens, Anthony. 1984. The Constitution of Society. Berkeley: University of California Press.

Hurd, Michael. 1989. The Economic Status of the Elderly. *Science* 244:659–663.

Kohn, Melvin, Atsushi Naoi, Carrie Schoenbach, Carmi Schooler, and Kazimierz Slomczynski. 1990. Class Structure and Psychological Functioning in the United States, Japan, and Poland. *American Journal of Sociology* 95:964–1009.

Lewis, Oscar. 1965. Five Families. New York: Mentor.

Lipset, Seymour. 1968. Social Class. Pp. 296–316 in David Sills (ed.), International Encyclopedia of the Social Sciences, Vol. 15. New York: Free Press.

Mills, C. Wright. 1959. The Power Elite. New York: Oxford University Press.

Mills, C. Wright. 1961. The Sociological Imagination. New York: Grove Press.

Pampel, Fred, and John Williamson. 1988. Welfare Spending in Advanced Industrial Democracies, 1950–1980. *American Journal of Sociology* 93:1424–1456.

Pampel, Fred, John Williamson, and Robin Stryker. 1990. Class Context and Pension Response to Demographic Structure in Advanced Industrial Democracies. *Social Problems* 37:535–550.

5

Transitional Conflict Theories

HISTORICAL PATTERN OF STABILITY AND CHANGE

The image of society underlying conflict theories includes ubiquitous change, but this does not imply that the change occurs at a constant rate or that the changes occurring at various times are equally significant to the structure of society and the lives of the people in it. The task of a theory of social change is not just to conceptualize change generically, but also to account for the patterns of change and stability that have actually occurred.

Teggart (1972)[1] argues that from the development of teleological explanations in the Socratic period until the mid-nineteenth century, change was addressed primarily as progress. Progress as a doctrine of the nature of change included the idea that social change has been in the direction of an advanced and knowable end-state. The progression from primitive to more advanced forms of civilization was conceived to occur through a fixed, natural sequence of stages. Existing societies were thought to represent different stages of development and comparisons among them were made to attempt to define the sequence through which all of them were passing, including hypotheses about their future course and often the scientific principles governing the sequence. The idea of progress also generally included a doctrine of gradual cumulative change through those stages.

The most scientifically influential example of a theory of progressive change has been Darwin's theory of evolution. Teggart's (1972) criticism of Darwin is especially interesting for two reasons, even though Darwin was not a social theorist. First, Teggart's criticism has been influential in recent developments in biological theory (see Eldridge, 1985). Second, it is an instructive example of the problems that arise when an interpretation is upheld on doctrinal grounds when the evidence does not support it.

Darwin assumed that evolution had a natural end-state, fitness, and that the development of species was the result of small changes accumulating over very long periods of time. The fossil record, which provides the data for studies of evolutionary change, is extremely incomplete and contains enormous gaps. The actual fossil record indicates long periods of time during which fossil forms remain the same, episodically interrupted by the sudden appearance of new forms. Defining the pattern of change requires an interpretation of the gaps, of what occurs in the periods for which there are no records. This methodological problem is identical to the lack of comparable records of various societies, especially in past epochs of developed and nonliterate societies. Darwin was aware of these gaps. He asserted the doctrine *natura non facit saltum*— nature makes no leaps—and interpreted the gaps as obscuring the orderly gradual change that he believed must have occurred.

Many of Darwin's critics within the scientific community accepted the general idea of evolution, but they argued that the process was more fitful than orderly and gradual. They held that species remain stable for long periods of time, now reckoned in hundreds of millions of years in some cases, and change rapidly when change does occur. During the periods of stability, adjustments occur within definable limits (cf., Eldridge, 1985). Thus, the modern evolutionary theory of change recognizes forces for stability as well as for change. The pattern it observes is a *punctuated equilibrium*—long periods during which negligible change occurs, punctuated by relatively brief periods of rapid change.

Teggart argues that historical social change displays the same pattern of stable periods punctuated by periods of rapid change, although much shorter in duration than the periods of time involved in biological evolution. He did not attribute the failure to appreciate this pattern to the deficiencies or gaps in the evidence. Rather, he saw the problem as the rigid adherence to interpretation of the record in terms of a doctrine of steady progress.

Teggart argued that there are multiple processes involved in the pattern of historical change and stability. He saw the creativity and intelligence of human beings as the origin of new forms of social life, but he argued that the impact of human creativity depended on existing social conditions. When these are stable, the life experience of an individual will occur within one cultural frame that will, in effect, dominate the individual's thought. The change possible through creative thought within one unchallenged framework will not profoundly modify the culture and structure of the society. On the other hand, historical events may occur that liberate the individual from his culture. Although he was not a conflict theorist, Teggart cited conflict as the essential liberating condition.

Teggart acknowledges that exposure to the conflict necessary to liberate thought patterns may occur in various ways, but he observes that exposure has historically resulted from migration and the collision of peoples with different culture bases. Migration itself is linked to a crisis of scarce resources. This contact, and the availability of conflicting idea systems to human intelligence releases the members of each group from the authority of their system of thought and in this context, new idea systems can be developed. Technological changes also confront societies and the individuals in them with ideas that contradict established ways of doing things.

Teggart viewed existing culture as a profoundly conservative force that operated by fixing ideas in action and reducing the raw materials for ever present creativity. He argued that episodes of rapid change occurred when this force was overcome and people were released by the presence of contradictory ideas. Rose Coser (1975) argued that the sheer complexity of modern life produced autonomy without necessarily confronting people with two conflicting cultures. This liberating effect occurs in several ways—the imposition of complex choices and the division of life into relatively separate spheres (e.g., home and work), creating both privacy with its freedom from social sanctions and inconsistent demands (a type of conflict) in the separate spheres. When the two arguments are combined, we can see that a crucial cognitive condition for release from authority is always met within modern societies, and we are directed to the process by which culture exerts its conservative force, even in the presence of conflict.

COSER'S TRANSITIONAL THEORY OF CONFLICT

Lewis Coser (1967) addressed conflict as a regular feature of social life and attempted to specify its functions with respect to both change and stability. His work is an explicit effort to utilize the method of functional analysis in a conflict theoretic framework. Conflicts of interests and values, and contradictions among alternatives existing within a culture, are recognized to be ubiquitous and to be expressed in the history of the society in a variety of ways. These modes of expression are conditioned by structural conditions, and each has its distinctive consequences.

Types of Change and Control Systems

Coser distinguishes between change *within* a system and change *of* a system in essentially the same way as Parsons. Changes *of* a system are profound, deep changes that result in the emergence of new systems following the destruction of the old. The transition from agricultural to industrial society is an example. Change *within* a system is perpetual slow change occurring in even the most static society. Periods of change *within* a system, correspond to Teggart's periods of stability, because changes of historical magnitude would be, in Coser's terms, a change *of* system. The development of a tourist industry by the Amish to supplement agriculture without basic changes in their way of life is an example of change *within* a system.

Assuming the ubiquity of conflict but varying patterns of change, Coser argues that structural conditions in the society determine whether conflict will result in change *of* the system or change *within* the system. In some cases, conflict may even serve to balance and preserve existing arrangements. In sharp contrast to Parsons, Coser attempts to address both changes *within* systems and changes *of* system in a unified conceptual framework. Parsons's argument that separate theories are required for these two explanations and that each of the theories can be developed without consideration of the other is rejected.

Coser argues that conflicts of interest and values or conflicts between interest groups prevent stagnation and preserve vitality. They prevent accommodations and habitual arrangements from stifling creativity. Coser accepts John Dewey's (1957) principle that conflict is required for creativity and reflection at the individual level. Applied to the social level, Coser argues that conflicts, through the human creativity they provoke or release, result in new norms and institutions. These may be essential to flexible responses.

Coser conceives of change *of* a system and change *within* a system as extremes of a continuum. The difference between the two is the extent of change rather than a qualitative difference of type or underlying process. The crucial structural variable that determines the degree of change is, in Coser's view, the rigidity of the control mechanisms of the society. Rigid systems suppress mild forms of change and adjustment and exert pressure toward radical cleavages and violent forms of conflict.

More flexible systems allow adjustments and shifting balances of power within the basic existing framework. It is not always clear whether changes should be classified as *within* or *of* a system.

An ambiguous case: The role of housewife. Glenna Matthews's (1987) history of changes in the role of the housewife is such an ambiguous case. During the colonial and revolutionary periods, the home was the locus of production in our society. People utilized more homemade instead of purchased goods, and production for commerce centered on farming and crafts performed at home. Economically, both men's and women's roles were home-centered. Chores were accepted in a matter-of-fact way, without identity implications. On the other hand, the home itself had a patriarchal authority structure and there was a strict division of chores by gender. In addition, men were connected politically to the external world, but women had no political role and were unconnected to the world outside the home.

The revolutionary war and the political philosophy of the new republic gave new importance to the home and gave women a role in external politics. First, the economic boycott of many British goods turned everyday household purchases into political statements. Women, who made these purchases, were thereby involved in the politics of revolution. Second, the philosophy of republican government required an educated citizenry. As a result, the education of children acquired political importance, and the home was conceived as the center of culture. Through raising children, women came to be regarded as the center of moral authority in the society. A cult of domesticity developed in which crafts as well as direct political education came to be highly valued. Even domestic arrangements, such as mealtimes, were conceived as opportunities to educate the children in terms of societal values such as civility and punctuality.

In some respects, the place of women in society was transformed. Their traditional role was invested with new and important meaning and their contribution to society became highly valued. To be a successful housewife, accomplished in crafts and child raising became a valued identity. On the other hand, women were still confined to their traditional chores and lacked suffrage and many property rights. How thorough was that change in the family system? With industrialization, men began to work out of the home, a large change in daily life, but patriarchy persisted. How do we assess that pattern of change and stability?

By the end of the Civil War, the women's movement was focused on suffrage and property rights and had separated itself from other social movements such as abolition when freed male slaves, but not women, were granted suffrage. As a result of economic changes, the interest in domesticity and the value placed on it also declined.

The economy came to be increasingly dominated by monopolies and professional organizations, undermining the ideal of individual self-determination. The power of the moral authority of the home seemed inadequate as a defense against a rapacious economic order. In addition, the way in which the middle class used household help changed. Available servants were primarily impoverished immigrants, typically unfamiliar with household tasks and standards. Although some training was done, more and more tasks were accomplished by appliances and technology—woodstoves instead of open hearths, sewing machines, refrigeration, indoor plumbing, canned foods. The middle-class housewife became more involved in doing chores herself, using labor-saving devices, rather than having them done by servants. The labor saved was not the housewife's—she did more—and the work was diminished in skill. Chores, not crafts, prevailed.

The Progressive movement further undermined the status of housewives near the beginning of the twentieth century. Home economics was established as a scientific discipline. The founders of the movement believed they were establishing a beachhead for women in science by creating a new discipline from which women were not excluded. However, the expertise of the home economist was promoted by attacking the expertise of the housewife. Traditional standards and practices were attacked and respect for the craft tradition and for unaided raising of children was shattered. World War I gave a major impetus to this trend. Food shortages required changes of diet and the traditions and knowledge of the home were no longer applicable. One cannot cook what one cannot buy and traditional diets and the knowledge that sustained them became less valued.

As a result of this series of changes and the secularization of the society, the home was devalued as a center of moral authority. The perceived skill of homemaking was reduced. The craft tradition was devalued. However, although the identification of women with their household role was not changed, the identification had become a negative one.

It is a matter of historical interpretation whether these epochal changes were changes *of* the family system or *within* it. Many women, of course, have been moving into other political and economic roles outside the home. The isolation of the housewife no longer equivalent to the isolation of all women. We have seen that the value placed on the housewife's role and the understanding of its political and economic implications have changed. On the other hand, many important aspects of the role have survived new technologies and value systems. This same ambiguity applies to interpreting the degree of change to the overall system. Many economic and technological changes have occurred, along with considerable reallocations of power. However, the reallocations of power have not included a breakdown of patriarchy.

In Coser's theory, this ambiguity in labeling the two types of change is not too problematic because he views the difference as a matter of degree. The nature of the change and its quantitative extent can be studied amid disagreement in the qualitative judgment concerning exactly how much change is required to constitute a change of system. The processes involved are the same. In other theories, however, in which the two kinds of change are considered different in kind, the methodological issues involved in naming the type of change is extremely important.

Termination of Conflict

In Coser's view (1967), termination of conflict is also related to structural conditions under which the conflict occurs. Absolute conflict is terminated only when at least one of the antagonists is completely destroyed. Conflict can be terminated prior to this destructive extreme if it occurs in the context of regulatory agreements. Sometimes, the antagonists agree on a terminal point that defines victory. When that point is reached, victory and defeat are recognized by both sides and conflict is terminated. Sometimes, definition of victory does not exist prior to the conflict. The status of the two sides, especially estimates of their ability to continue, may then be quite ambiguous during the conflict. Sometimes, a group will suffer damage because it is unable to recognize that it has lost. At other times, the ambiguity will allow compromise because neither side will feel confident enough to continue the conflict. In all cases, the manipulation of symbols is essential to the termination of conflict short of the total annihilation of one side.

Violence

Violence, one form in which conflict may be expressed, is singled out for analysis. Coser argues that although violence is destructive in the short run, it may have long-term favorable consequences for the system in which it occurs. First, violence may be the only means of political expression and action available to groups that have been denied access to nonviolent legitimate political mechanisms. In such cases, violence can begin a process by which excluded groups enter the political life of a society. Related to this, the appearance of violence serves as a warning symbol of important systemic problems. That is, violent actions that are unsuccessful in taking power by force may alert powerful groups that other steps need to be taken to deal with the interests of the violent group. When violence is initiated by agents of control, it may provoke outrage and insistence by segments of the society that other means be found.

The Communist Bloc: A Case Study

Coser discusses the relationships among nations within the Communist bloc as an example of conflict between parts of a larger whole. Coser conceived of the relationship between the Soviet Union and its satellites as one of domination by rigid and forceful means of control. He argues that changes within the satellites themselves altered conditions so that the means of dominance were no longer adequate. Thus, he foresaw (by 1967) the breakup of the Soviet bloc. This successful application to a complex empirical case lends credence to his method of analysis and conceptual scheme.

Nationalism. The first factor leading to the breakup of the Soviet bloc was, in Coser's view, the persistence of nationalism. Communist ideology included the belief that nationalism would fade as an important force due to the standardizing effects of participation in global political and economic networks. Within the bloc, it was assumed that fraternal ties, organized within an international socialist framework, would reduce national forces to insignificance. When Stalin achieved power over the satellites, he believed that they could be brought into the same relationship to the centralized power of the Kremlin as the republics in the USSR.[2] Heads of state in the satellites and top party officials were nominally independent. However, they were installed by Soviet means and received resources from the Soviets for the reconstruction of their countries after World War II.

The bloc remained coherent for a time. However, as the economic and political life of these countries returned to a degree of normalcy, national and separatist tendencies emerged in all of them. Coser (1967:232) characterized a centralized Soviet empire in Eastern Europe as a pipe dream. He anticipated a possible drift toward a series of federated national states following divergent paths toward development. This may yet occur. However, in line with Coser's theory, the last 25 years before the breakup had been characterized by very rigid attempts to suppress the conflict between national forces and international communism.[3] The result may have been a more drastic change than might have occurred if conflicts had been managed flexibly.

In addition to the conflicts that characterized relations between the Soviet Union and the Eastern European bloc, the conflict between the Soviet Union and China was also fueled by the differences in their stages of development. China has not yet industrialized. The population must be induced to extraordinary efforts to accumulate the resources necessary to begin rapid industrial growth. In China, the traditional nationalism, isolationism, and mistrust of the West are combined with communist ideas to motivate the population. China had not only expressed distance from the Soviet Union, as well as the rest of the West, but also claimed leadership of the communist movement for itself. In the long run, this may be credible as resources grow; in the short run, it is a potent motivating ideology. Thus, as Coser analyzed the communist bloc, nationalism was a potent disruptive force in all cases, but it was expressed differently in different countries due to historical circumstances and structural conditions.

Size.   Modern means of communication and transportation have expanded the possibility of central control. For a time, Coser argued, it seemed that this kind of control could be enlarged indefinitely. However, this turned out not to be true. As the size of an organization and the number of elements in it increase beyond certain limits, reorganization becomes necessary and centralized decision making becomes increasingly ineffective. Coser argues that although forces in the Soviet satellites and in China became less willing to be controlled, there was a simultaneous loss of effectiveness in control due to the increased size of the organization.

I should like to add an observation about modern electronic communication media. When they were first developed, they were expensive and available only to central governments and to the largest corporations. Their utility in propaganda, domination through increased efficiency of disseminating messages, and monopoly control over communication channels was frightening. Our predictions of their consequences emphasized their potential for domination as centralized, monopolized tools of elites in mass society. They were regarded as tools of centralization, as reflected in the work of Mills and Coser. However, as they have become less expensive and more widely available, their decentralizing potential has also become apparent. Anybody, anywhere can communicate globally, process information, and so on. The consequences do not follow from the technology per se but rather by its relationship and application to the conflicts within the society.

Transition

Coser views social conflict in all its forms of expression as a ubiquitous social regularity to be subjected to functional analysis. Structural conditions determine whether change resulting from the conflict will be profound or trivial, whether the expression of conflict will be violent, how the conflict will be terminated, and so on. Various consequences are considered. Coser's form of argument is sociological in both its attention to the implications of social structure and its utilization of functional analysis, a codification of a methodology for studying social structure and its implications.

However, when we consider measurement, Coser's approach resembles historical interpretation more than modern sociology. The key variables are not operationally defined. That is, there are no specifications for how societies or historical epochs are to be categorized or measured in terms of the variables. The specific dimensions of "rigidity of control" are not made explicit. The distinction between change *of* system and change *within* system is not clear-cut. The concept is straightforward enough to be applied to major historical events and truly trivial change. But in the middle ranges of the continuum, application is difficult.

This methodological issue arises when we take a historical perspective and attempt to consider different societies and epochs in a common framework. Within a systems approach, such as Parsons's, each society or epoch is treated in its own terms. The practical problem of creating indexes appropriate for each society is present, of course, but there is little need to relate one set of indices to another. We see in Coser's approach the application of sociological reasoning and theoretical interests to historical problems. The measurement technique in his case studies is historical interpretation. Conceptually, "rigidity of social control" can be applied to any historical epoch or society. However, to measure it, we must make an overall detailed assessment of the society or epoch in the historical manner.

The difficulties inherent in the measurement of sociological variables in a variety of historical contexts do not have a general solution. Different indexes of the same underlying variable may be required in each society or epoch, raising many questions of validity. The study by Kohn et al. (1990), reviewed earlier, is an example of a successful resolution of the problems of measuring the variable "self-direction at work" in three countries during one historical epoch. Separate indices were developed in each country studied and the validity of the concept was established, at least in contrast to stratification measures. Of course, the study of a larger sample of countries or epochs would require the development of indices particular to each for each variable. Coser's approach allows historical methods to be used while the practical problems of applying sociological measurement techniques are being, if not mastered, at least managed.

DAHRENDORF'S MIDDLE-RANGE THEORY OF CONFLICT

Dahrendorf's (1958, 1968) discussions of social conflict mark an important stage in the transition of dominance from functionalist to conflict imagery of society. Initially, functionalist theory was criticized for being incomplete and for omitting various topics. The early critical theoretical statements were directed to supplementing functionalist thought, rather than replacing it. It was only later that the idea of a general theory of society developed from consistent conflict theory principles gained influence. Dahrendorf's theory of conflict is an explicitly middle-range theory of conflict and change, designed to supplement a separate theory of integration.

Range and Tasks of Conflict Theory

After explicating the contrasting essential imagery of structural functional and conflict theories, Dahrendorf observed that the two are not logically contradictory. That is, it is possible for a society to be stable and changing at the same time, so long as the stability is not absolute nor the change total. Similarly, society can include elements of coercion and of voluntary compliance. Dahrendorf (1958) regards the two images as reflecting equally valid aspects of every conceivable society. Both, he argues, are necessary to a description of society and might be incorporated in a more general theory. But in the absence of such a theory, he argues that the double aspect of society must be respected theoretically by adopting the more fruitful imagery for each question addressed. His criticism of structural functionalism is that it is not a general theory. Within its appropriate range of application, he explicitly accepted it as a theory of integration. By the same token, he recognized that his theory of conflict and change was not a general theory of society.

Within the general imagery of change and conflict, Dahrendorf specifies specific tasks for conflict theorists. Conflict theorists stress the coercive and dysfunctional aspects of existing social structures; therefore, the origin of conflict and change is sought in the structure of society itself. He argues that the structural origins of conflict can only be understood if the conflicts can be characterized as struggles among groups within the society. Thus, conflict theory becomes the structural analysis of conflicting groups. Dahrendorf identifies the origin of these groups, the forms of struggle among them, and the process by which group conflict effects change as the specific interests of conflict theory.

Dominance and Conflict

In every social organization, Dahrendorf argues, the occupants of some positions have powers of command over the occupants of other positions in some circumstances. Therefore, every social organization is, in part, an imperatively coordinated association. The structural basis of conflict is to be found in these relationships of unequal power. In contrast to such values as income or prestige, dominance is not distributed in continual gradations. Rather, a dichotomy exists between those who dominate and those who are dominated. Within the dominant group, there are differentiations representing a division of the work of command. The process of conflict and change begins with an integrated system and includes several steps, each determined by structural conditions.

1. Those people holding dominant positions and those holding subordinate positions constitute quasi-groups with opposing latent interests in the preservation of the dominance relations. It is in the interests of those with power to preserve the system of dominance relationships. It is in the interests of their subordinates to alter the system of dominance relations. These groups, whose opposing interests are implied by the structure of dominance are quasi-groups when they are organized, but they are merely an aggregate of people in similar positions when they are not. The interests are latent when the individuals are not conscious of them.

2. The quasi-groups organize themselves into interest groups such as labor unions or political parties with manifest interests. Conditions of organization intervene in this step.

Dahrendorf divides the conditions of organization into three types. *Social conditions of organization* include the means of communication available within the quasi-group and the manner of recruitment into it. *Political conditions of organization* must be met for an organized interest group to form. Most important is the right to form coalitions. *Technical conditions of organization* include material means, a founder, a leader, and an ideology or expression of interests.

3. Interest groups are in constant conflict in pursuit of their divergent interests. Conditions of conflict determine the form and intensity of the conflict. *Conditions of conflict* include the degree of social mobility and the presence of mechanisms for regulating conflicts.

4. The conflict leads to changes in the structure of social relations. The kind, speed, and depth of change are determined by conditions of structural change. *Conditions of structural change* include the ability of

leaders to retain power and the degree of pressure that can be exerted by the subordinate group.

Dahrendorf's discussion of social conflict suggests that the relationship between the organization of interest groups and social change is complex and somewhat different than we might have expected without the theory. In Dahrendorf's view, the greater the failure to meet the conditions of organization, the more intense and violent the conflict will be. In addition, when the minimal conditions for forming conflict groups have been met, the ability of the group to develop regulatory agreement varies inversely with violence of conflict (e.g., a union strike as opposed to a wildcat strike). The intensity of the conflict varies directly with the amount of structural change it will generate. The violence of conflict varies directly with the speed of structural change. We must conclude then that forming interest groups and organizing the attempts to bring about structural change actually slow down the pace of change and reduce the amount of change achieved.

This conclusion, of course, only refers to structural changes in the society, the kinds of changes that Coser calls changes *of* system. The ability of groups to organize in pursuit of their interests within a system leads to stability *of* the system. This tells us that the inability of interest groups to form is an important component of rigidity in control systems. It also indicates that the power of interest groups to initiate change within a system is not taken only from more powerful interests, but at least in part by transforming their constituencies' power. With respect to changes *of* a system, the most potent force is randomness—unorganized, violent conflict initiated by uncoordinated members of the system.

Consensus and Integration

In his acceptance of structural functionalism as a theory of integration, Dahrendorf (e.g., 1968) equated human society with the regulation of conduct by norms. The application of sanctions to enforce the norms was seen as the intersection of the divergent interests of conflict theorists and structural functionalists—of the use of power and voluntary compliance. This acceptance of norms as the basis of integration clearly defined the task facing conflict theorists who attempt to develop a unified theory of change and stability on consistent principles. Norms must be replaced as the organizing principle in society. Norms are present implicitly and explicitly in the conduct of members of society. However, voluntary compliance with consensually held norms must not be an explanatory principle. Much of conflict theory has been concerned with extending conflict principles to the study of integration and specifically with norms.

In this context, Anthony Wallace's (1961:31–39) proof that cognitive consensus is not required for societal integration is worthy of review. Wallace considers ritualized or routinized exchanges among members of a society. He raises the question of what each participant must know to successfully participate in the routine. Essentially, must they all know the same things? He demonstrates formally that they need not. A variety of cognitive maps are adequate to maintain rituals. For example, parent and child can engage in the "tooth fairy ritual" while the child believes in the fairy and the parent does not. As the child grows, she can continue in the ritual while no longer believing in the fairy. The parents may or may not know accurately whether the child believes in the fairy. As a result, sometimes the child and sometimes the parent will have the more accurate map of the overall situation. All that is required for successful participation is knowledge of enough contingencies of the ritual to generate the sequence. Many understandings of the situation will work to sustain the sequence.

Formally, the tooth fairy illustration includes all of the elements of Wallace's argument that social life can be based on organized diversity rather than consensus. However, although formally adequate, the illustration lacks any apparent connection to larger problems of social life, and its import may be missed. Two additional illustrations may help clarify why consensus is not necessary to social integration. First, consider interpersonal relationships. These can be begun and sustained for quite lengthy periods and can involve considerable commitment and risk without agreement on the rules underlying them, the worth of the participants, and so on. When people initiate a relationship with the potential for sexuality, in particular, it is common for one to mislead the other about such things as one's past, other commitments, income, state of health and contagion, plans for the future, opinion of the other person, birth control practices and so on. The understandings and strategies of the people involved may be very different. The state of affairs is summed up in the expression "all's fair in love and war." Nonetheless, relationships are formed and sustained, although it is not surprising that so many of them are terminated with so much hurt. What is true of our sexual relationships is only slightly less true of most of our interpersonal lives.

Second, it is possible for us to participate in our highly complex technology with limited and specialized knowledge of how it works. We can, for example, turn on the lights without the slightest idea about how electricity works or the politics of the utility company. In fact, it is clear that in our complex technology, complete knowledge is impossible. This implies that the knowledge bases of individuals must be different. If I am to operate electric appliances without knowledge of how they are made or work, someone else will be required to have that knowledge on my behalf. We will have to interact despite this difference. Wallace, in fact, argues that diversity is necessary, not just possible, in all societies.

Logically, then, there is no reason to assume that stability, predictability, and order are achieved by cognitive or normative consensus. Logically, it is possible to have order without consensus. Lewis (1969) analyzes a useful generic basis for order without consensus, which he calls a conventional order. In Lewis's analysis, each individual must coordinate his conduct with that of others because the success of each person's own plans is contingent upon the conduct of others. Thus, each individual faces a coordination problem—the need to recognize regularities in the social environment and to choose a course of action that will succeed. Each individual's action will become repetitive (habitual or routinized) and, therefore, predictable to others when she perceives that changing the conduct will be less successful, given the expected conduct of others. The system will stabilize to the extent that the individuals remain predictable to one another, and each has adjusted her conduct to the conduct of the others. Once regularities are perceived, the individuals will come to expect others to continue to conform to the established pattern and will enforce the regularity with sanctions. In a perfectly stable system, no one could conceive of a new course of action worth trying, and, therefore, everyone's routine would continue to work. Sanctions add to the cost of trying something new.

Lewis calls these routinized, coordinated patterns of individuals' action *conventions*. The individuals do not necessarily have knowledge of the entire system. Nor do their partial cognitive maps have to be identical. All that is required is that the individuals perceive that changing their own conduct will decrease their success in meeting their own objectives, given the preferences displayed by others. Under these circumstances, individuals will prefer to conform so long as others conform without necessarily agreeing with one another or liking the arrangement. In this model, power applied as sanctions in defense of order could stabilize a system by discouraging the disadvantaged from altering their conduct. In agreement with the explicit conflict models, solidarity and awareness of one's group interest would encourage innovative behavior among disadvantaged groups in a conventional order.

We can conclude, then, that the explanation of stability need not rest on the existence of a moral or cognitive consensus. Mutual dependence among individuals in the pursuit of their own interests can provide a basis for stability. This reopens the question of whether a conflict theory must be supplemented by a separate theory of integration or stability, as well. Whether explicitly combined in one statement, or developed piecemeal in the work of a variety of theorists, integration/stability and conflict/change can be logically accommodated in a single coherent framework.

NOTES

1. Teggart's book is a reissue of two very influential earlier works. The actual publication dates are 1918 (*Processes of History*) and 1925 (*Theory of History*).
2. Coser's analysis refers only to the disintegration of the Soviet bloc by the defection of satellites. However, from the vantage point of 1992, we know that the core republics of the USSR have also abandoned the central communist government. In effect, Stalin was correct. The relationship between the satellites and the central government turned out to be quite similar to the relationship between the core republics and the central government. Both have broken down, and for similar reasons.
3. Coser does not acknowledge religion as an important force in the conflict. This is probably an important substantive omission.

REFERENCES

Coser, Lewis. 1967. Continuities in the Study of Social Conflict. New York: Free Press.

Coser, Rose Laub. 1975. The Complexity of Roles as a Seedbed of Individual Autonomy. Pp. 237–264 in Lewis Coser (ed.), The Idea of Social Structure. New York: Harcourt Brace Jovanovich.

Dahrendorf, Ralf. 1958. Toward a Theory of Social Conflict. *Journal of Conflict Resolution* 2:170–183.

Dahrendorf, Ralf. 1959. Class and Class Conflict in Industrial Society. Stanford: Stanford University Press.

Dahrendorf, Ralf. 1968. Essays in the Theory of Society. Stanford: Stanford University Press.

Dewey, John. 1957. *Human Nature and Conduct.* New York: Modern Library.

Eldredge, Niles. 1985. Time Frames: The Evolution of Punctuated Equilibria. Princeton, NJ: Princeton University Press.

Kohn, Melvin, et al. 1990. Class Structure and Psychological Functioning in the United States, Japan and Poland. *American Journal of Sociology* 95:984–1009.

Lewis, David. 1969. Convention. Cambridge: Harvard University Press.

Matthews, Glenna. 1987. Just a Housewife. New York: Oxford University Press.

Mills, C. Wright. 1959. The Power Elite. New York: Oxford University Press.

Mills, C. Wright. 1961. The Sociological Imagination. New York: Grove Press.

Teggart, Frederick. 1972. Theory and Processes of History. Gloucester: Peter Smith.

Wallace, Anthony. 1961. Culture and Personality. New York: Random House.

6

Conflict Theories
of Integration and Change

Conflict theory has developed in the direction of unified theoretical explanations of stability and change. The emerging theories are not grand ones in the sense of including explanations of all social processes. However, they are considerably broader than theories of change alone and are intended to replace, rather than supplement, specialized theories of stability and integration, especially structural functional ones.

GIDDENS'S THEORY OF STRUCTURATION

Generality and Structure

To understand Giddens's (1984) approach, it will be helpful to reconsider the difference between changes *of* a system and changes *within* a system. To Coser, as we have seen, the difference is one of degree, and there are no criteria for distinguishing between the two. If the difference is one of degree, a firm criterion must be arbitrary, amounting to no more than a line drawn on a scale. For an analogy, consider height. It can be measured as a matter of degree, and it makes good descriptive sense to also distinguish between categories such as "average height" and "tall." It is partially arbitrary where the category boundaries are drawn, but drawing the boundary at 5'3" would be silly. However, the exact placement of the boundary is not dictated and, in fact, can be placed anywhere in a fairly broad range. All that is required for clarity is to indicate where the boundary has been placed so that the definition is known.

But suppose that changes *of* system are qualitative changes. Suppose that a change *of* system transforms all the relationships, routines, distributions of resources, and institutions within the system. In effect, a change *of* system would destroy one system and replace it with a new one. In that case, there would be a discontinuity and a redefinition of the surviving elements of the system. For an analogy, consider race or gender. In otherwise similar biographical circumstances, the difference between being a male or female or between being black or white fundamentally alters how one is expected to act, how one is treated by others, and the opportunities available. Giddens (1984) takes the view that the transition from one historical period to another is a discontinuity, a reorganization.

In this context, we will need to reconsider what sorts of regularities of social life could be universal or necessary, that is, not restricted to the discrete system in which they were recognized. Giddens (1984:343ff.) argues that the regularities existing within any system will not be necessary because they are contingent upon the regularities of thought and habit peculiar to that system. Therefore, different systems will display different regularities, summarized as expressions of different cultures, and none will be universal. For example, physicians in the United States are overwhelmingly male, while in other countries more physicians are female. The regularity within each system, concerning the kind of person found in particular careers, is not a necessary one, not a general law of social life. In fact, our attempts to change any arrangement within the society are based on faith that the arrangement is not necessary. In this, Giddens is in agreement with structural functional theories that consider regularities only within a cultural context.

But Giddens is more thorough in rejecting the possibility of general laws in the social sciences. A law might be based on regularities of unintended consequences and thus not be affected by changes of the culture. For example, the relationship between self-direction at work and values and cognitive style has already been documented (Kohn, et al, 1990) in three countries and might prove to be a general regularity. But Giddens argues that causal relationships are altered by knowledge of the causal relationship (1984:346) Therefore, even when the regularities appear to be independent of culturally based knowledge and potentially general, he argues that if they became manifest they would be changed and lose universality. Lack of knowledge, then, even in all known societies, is an alterable condition and disqualifies the regularity as a general law.

This argument is explicitly intended by Giddens to disqualify any structural regularities as general explanatory principles. This would include Durkheimian arguments of the social factual type[1] and arguments concerning historical structural regularities such as those proposed by many conflict theorists. It is worth noting that the argument rests entirely on the doctrine that knowledge of a regularity alters the regularity in every case. There is no compelling reason to accept that doctrine. One might, in fact, see the doctrine itself as a proposed general law of a paradoxical nature.

Although the primary substantive interests of conflict theory concern the large-scale structure of society, the doctrine that there are no *general* structural laws resolves important difficulties in the conflict approach. First, it provides that no injustice, no maldistribution of power, no fault in society is inevitable. Any regularity can be changed. This disarms political defenses of systems that include the acceptance of necessary evils and critiques of plans that include the idea that certain transformations of society that they require are impossible. Second, it is an implication of another doctrine—that humans enjoy free will in some form. Once the position is taken that the behavior of the human being is not determined by circumstances, that an element of choice or will is involved, one must logically accept that social structural regularities can always be changed by coordinated acts of will.

Free Will: The Actor Who Could Do Otherwise

Much of Giddens's (1984) work is driven neither by empirical results nor by theoretical sociological arguments, but rather by the implications of philosophical doctrines he adopts. The most crucial of these is the doctrine of free will. Giddens (1984:9) adopts the doctrine that the human is an agent. By this he means, among other things, that the individual is responsible for his or her conduct, both morally and in the sense of causing it by exerting power over the environment. It is essential to agency, in Giddens's approach that "the individual could, at any phase in a given sequence of conduct, have acted differently(1984:9)."

Although we experience our conduct in the world as if we are able to make choices, there is no empirical test for whether this is true or not (cf., Dennett, 1984). Our behavior may be fully determined by external and psychological causal factors, which also impose the perception of control. The doctrine of agency or free will has been explicated in a number of ways, each with distinctive provisions and implications.[2] Giddens does not become embroiled in the philosophical issues by offering a detailed explication of the nature of agency, focusing rather on the very common core provision of "being able to do otherwise" and some of its most important implications. The first is that there can be no general causal law governing individual conduct with respect to those behaviors in which agency is implicated. No matter how precisely we identify the causes and no matter how predictable the conduct has been, because of free will, we assert that the actors could always do otherwise. Their behavior is not explained by the law, although it can be described by the law. Changes in the actors' knowledge can always result in changed behavior. In other words, *individual* conduct is not fully determined.

The second implication is that dominance is not complete, but rather it involves willful compliance of the dominated. Giddens (1984:16) asserts that influence, while asymmetrical, is always mutual. Subordinates can always influence their superiors. Although willful, compliance in one's own domination may be misinformed. In general, the coercive power of social structures is undermined. We see again the importance of human mind in social life, now more technically expressed.

Agency, regularity, and culture. The absence of general causal laws does not imply a lack of order in conduct. The agent is generally conceived to be purposive—to have preferences and to exercise his choices in order to achieve goals defined by those preferences. The exercise of will is free in the sense that it is not fully determined, but it is not free in the sense that it is without cost. The actor learns the contingencies linking existing situations, her own options for action within them, and outcomes. These contingencies, insofar as they are orderly themselves, order conduct without removing the element of choice. So long as actors maintain their preferences and their understanding of the contingencies, their behavior will be predictable. However, the regularity is vulnerable to changes of both preference and knowledge of the contingencies. In most versions of agency, real circumstances greatly, but imperfectly, influence the actors' knowledge of the contingencies of choice through evaluation of the consequences of prior choices.

Culture and social structure are special cases of orderly contingencies. Among the contingencies in the world are the actors of others. To the extent that actors define their personal preferences and knowledge of contingencies in terms of the culture, their choices will tend to be coordinated and predictable. This success will tend to reinforce the cultural values and knowledge base as the basis for future decisions. As a result, the culture will tend to reproduce itself through the choices of those who utilize it. This self-reproducing character of cultures is the basis for the success of those explanations that, although not general, apply within a historical epoch. The culture is not a "real" entity, but an organized system of knowledge and values operating through the choices of people. In Giddens's view, the culture exists only in human memory and in its instantiations—his term for the occasions of its use. The core process, then, is not the regularities occurring within one cultural framework. Rather, it is the process of assembling and utilizing versions of the culture in coordination with others—*structuration*, not structure.

Individual choice cannot, however, alter the culture in the sense that sociologists usually mean. I (and you) am free to act contrary to cultural expectations—my own and those expressed to me by others with whom I interact. However, depending on the results, even my own expectations may be strengthened rather than changed and the expectations of others need not be affected at all. My contrary behavior will be an instance of imperfect reproduction of the system, but sociologists refer to change of the culture or the regularities they support as changes in the conduct of many people. Although the culture can be changed only by changes of mind, these must be numerous. This is why doctrines, in addition to free will, are necessary to deny the possibility of general social scientific laws in principle. There may be regularities in the process of coordination (or conflict or control) that are not altered by knowledge of them.

Agency, power, and mutual influence. Giddens (1984:15) utilizes the term *power* to refer to the ability of the actor to intervene in the flow of events. Thus, for example, my ability to tap the keys on the wordprocessor is power in his sense. Usually, sociologists refer to the ability of one person to compel or coerce another to behave against his or her will as power. This more restricted definition is a special case of power in Giddens's sense. Giddens's statements about power should not be taken as competitive or as conflicting with those of other sociologists because they are about a very different subject matter.

The exercise of power in the restrictive sense is a boundary of Giddens's theory. When power is applied, the compelled individual loses his choice and ceases to be an agent with respect to the areas under compulsion. The structuration theory, which assumes agency, does not apply to those cases. Thus, to the extent that power in the narrow sense is implicated in behavior, the structuration theory must be supplemented with another. The boundary and the underlying distinction are clear in cases of straightforward physical constraint. If my children, given their usual free run of our house, play in their rooms, they act as agents, and their conduct tends to replicate the knowledge and values on which it is based. If I lock them in their rooms as a disciplinary measure, they are no longer agents with respect to location. In either case, they are in their rooms, but the implications for future conduct and belief systems are different. The true difficulty with this distinction arises in intermediate cases. Suppose I order my children to their rooms as a disciplinary measure but do not lock the doors. They remain there, but not fully voluntarily. To what extent does a theory assuming agency apply to such intermediate cases? What must be added to it?

Among the agent's powers recognized by Giddens is the ability to influence other agents. It is not clear whether compulsion by the exercise of coercive power should be counted among the means of influence or whether it is different in kind. However, I think it is truer to the notion of agency to distinguish between influences upon the agency of another and removal of that agency. Giddens's discussion of influence focuses almost exclusively on the means for influencing other agents in interaction, especially the dramaturgical devices and negotiating identities outlined by Erving Goffman (discussed in Chapter 8) and the conversational methods proposed by the ethnomethodologists (discussed in Chapter 10). In interaction, the knowledge and value premises held by the actors are confronted with a new situation. Each actor will try to influence the others to act in ways that serve his own preferences and to seek assurances that they will do so.

Giddens's focus on interactional means of influence is principled. He distinguishes between the agent's motivation and purpose for action and her ability to provide discursive reasons for them to others. Conduct, in this view, is a continuous stream. Specific acts are made discrete by attending to them in a way that isolates them as meaningful episodes. That is, the discursive definition is not something that is applied to an already existing act. Rather, discursive attention is an essential element of the act itself, without which it is not an act. The interactional means of influence discussed by Giddens direct the attention of others. By these means, acts are constituted for others as attention constitutes them for the individual. It is crucial to note that the continuous stream of conduct occurs independent of the application of discursive attention that constitutes acts. The organization of that stream of conduct requires a separate theory and imposes limits on the actors' ability to do otherwise, except in the sense of redescribing conduct that they cannot actually alter.

Action and external contingent outcomes. In Giddens's approach, the knowledge and values underlying action reproduce themselves in and through that action. They are the culture but exist only in instances of use rather than as an external coercive force. In everyday experience, this culture is perceived as an external reality—a parameter for decisions—and people are not aware that it is constituted only in their actions. Constituting the society or its culture is a latent consequence of action.

Giddens explicitly attributes such latent consequences to acts, as opposed to nonaction behavior, even though they are not expressly constituted. He argues that latent consequences feed back into action as unacknowledged conditions. Thus the success of actions constituted in a given way will result in the replication of conditions that are not recognized. This argument is similar to Wallace's formal argument that many different perceptions of a system of relationships and routines are adequate for participation in the system, and for the maintenance of the system.

However, not every consequence to which an act can be linked retrospectively (in hindsight) is attributed to that act. The principle applied by Giddens is whether a resulting occurrence "depended on too many other other contingent outcomes for them to be something the original actor 'did' " (1984:11). Giddens illustrates this boundary with a hypothetical case. A homeowner turns on the lights, alarming a prowler who flees, is caught by a policeman, and is placed in jail for a year. Even though none of the elements in the sequence might have occurred without the lights being put on, Giddens would call turning on the light and "probably also alerting the prowler" things the person did. He would not, however, call causing the prowler to get caught or placed in jail things the person did.

This principle defines another boundary of Giddens's theory. There are consequential and orderly events occurring that cannot be attributed as consequences to acts in the sense required for this theory, even when the acts are necessary for their occurrence. There are too many other factors contributing to the occurrence for them to be constituted in and through the act. The arrest and imprisonment of burglars, as a societal routine practice, is not constituted or replicated by the knowledge base underlying turning on the lights. This distinction is related to fate in Mills's sense.

The issue to be considered is what this principle excludes from explanation in terms of agency alone. Personally, I think that lighting a room by flicking a switch is dependent upon a great many other contingent outcomes. I believe that it is correct to say that *I* flicked the switch, but that *we* lit the room. *We* refers to all the people and their activities involved in completing the circuit. When things become routinized and we come to depend on them and take them for granted, we sometimes lose sight of how complicated they really are. We incorrectly perceive that intended results of our acts are actually the results of that action, when, in fact, they are results of a great many coordinated actions.

Agency, it seems to me, is always exercised in sociologically interesting cases, in the context of the ongoing contingent outcomes that are usually called the "system" or the "society."

The theory of structuration, based on agency, has a boundary that requires it to be combined with other theories that account for these patterned contingent events. The knowledge and values underlying the act of turning on the light will only be replicated through instances of flicking switches if the lights actually go on. That much is implied in the purposiveness of action. Structuration must be combined with an explanation of how the lights are made to work, how jails come to exist, and so on.

Structuration: The Core Process

Much of the core process in Giddens's theory has been indicated in a piecemeal way in the context of developing the implications of agency. It will be worthwhile, however, to state it in a straightforward way, using Giddens's distinctive terminology.

The person is conceived as a purposive agent who is able to constitute actions in the flow of behavior by the direction of discursive attention. Each agent is also able to discursively constitute her own and others' actions for others in interaction and to influence the others in the exercise of their agency. These discursive accounts often invoke, and thereby constitute, a societal context for acts, as well as a biographical context. Discursive attention is essential to the existence of acts, not added to acts already existing in their own right. Thus, acts are not redefined. Instead, one act ceases to exist discretely in the flow of behavior and another comes to exist. Characterizing historical or societal epochs as context for events within them and contrast to alternatives is a special case of this process of constitution.

Activities are ordered across time and space. They are conducted routinely and repetitively in similar situations. To a large extent, these regularities exist as a result of the constitution of acts by agents—insofar as the regularities are not general, but rather specific to the context in which they are constituted. The exercise of coercive power and the operation of other contingencies in concert with agency require supplementary theories. Most routine conduct is ordered by habit and not separately motivated, that is, not constituted as action. Types of conduct other than action could include transcultural regularities.

A system is a patterning of social relationships across time and space. The degree of patterning varies. Insofar as patterning exists, it exists as practices reproduced by the recursive organization of structure. Giddens defines structure as rules and resources that exist only in human memory and as instantiated in action. (This means that *resources* refer to skills and not to such things as guns that exist physically and between acts. Although analytically distinct, skills and equipment are interrelated in practice.) These structures are the substantive terms in which events and the flow of behavior are rationalized or constituted. By *recursive*, Giddens means that the action constituted by these rules will tend to reproduce the rules while instantiating them. The imagery seems to be formally analogous to the biological idea that DNA reproduces itself, using the body as its vehicle. There is not necessarily consensus on the rules, and individuals, for their own purposes, may invoke them insincerely. The invoked rules are used in a variety of purposive ways.

By acceding to a characterization of what rules are relevant and appropriate, the individual contributes to the reproduction of those rules. If he is in a position of subordination, he is compliant with it and contributes to its continuation. Contributions to the reproduction of structure are not necessarily equal nor decentralized, however. There are strategic positions in which certain actors can take greater reflexive control of this process. This is a major point of intersection with those conflict theories that deal with the distribution of power within a given system and its consequences. The potential for change or liberation is guaranteed by the doctrine that "there is no mechanism of social organization or social reproduction identified by social analysts which lay actors cannot also get to know about and incorporate into what they do" (Giddens, 1984:284).

COLLINS'S CONFLICT SOCIOLOGY

Randall Collins has developed two distinct but interrelated theories. The first (Collins, 1975) is a partially deductive conflict theory, not restricted to the societal level, but focused on relatively large-scale social organization and change. The second (Collins, 1981), which we will summarize in the next section of this chapter, addresses action and small-scale interaction in a way that attempts to bring existing work on those topics to bear on theoretical problems raised by the theory of larger-scale structure. Collins addresses societal integration by placing structural functional arguments about the integrative function of rituals in a conflict theoretic context. His theory of interaction ritual change further specifies how ritual is implicated in societal integration.

The theory of larger-scale phenomena includes hundreds of propositions and deductive steps and, for that reason, cannot be summarized in its entirety. We will review a few of Collins's arguments to illustrate his approach and to provide a basis for discussion. Collins's (1975) theory has three distinctive characteristics, relative to the other conflict theories we have reviewed. It is presented in modern scientific form as a set of related deductive arguments that are testable, at least in principle, at each step. Second, it derives conflict sociological principles from selected species characteristics. Third, fundamental relationships concerning societal integration and originally reported by important functionalist theorists are derived within a conflict framework. Thus, his theory does not require a separate theory of integration based on nonconflict principles.

Collins presents his conflict sociology as a theory under construction rather than as a coherent and basically finished product. The theory is intended to be tested, revised as needed, and completed. Completion of the theory requires two processes—its extension into aspects of social life not now included and further explication of the theoretical arguments. The logical connections among the propositions in the theory are loose, and Collins characterizes them as sketches rather than formal arguments. The presentation of theory in partial disarray is part of the theoretical strategy we will discuss later. It reflects a general view that theory is successful when it organizes existing empirical research and promotes further empirical research, even when it is not elegant in the philosophical sense. Of the two values—elegance in argument and interaction between theory and empirical research—Collins clearly prefers the latter when there is conflict between them.

Deductions from Postulates

Collins's conflict theory is presented in the form of loosely integrated deductive arguments. Many of the propositions, if not most, are based in empirical research regardless of how they are used in his argument. That is, the deductions and the propositions from which they are deduced are approximately equivalent with respect to empirical verification. The sense in which some are more fundamental than others is not related to whether their basis is in fact or assumption, but rather in how they are used in argument.

This approximate equality of empirical standing applies to those few propositions that Collins identifies as postulates. *Postulates* are defined as fundamental propositions that are taken for granted without proof for purposes of argument, and the identification of a few propositions as postulates bears consideration as the first substantive issue in Collins's (1975) theory. The propositions identified as postulates (1975: 73, 152–153, 281) are premises for sociological arguments in the conflict tradition. However, for the most part, they are not themselves sociological. Rather, they identify assumptions about human beings as human beings, independent of the society to which they happen to belong. They are focused on such species characteristics as cognition, emotion, and bonding; strength of drives; and social responsiveness to fellow humans. But they are not an exhaustive catalog of well-established biological and psychological facts. Rather, they are selected on grounds of usefulness in a conflict theory and tend to ground conflict sociology in the biological characteristics of human beings. As illustrations, we can consider how the omnipresence of conflict in society and male domination of females are derived.

Social conflict. The presence of social conflict is derived from a very few basic premises (1975:73). Each individual constructs his own subjective reality, but individual cognition is constructed from social communications. Therefore, each individual has power over others' cognitions through communication. Each individual attempts to maximize his own subjective status to the extent allowed by the resources he controls and his contact with others. Each individual will seek status-favorable and avoid status-unfavorable contact with others. When individual resources differ, inequalities of power are involved in defining subjective reality. When differential power is exercised and withdrawal or avoidance is not possible, conflict is implied.

Conflict, then, is implied by species-characteristic conduct in the presence of unequal resources. No aggressive or territorial impulse is assumed. In fact, the postulates imply that our first inclination as a species is avoidance, because conflict will occur only when avoidance is impossible. Only conflict over subjective status is mentioned. If conflict over biological necessities such as food, water, or shelter is partly independent of issues of subjective status, additional theoretical arguments would be required to explain those conflicts.

Sexual domination. Three species characteristics are postulated in the explanation of sexual dominance—strong sex drive, strong resistance to coercion, and typically greater size and strength for males than for females. Neither gender is conceived to have a stronger drive, nor is a difference postulated between the territorality or aggressiveness displayed by the two genders. Insofar as these exist, their implications would have to be added. Again, the selection of specifically useful species characteristics creates a boundary for the theory. Patterns of sexual domination are attributed to social circumstances rather than biology, insofar as it is possible that society could be transformed to remove them.

Collins's approach treats sexual dominance as a special instance of domination of the smaller and weaker by the larger and stronger. The postulated strong sexual drive implies that sexual access will be sought after and will be a commodity exchanged in many bargains. Because the drive is postulated for both males and females, the pattern of sexual access and conflict over it is determined by the pattern of resources available for bargaining. Thus, male sexual domination of females is attributed not to the biology of the genders, but to social structure as reflected in the distribution of resources available to trade for sex or to influence others to be sexually accessible.

The details of the theory of sexual dominance are expressed in a series of casual relationships, some of which are derived from theoretical considerations and others from empirical research. Males dominate because the more one gender controls the means of violence and material resources, the more it controls sexual activities and the more auxiliary services can be demanded from the subordinated gender. Men tend to control the means of interpersonal violence in private, because of size and strength and tend to control the other material resources of the society. However, Collins argues, the more force is monopolized by political agencies outside the household, the lower the power of men over women because the advantages of size and strength are reduced.

Sexual aggression and violence are linked to the absence of other material resources. When other resources are absent, size and strength remain as the resources of last resort for the larger, stronger gender. But these resources, unless they are valued in mate selection, are expressed in aggression and coercion, not friendly bargaining. The smaller sex attempts to avoid sexual access to avoid coercion.

When we consider these two kinds of resources—material and coercive—together, we must draw this conclusion: When the males of our species control the material resources of the society, they will use it to advantage in sexual bargaining. When the males do not, they will utilize sexual coercion unless females avoid contact that affords sexual access or the society politically monopolizes violence. Thus, unless women are to be permanently disadvantaged materially or segregated from men, the political control of violence is necessary to prevent sexual domination. Note that if the female sex drive is strong, rational conduct to avoid coercion may be undermined. If the male sex drive is strong, the political control of violence required to prevent sexual coercion may be quite repressive.

The complex relationships among family structure, political structure, moral values, distribution of resources, and sexual access are expressed as a series of causal relationships. For example, the less surplus a society produces beyond what is needed for members' survival, the less work can be imposed in sexual bargains. The conditions that correlate with the degree of surplus production beyond bare survival needs are not identified in this theory. The more material property is controlled by one sex, the more the other sex must withhold sexual access as a bargaining chip in long-term economic exchanges, such as marriage.

Collins's theory does not include interaction among these causal relationships and those involving other societal institutions nor among the causal factors. For example, is there a relationship between the extent to which production exceeds absolute survival needs and the control of material property by one gender? Does the relationship between control of property by one gender and the withholding of sex as a bargaining strategy by the other occur regardless of the degree of production in excess of survival needs?

Deriving functionalist propositions. Rejecting structural functional theory as an explanation does not imply rejecting all of the relationships and predictions organized by the theory. Many of them are empirically sound, and it is a task of the conflict theorists to provide alternate explanations of them if the structural functional theories are to be replaced rather than supplemented. Collins approaches this challenge by deriving specific functionalist propositions originally found in the works of Emile Durkheim and two functionalist anthropologists—Malinowski and Radcliffe-Brown—from principles unrelated to societal functionality. Collins's does not derive these propositions from conflict principles, but rather from the species characteristics of humans.

Collins (1975:152) postulates that (1) all animals have automatic emotional responses to certain gestures and sounds made by other animals; (2) the basic social ties among animals consist of mutual arousal of signals for alarm, recognition, affection, sexual arousal, antagonism, and play and the asymmetric arousal of threat and defense signals; (3) human beings are animals and human social ties, therefore, are fundamentally based on automatically aroused emotional responses; and (4) human beings have the capacity for symbolism.

Collins then suggests a series of correlations concerning the arousal of social ties. The longer people are physically copresent, the more signals will occur and the greater the level of emotional arousal will be achieved. The more people are copresent, the more intense the emotional arousal. The greater the common focus of attention, the more likely people are to experience a common mood or emotion. The more people use stereotyped gestures and sounds, the greater the common focus of attention. The more people use stereotyped sequences of gestures and sounds, the more likely they are to experience a common mood. The stronger the emotional arousal, the more real and unquestioned the meanings of symbols people think about during the experience.

The next step in Collins's reasoning is characterized by Durkheim's principle of social density. Longer physical copresence and more focus of attention by stereotyped gestures and sounds are associated with experiencing the symbols as real and unquestioned. The stereotyped gestures are rituals and their use makes the society and relationships symbolized in the gestures seem real. The more these conditions for strong ritual experiences are met, assuming they do not arouse antagonism or threat deference, the greater the interpersonal attachment and feeling of security. The greater is the past solidarity, the more painful a change. Thus, the emotional arousal will tend to integrate the society by linking changes in its rituals to emotional threat. As stress increases, the greater is the incentive to invoke ritual solidarities for their emotional comfort.

This argument grounds solidarity rituals in the emotional life of individuals rather than in their function for the society. The rituals have the function of promoting solidarity and preserving the institutions and symbols of the society, but they are not explained by those functions. Instead, the societal functions are explained by the characteristics of humans as a species when placed in specific situations. Thus, the empirical observations of structural functional theory are explained in a new way.

Collins observes that his argument is not complete. The omission of two steps is troublesome, because they are complex and controversial. The first omitted assumption is that the learned stereotyped gestures and sounds are quite similar to automatic species signals with respect to their emotional significance. The second omission is that there is no explanation for the existence of the system of shared stereotyped gestures and sounds in the first place. They are not species characteristics, but rather peculiar to each society. How and why does a system of learned rituals arise? This question is important because it is hard to answer without reference to systemic functions.

Ritual Interaction Chains

Ritual interactions are the core of Collins's explanation of social integration. Collins (1981:990) argues that the large-scale structure of society has its effects by impinging upon the individual actors' motivations. The actor's strategy for achieving her goals in a situation often depends on her perception of contingencies external to that situation. In a simple case, my decision to accept a check rests on my estimate of the future actions of my bank. These estimates are conditioned by the actors' past experiences.

In part, these estimates are impersonal and are concerned with the operation of institutions in general. Such estimates define, in effect, the background of contingencies or probabilities of many occurrences in the society—how long will mail be delayed, what products will be in the market, and so on. Other estimates are personal to the individuals in the particular interaction. To what extent and how do others in interaction respect and participate in the institutions of the society as the estimating person understands them? For example, if you offer to drop my letter in the corner mailbox for me, I must decide whether the postal service will be quick enough for my purposes if I use that mailbox instead of driving to the post office and I must also decide whether you will actually drop my mail in the box.

These estimates of other individuals in interaction are made through ritual interchanges as described earlier. They are emotionally based, rather than cognitive, and express the person's participation in and loyalty to social institutions beyond the interaction, insofar as the institutions are validated and security in their operation is experienced. The institutions are invoked by these gestures as a strong and unquestioned reality.

Collins observes that the social structure is composed of the activity of individual actors dispersed in time and space. This activity often takes place in the presence of others, that is, in social interactions. It is in these interactions that the ritual interchanges occur. Collins argues that the individual's life can be conceived, in part, as a chain of interaction rituals. In each interaction, the person conducts the business of the current interaction and, through ritual, expresses her own and the interaction's connections to the broader social circumstances. A common reality, or definition, is invoked by the ritual exchanges, including, most especially, attitudes toward the society and coalitions within it.

FEMINISM: AN EMERGING PERSPECTIVE

During approximately the last 20 years, closely related variations of a feminist perspective have become almost universally accepted in sociology. At the core of the feminist perspective is the recognition that as a gender, women are subordinate and disadvantaged (some would say oppressed) in the dominance relations and economies of all known societies. The crucial importance of gender in determining life chances has long been recognized. Men and women have traditionally entered different careers with different economic rewards, had different property and political rights, and had different obligations in the family. In fact, gender is among our most important life-controlling characteristics. However, many of the differences had been regarded as special protections and benefits to women, often justified by supposed innate differences of ability between the sexes. The opponents of feminism as a social movement still argue for the continuation of many traditional arrangements as protections for women.

The most obvious and profound impact of feminist thought in sociology has been in those aspects of social life in which men and women relate to each other primarily in their roles as men and women—the family, sexual relationships, and interpersonal relationships between men and women in general. Gender roles have been redefined in terms of the dominance relations in society. As result, these areas of interpersonal relationships have been reconceived in terms of how they reflect and contribute to those dominance relations. In these areas, research that has been substantially influenced by the feminist perspective is now the sociological mainstream.

The study of other social institutions and processes—for example, the workplace, criminology, education, and deviance—has also been greatly influenced by feminist thought. In these areas, gender issues interact with those raised by other roles that simultaneously apply. The politics of domination by gender is superimposed, for example, on relationships in the workplace, career lines, opportunities for training, and so on.

However, as Stacey and Thorne (1985) argue, the feminist influence in sociology has not culminated in a theoretical revolution. A feminist contribution has been added to the existing theories of specific institutions and processes and has reduced the bias toward emphasizing the male experience in them and accepting male perspectives about them. But no new explanations of these institutions truly reorganized around feminist themes have been developed. In addition, no widely accepted feminist theories have been developed at the greater level of generality characteristic of the schools of thought considered in this text.

Stacey and Thorne (1985) attribute the truncated development of feminist thought to three main factors: (1) Its grounding in gender roles has left unbroken links with functional theory and imagery that have slowed the transition to thinking of gender in politicized structural and historical ways. (2) Gender has been construed as a variable in various theoretical approaches, rather than as a basic theoretical category. (3) Feminist work has been "ghettoized" within other theoretical frameworks, especially Marxism. Hybrids of feminism and other approaches have developed, but the work has been circulated in specialized sources and not integrated into the mainstream of theory.

At this time, then, despite the profound influence of feminist thinking on sociological research and analysis of specific institutions, there is not yet a body of feminist sociological theory per se. The theoretical and empirical contribution to the study of specific institutions has been within existing frameworks. More general feminist reorganization of theory has not yet been proposed.

SUMMARY

Conflict theorists attempt to explain both the stability and change of large-scale social structures, which they conceive as characterized by relationships of domination and subordination and the exercise of power. Initially, conflict theories such as Coser's and Dahrendorf's were developed as theories of social change to supplement a separate theory of integration and stability. Structural functional principles were adopted, sometimes explicitly, for the theories of integration. Later, attempts were made to construct conflict theories of integration. Giddens's approach was to proceed analytically, developing the conceptual implications of philosophical doctrines, especially agency. Collins developed a less conceptually integrated theory, but one that is testable and closely tied to existing empirical evidence from a large variety of sources. Within the loose structure, specific arguments can be revised to accommodate changing empirical information. Thus, Collins is able to use important structural functional insights, especially those of Durkheim, within his framework. In addition, evidence concerning topics not addressed by Collins, such as the factors leading to production beyond the minimal survival needs of members of a society, could be simply added to the theory without necessarily revising any important arguments within it.

LOOKING AHEAD

There is a peculiarity in Collins's discussions (1981, 1989) of interaction ritual chains. One major focus, of course, is how dominance and subordination are expressed in interaction. We saw this specific concern in his analysis of gender relationships, and it also occurs throughout his theory. Despite this, and despite his postulation that threat/deference emotions are evoked asymmetrically, he argues that these interaction rituals invoke a common reality and create a common mood.

We have seen, in our discussion of conventions, that this is not logically necessary. Empirical evidence exists, at least for verbal expressions, that individuals publicly avow moral sentiments that they do not hold and that they violate in private in order to avoid community censure and complications (cf., Warriner, 1958). The rituals could do their integrative work even if the participants did not share a common image of reality or a common mood. The rituals could merely express convention-ally individuals' willingness to participate in the societal routines so long as others did so. But if we raise that objection, we must answer another question: Why are they willing to participate? For example, why is a person willing to ritually indicate his own subordination and show defer-ence if he does not agree that this is appropriate and does not like it?

It is appropriate to think of the rest of this book as addressing the family of questions implied by disagreement and unshared mood. We present Merton's conflict model of social roles, in which conduct is coor-dinated in time and space without cognitive or moral agreement by the distribution of resources. Subsequently, several processes are identified through which the resources are mobilized in interaction. In effect, the several theories taken together partially develop a theory of conventional behavior appropriate to a conflict sociology of the large-scale social struc-ture.

NOTES

1. Durkheim (1966) argued that sociology could be built upon statistical regu-larities of conduct, considered apart from the psychological reality of the participants. The structure of the society, indexed by these regularities, was conceived to impose itself coercively upon individuals. Giddens's argument would deny the generality of these regularities. Within a society, they would remain descriptive, but their explanatory power is removed. Seeing, for example, a correlation between self-direction at work and valuing flexibility, Giddens's approach is to seek an explanation in the process of actors' making decisions and coordinating their conduct in interaction.

2. See Dennett (1984) for a review, analysis, and critique of many doctrines of free will and a defense of important provisions.

REFERENCES

Collins, Randall. 1975. Conflict Sociology. New York: Academic Press.

Collins, Randall. 1981. The Microfoundations of Macrosociology. *American Jour-nal of Sociology* 86:984–1014.

Collins, Randall. 1989. Toward a Neo-Meadian Sociology of Mind. *Symbolic Inter-action* 12:1–32.

Dennett, Daniel. 1984. Elbow Room: The Varieties of Free Will Worth Wanting. Cambridge: MIT Press.

Dewey, John. 1957. Human Nature and Conduct. New York: Modern Library.

Durkheim, Emile. 1966. The Rules of the Sociological Method. New York: Free Press.

Giddens, Anthony. 1984. The Constitution of Society. Berkeley: University of California Press.

Kohn, Melvin, Atsushi Naoi, Carrie Schoenbach, Carmi Schooler, and Kazmimierz Slomczynski. 1990. Position in the Class Structure and Psychological Functioning in the United States, Japan and Poland. *American Journal of Sociology* 95: 964–1008.

Stacey, Judith, and Barrie Thorne. 1985. The Missing Feminist Revolution in Sociology. *Social Problems* 32:301–316.

Warriner, Charles. 1958. The Nature and Functions of Official Morality. *American Journal of Sociology* 64:165–168.

7

Social Roles: A Middle-Range Conflict Theory

The conflict theory of roles to be developed in this chapter regards "social role" as a unit both of social structure and of individual cognition. As a unit of social structure, the expectations, rights, obligations, and resources of the role persist, independent of changes in personnel. However, each individual also has his or her own perception of the social world, usually called a *cognitive map* or *model*. In Parsons's approach, the social structure itself is internally consistent and the individual perceptions of it are accurate enough so that conduct in accord with one's own perception of social structure will contribute smoothly to the tasks regulated and organized by that social structure.

The conflict model, because it assumes internal conflicts or contradictions in the social structure, requires a fundamentally different explanation of the connections among social norms, the individuals perception of them, and the resulting conduct. What will an individual who acts in accord with his own perceptions do if the applicable rules contradict one another? The answer is not predictable from the rules alone. If the individual acts on his own understanding of the rules, *whatever* is done will violate the expectations of others with different perceptions. That is, although the individual's value preferences remain important in the social psychological process, their result cannot be conformity to the social structure. In fact, if the normative structure is characterized by internal conflicts, conformity to it is impossible. To the extent that normative expectations are in conflict, every action will be approved by some and disapproved by others and will conform to some versions of the rules and deviate from others. The rational and moral considerations of the individual cannot be mutually reinforcing. Other factors must enter the process to coordinate the conduct of individuals' acting on their own perceptions.

MARGINALITY AND AUXILIARY CHARACTERISTICS

Ironically, the phenomenon that most fundamentally discredits role theories based on conformity to consensually held norms was observed at least as early as the 1920s, before the conformity/consensus theories dominated sociology. Park (1928) described an instance in which conformity to norms was not possible as an explanation or description of social conduct. He observed that human migration resulted in people of different racial and ethnic backgrounds living in close proximity to one another. The processes of acculturation, assimilation, and interbreeding take place at different rates. When these processes occur slowly, the different groups participate in the economic life of the society and live in close proximity but maintain somewhat distinctive customs and participate differently in the communal portions of social life.

As interbreeding occurs, the racial or ethnic hybrids are *marginal people*. They are not fully members of either group, nor are they fully excluded from the obligations and rights of either. Both sets of group norms apply partly to them and neither set applies fully. If the marginal person conforms to one set of norms or insists on treatment appropriate to one group, she violates those appropriate to the other. Park was concerned with the resulting process of choice and change as the microprocess of social change and with the burdens it imposes on marginal people. For our purposes, though, a technical point is most crucial: *Whatever* the person does will simultaneously conform to and violate applicable norms. Conformity cannot describe nor explain the resulting conduct. Some manner of choice and active construction of a personal life is required.

In principle, this type of marginality would no longer exist if discrimination on the basis of race or ethnicity were eliminated. The rules applying to the two (or more) racial or ethnic groups to which the hybrid belongs would be the same. In such a world, perhaps conformity to norms, rationally applied, could explain social conduct. But that process cannot explain social conduct in this world, where another kind of behavioral process is needed. We know, then, that at best the analytic theory of action is incomplete. At least some human social conduct is not organized by conformity to consensually held norms and values.

In Park's discussion of marginality, the ability to act by processes other than conformity to norms, rationally applied, is established, but it is linked to a specific circumstance in which people cannot be unambiguously categorized. The categories themselves are clear-cut. But Hughes (1971/1945) recognized marginality as a specific instance of a broader phenomenon that he called *dilemmas* or *contradictions* of status. Hughes distinguished between the determining characteristics of membership in a social status and auxiliary characteristics that are associated with it. The distinction resembles that between universalistic and particularistic criteria for membership or between rational, merit-linked criteria and nonrational, prejudicial ones. Characteristic examples of determining characteristics are the license of the physician or automobile driver, the employment of a person for a specific job and the assignment of its responsibilities to him, education, and competence. Some important auxiliary characteristics are gender, race, ethnicity, and religion.

Hughes observed that a set of these secondary expectations is typically associated with statuses so that we expect doctors to be males and nurses to be females, most professionals to be white, and so on. This influences recruitment and entry to the positions. In addition the activity of people in the position (doctors, for example) is governed by multiple sets of norms—those applicable to doctors, those applicable to men, those applicable to whites, and so on.

In traditional societies, those that do not change rapidly, this simultaneous application of multiple sets of rules causes no problem. All the status holders meet both primary and auxiliary criteria and the rules are suitable for all the incumbents. But when recruitment for positions changes, such as when women enter workplaces formerly reserved for men or when a society begins to recruit minorities for positions from which they had previously been barred, the rules governing some people by virtue of their secondary characteristics may conflict with customs of the position. For example, engineers customarily hold a party to celebrate project completion. Traditionally, engineers have all been men and the party has been a stag party. When women enter the profession, they must make some accommodation between the customs surrounding the engineering profession and those surrounding gender.

This accommodation cannot be simple conformity because two sets of conflicting rules are involved. But now we see that the conflicts must occur whenever there is social change, including the appearance of new technologies that create new jobs with undefined auxiliary expectations or that change the nature of existing ones. A world governed by conformity must either make no auxiliary distinctions or experience no social change, including technological change. It is an unlikely world.

During the 1950s and 1960s, Erving Goffman (1959, 1961, 1967), whose work will be discussed in more detail in the context of symbolic interaction theory, extended this line of reasoning still further. He argued that *every* role had a more or less detailed set of secondary characteristics that defined an expected identity for incumbents associated with it. As a result, all role-organized behavior is characterized by tension between primary and secondary characteristics and by their manipulation to control identity. In Goffman's work, then, the explanation by conformity had been replaced by an explanation in terms of the active management of circumstances by individuals in interaction. Conformity was regarded as a mere option and the norms were regarded as contingencies in this active process—facts to be reckoned with, but not a compelling consideration in the application of rationality. In other words, conformity to norms and values, rationally applied to circumstances, is not the exclusive process of social conduct, nor the fundamental process to which there are a few exceptions.

INTER- AND INTRA-ROLE CONFLICT

Simultaneously, research into the structure of the roles themselves was radically transforming our understanding of them. At roughly the same time that we were discovering that people were not basically conformists to, but rather active managers of, their normative environment, we were also discovering that the normative environment could not be reasonably construed as a well-integrated system of norms. Research indicated that the normative structure was characterized by both conflicts among the requirements of different roles (interrole conflict), of which the primary/secondary characteristic conflicts are a special case, and conflicts among the requirements of a single role (intrarole conflict). (Preiss and Erlich (1966) provide a case study, discussion of the theoretical issues, and extensive bibliography.)

Different, even conflicting, normative requirements in different roles do not, in themselves, imply a system of norms that is malintegrated. In fact, many of the conflicts improve the functioning of interrelated roles. Schwartz (1974) observes, for example, that higher status individuals normatively expect to be shown deference by lower status individuals.

This deference can take the form of normative specification that the lower status person must wait for the higher status person. These differences between roles—one showing deference, one expecting it; one waiting, one expecting others to wait—help coordinate activities that involve both roles, for example, by regulating scheduling. System integration is reduced, however, when the same person holds two or more positions with conflicting norms. When the (lower status) patient who must show deference to a doctor is also a (high status) lawyer, the pattern of deference is problematic. Various lawyer/patients will resolve the conflict differently and the patient/doctor relationship becomes less predictable and less coordinated.

Everyone holds multiple roles. We are simultaneously members of families, groups of friends, and voluntary associations. We must reconcile the requirements of these various memberships with each other and with the requirements of jobs, school, and so on. Because the combinations of requirements are so diverse, the resolution of the conflicting requirements is accomplished biographically to some extent—accomplished by each person's balancing the demands upon him or her in a personalized way. As in the example of the relationship of the lawyer/patient to the doctor, these individual solutions are somewhat unpredictable and reduce the coordination among the various roles.

Interrole conflict is still logically compatible with the idea of well-defined single roles to which one could conform, barring external complications. However, the sheer variety and quantity of conflicts imply that coordination of the roles in a system is not accomplished by consensual values because our multiple roles virtually guarantee external complications as a matter of fact, even though they are not logically necessary. The normative structure itself contributes to change and instability and an integrating mechanism of another kind is required to explain stability.

Intrarole conflict, conflicts within the requirements of a single role, pose an even more fundamental problem for explanations based on conformity. If a role has internal contradictions, it is impossible to conform to it even if all the issues surrounding incumbency in multiple roles could somehow be resolved. In the conflict approach to norms, intrarole conflict is ubiquitous. Normally, a role requires one to interact with diverse others holding different roles that relate to one's own. For example, a student must coordinate activities with fellow students, instructors, librarians, and administrators. These diverse other positions impose different requirements on the student that are typically in partial conflict, even if no other roles in the student's life are taken into account. Intrarole conflict eliminates conformity as a possible explanation of systemic stability and coordination.

TOBY'S SUPERNORMATIVE APPROACH TO INTEGRATION

By the early 1950s role conflict and the strain it produced were regarded as inevitable. Normative conflict was recognized not only as a useful mechanism for promoting change, but also as a source of anomie and disruption. Consequently, theorists turned to the question of what protected the stability of societies from the conflicts within their own normative or institutional structures. Toby's (1952) early treatment of this theoretical problem incorporated elements based on the principle of conformity to norms as well as some elements based on different behavioral dynamics.

Toby (1952) recognized that the rights and obligations associated with roles are inconsistent. He likened the situation to a jurisdictional dispute in which different parties advanced different claims on the individual, based on different role relationships. For example, a family member/worker suffers a death in her immediate family. Will she follow the family obligation to stay home or the work obligation to do her job? Toby proposed that additional norms existed besides those defining the separate role obligations that established priorities among them. Thus, by staying home, the person would not be choosing idiosyncratically between two obligations, but would be conforming to a third norm, superior to the others in a hierarchy. Conformity to the integrative, priority-setting norm governs the choice between the conflicting norms of the two roles. If we were willing to accept the premise that our normative structure is quite complex and detailed, the hierarchy of norms would resolve many instances of conflicting norms at a lower level without rejecting conformity as the basic way that people orient themselves to roles.

But Toby also proposed that types of conduct that were not based on conformity to norms had an important role in social life. He proposed that several mechanisms ameliorated social conflict: While some were based on a hierarchy of norms, others were not normative. Toby suggested that *rituals* existed to smooth over disputes without agreement on underlying normative priorities and without the parties' agreeing about where fault lay. For example, people who collide on the street, thus denying one another the right of way, can both excuse themselves. In doing so, both ritually accept blame and allow the other to forgo hostilities without losing face. However, as Toby makes explicit, both may believe the other is at fault, while ritually accepting the blame. It follows from this, although it is not mentioned explicitly, that in less transitory cases, those felt hostilities may be expressed later in a variety of ways. A related device is *tact*, which Toby conceives as socially required lying to avoid hurting others with the truth. Tact, then, ritualizes lying.

A third related mechanism is the *segregation of roles*. The problems caused by conflicting rules can be reduced by temporal and spatial segregation of the role performances. Each set of demands can be honored at the appropriate time and place. This separation will stabilize systems, however, only if others agree on which role is to be honored at any given moment or if some or all of them are ignorant of activities contrary to the ones they prefer.

These mechanisms have several common aspects. They require a strategic choice by actors: to blame and retaliate or to withdraw ritually, to hurt with the truth or be tactful, to perform one role or another. All three require a strategically manipulated difference between reality and appearances. Real feelings, real reasons for actions, and real conflicting obligations are not exposed. Consequently, all three ameliorate conflict by promoting ignorance of matters, knowledge of which would lead to conflict. Considered together, these devices are not harmonious with a model of conduct based on conformity. The conforming actor determines what to do by considering how norms apply to his particular circumstance and then following them. But to utilize these mechanisms and to avoid being disadvantaged by others' use of them, one must attend skeptically and manipulatively to the particular others with whom one interacts.

This manipulative theme becomes more pronounced in other means available to individuals to deal with role conflicts. Toby proposes that individuals may be able to *play off groups* that are pressing conflicting demands. An individual might *stall* until temporal conflicts are removed. He might redefine the conflicting roles. He might lead a *double life*. In these areas, there are no institutionalized justifications for the resulting arrangements. The problems are solved by "personal skill in negotiation and his ability to communicate his plight and invoke sympathy" (Toby, 1952:327).

Toby's treatment of role conflict is transitional. The significance of role conflict as an intellectual problem in theories based on conformity is recognized. New mechanisms of social conduct are proposed to explain conduct in structural situations in which conformity is not an appropriate explanation. However, there is neither a theory of role conflict per se nor a recognition that role conflict should be the core phenomenon in role theory rather than a difficulty within a role theory based primarily on consensus.

In addition, Toby did not fully realize the changes in the view of human conduct implied by the new behavioral dynamics. At the very least, if humans sometimes conform and sometimes manipulate and bargain, we must understand how we switch from one type of behavior to the other. More profoundly, we must recognize that the occasions of conformity are strategically chosen and that conformity is one way of manipulating and bargaining. The changes in our idea of normative structure require a profound change in our idea of human conduct. Strategy, manipulation, and bargaining have become the central phenomena of social conduct to be explained rather than difficulties in a model based on conformity. In the developing modern view, the social structure is characterized by conflicts of interests and values and by the uneven distribution of resources for getting one's way. Individuals behave within this structural context by strategic manipulation and negotiation, using conformity or the appearance of conformity as one tool among others.

MERTON'S SOCIAL FACTUAL CONFLICT THEORY OF ROLE SETS

Unlike Toby, Merton (1957) did not conceive of role conflict as a theoretical problem within an action theory based on conformity to consensually held norms and values. Rather, he took a fundamentally different approach in which conflicting norms were regarded as an essential characteristic of role structures. A social status, Merton argued, does not impose a single set of expectations on its incumbents. Rather, each status (or position in a social structure) held by a person involves her in a variety of role relationships with the person(s) in each of the diverse statuses with which she interacts because of her own status. For example, the status of teacher imposes role relationships with students, parents, boards of education, principals, and so on. Merton calls the array of other positions that are regularly associated in role relationships with any given status the *role set* of that status.

If the expectations imposed by the various members of the role set were the same, the substitution of the role set for the unitary role would be relatively inconsequential. But Merton (1957:112) explicitly aligns himself with the conflict theoretical tradition and argues that because the members of a role set have different positions in the social structure, they will typically have different interests, sentiments, values, and moral expectations from one another. Thus, when a person enters a position in the social structure she will typically be confronted by expectations for her conduct that differ from one another and from her own preferences.

This set of theoretical assumptions about the role set suggests two obvious social psychological questions: (1) How does the individual select a course of conduct, and (2) how do people adjust to one another's preferences in interaction? We will review answers to both of these questions later, but Merton's theory of the role set is sociological, not social psychological, and addresses a different kind of question. If each *position* in the social structure has a characteristic set of interests and moral expectations, to what extent does each *position* get its way? Which interests and values prevail, not in any particular case, but as a standardized feature or stable rate of occurrence within the social system?

A role set is not a set of interpersonal relationships among particular people who interact with one another in complementary roles. A role set is not a collectivity. Rather, the role set is the set of standardized relationships that exist among the complementary positions, abstracted from particular interpersonal relationships. It is possible, for example, to conceive of the standardized roles of the man and woman in the family unit but also to recognize that each particular man/woman pair develops its own variation on the theme. These variations may be unique if examined in enough detail, but they have common and quantifiable features as well. If there are children, and if the pair dissolves, the woman typically has custody of the children. While the pairs are together, there is a division of household chores that can be typified in terms of areas of responsibility or quantified in terms of hours spent. Merton's theory of the role set is an attempt to explain such regularities in the outcomes of interpersonal relationships in terms of structural regularities in the role set.

The normative expectations and preferences are assumed to differ among members of the role set. Thus, conformity to the normative structure as a whole is not possible. But the different sets of expectations and preferences do not exist abstractly as equally compelling moral alternatives. Rather, each set of preferences is associated with one of the positions in the role set. Merton proposes that structural conditions within the role set are parameters for resolving the moral disputes, helping to determine which position's value preferences and expectations will prevail. People in each position would like to impose their characteristic preferences. Structural conditions, primarily the distribution of resources and the ability to mobilize them by virtue of holding a position, influence their ability to do so. Merton identified a few variables that influence which position will prevail in cases of normative conflict.

Relative importance of statuses to one another. The various members of the role set do not care equally about one anothers' activities. Those with greater concern about a subject should, then, press harder and more consistently to impose their views on that subject. Consequently, assuming that the positions have similar resources in other respects, the resultant conduct should reflect the preferences of the position with greater concern more often and more fully than the preferences of other positions.

Relative differences in power.   Different members of the role set have different amounts of power or authority to influence specific behavioral choices. A position with relatively greater power will have a greater influence than one with lesser power. To the extent that the power underlying different sets of expectations is equal, its effects are negated, and other factors, such as degree of concern, become more important. The relative influence of different structural conditions, such as power and concern, is an empirical question and is not prejudged in Merton's theory.

Secrecy.   Different positions have different access to information about conduct. The more information available to those in a position, the more effectively they are able to respond to and influence that conduct. In the extreme, conduct that is completely concealed from incumbents of a position cannot be sanctioned by them at all. They would not know it had happened.

Observability of conflict.   Sometimes, members of a role set are aware of the conflicts among their respective expectations. To that extent, they tend to reduce their efforts to impose their own expectations. In effect, the problem of resolving conflicting demands is assumed by the conflicting members of the role set. The accommodation among the conflicting members of the role set can then be enforced as if there had been agreement concerning preferences.

Solidarity.   The degree to which persons in a position agree on particular issues varies. Insofar as they agree and have solidarity, their separate efforts will be to the same effect and the position will maximize its influence. As disagreement increases, the efforts of the separate persons who hold the position will tend to cancel one another out. The position will not have a clear influence.

Abridgment.   Occasionally, it is possible for a position that imposes a conflicting demand to be eliminated from the role set, thus reducing the conflict.

Articulated Role Sets

Merton refers to the operation of these structural conditions upon conduct as the articulation of the role set. The degree of articulation is variable. The articulation of the role set does not alter the underlying conflicts of interests, expectations, and values. Neither does it alter other structural conditions, such as the uneven distribution of power and information. If we think of the alternative preferences for how to behave in a repetitive situation as defining a set of options, the other structural conditions tend to influence or coerce (to use Durkheims's term) the choice among them. If it were not for the uneven distribution of power, concern, information, and other variables related to sanctioning the conduct of others, all the alternatives would be equal in their consequences. The choices would be individual choices and they would be relatively unpredictable without detailed knowledge of individual preferences. However, when the diverse people in a position are subjected to characteristic structural pressures such as the threat or use of power against them, their decisions become less influenced by their own preferences and more influenced by the structural context. Their conduct becomes predictable on the basis of a position that is, socially rather than biographically ordered. It is not the result of agreement with the version of the norms being followed. Rather, it results from the greater resources mobilized in favor of that version of the rules, relative to others.

Articulated role sets and institutions. Recently in sociology, the term *institution* has been used to refer to any subsystem of a society. The term does not imply a specific explanation for how the subsystem is integrated or stabilized. But to Parsons, the term *institution* referred, *by definition*, to a social system integrated by consensual social norms and a realization of those norms and values in collective action. Although conflict sociologists recognize the existence of reasonably stable subsystems, no institution, *in the sense defined by Parsons*, can exist in a society characterized by normative conflicts. Although the word *institution* remains in use, the phenomenon called an institution by Parsons is no longer recognized to exist.

Merton resolved this terminological confusion in a different way. He apparently conceded the term *institution* to Parsons. Instead of using it with a new definition, he coined his own term—the *role set*—for societal subsystems. The term *articulation* refers to the dynamic aspect of integrating and stabilizing a role set, or system of interrelated roles, by ameliorating the consequences of conflicts within it. The term *articulation* is parallel to the term *institutionalization*, which is the dynamic aspect of integrating a system of interrelated roles by normative consensus.

In terms of its substance, Merton's theory of role sets is clearly and explicitly in the conflict theoretical tradition and fundamentally opposed to Parsons's approach. But at the time of its development, in the late 1940s and early 1950s, the attention of the conflict theorists was focused on processes of change. At that time, processes of stability and societal integration were still understood in Parsonian terms. Because it concerned roles, systems, and normative expectations, Merton's role set theory was regarded as a modification or friendly amendment to Parsonian action theory. This error of classification became important as conflict theorists began to address processes of integration and stability as well as change and ignored this important resource. As we will see, however, although Merton's terminology has gone out of use, the role set imagery is essential to the microsociological theories of interaction.

Too much can be made of whether a theory purports to explain stability or change, order or conflict, and so on. In theories that recognize such pairs as extremes of a continuum of rates of change (or degree of conflict, etc.) and develop variable relationships to account for the placement of societies along the continuum, naming the theory after one end of the continuum rather than the other does not affect the substance of the theory. Whatever variables correlate positively with relative stability will correlate negatively with rapid change, and vice versa.

Limits and Use of Merton's Theory of the Role Set

Merton's analysis of the role set is an example of middle-range theorizing. As such, it treats a limited range of phenomena, leaving related matters to other theories. This analysis of the role set begins with the observation that the social structure confronts incumbents of a role with a relatively small number of alternative courses of conduct, each associated with another role in the role set. The characteristic set of alternatives that is imposed on each role is one variable aspect of an existing social structure. The distribution of conduct among these alternatives is explained by other differences within the role set—uneven distributions of power, information, solidarity, and so on—among the positions in the role set. As Stinchcombe (1975) has observed, Merton's theoretical analyses of many topics are similar in their reasoning. All try to explain the distribution of choices among socially structured alternatives in terms of social structural characteristics.

But each middle-range theory makes specific assumptions and addresses specific issues appropriate to its empirical focus. Thus, for example, the theory of the role set does not explain how particular sets of choices come to be associated with particular roles. That is, the theory does not explain the origin of the division of labor in the society. It also does not explain how the structural conditions that articulate the choices originate and change. That is, it is neither a theory of social stratification nor a theory of change of the basic structural conditions in the society. It does not explain how different societies come to impose different sets of choices. A complete theory of social structure beginning with this analysis, then, would require the combination of the theory of the role set with compatible explanations of other phenomena. Two substantive characteristics requirements for compatibility are immediately apparent: (1) the recognition that interests, values, expectations, and so on vary with position in the society and (2) the recognition that the resolution of these moral disputes is patterned by the distribution of resources in the society. These two criteria are met by any of the conflict theories previously discussed.

Theories that do not address social structural issues concerning societal scale events and long temporal periods are called *microsociological*. Social stratification and change, the issues previously mentioned, among others, are macrosociological. Merton's analysis of the role set is a microsociological theory and must be combined with explanations of macrosociological phenomena. But even as a microsociological theory, the analysis of the role set is not complete. It attempts to explain the distribution of conduct favored by the various members of the role set. It does not explain how the incumbents of a role decide what to do. That is, it is a sociological theory in Durkheim's sense, not a social psychological one. The social psychology of role performance, the link between the social structural distribution of events and individual conduct, is addressed in other theories, which must be combined with Merton's structural theory of role.

GOODE'S THEORY OF ROLE STRAIN

Goode's (1960) theory of role strain is an attempt to explain individual conduct within the structure of social roles. Goode characterizes the role structure as making excessive demands on the individual, largely because conflicting demands cannot all be met. The individual chooses which demands to meet and how well to meet them. The individual does not, of course, confront the system of roles as a statistical distribution of resources by position. Rather, each individual, by virtue of the role he or she is in must deal with particular other people because of the roles they are in. Each person's particular expectations define his or her options, and each one's particular resources are the contingencies of choice.

Goode treats these contingencies as subject to change, but also as parameters (fixed conditions) at the moment of choice. Goode's primary concern is how these parameters are analyzed cognitively and motivationally by the individual in the process of choice. In subsequent chapters, we will consider theories of how individuals interact in the process of coordinating their choices. Relative to those theories, which can be characterized as treating conduct as the outcome of negotiations or bargaining among individuals, Goode's theory describes how each individual selects and modifies his or her bargaining position.

Nature and Sources of Strain

Role strain is the felt difficulty in fulfilling role obligations. It does not serve as a challenge in the way that the felt difficulty of doing sit-ups does, for example. Rather, it is conceived as an unpleasant state that the individual is motivated to reduce. Mastery of a task so that it becomes easier might reduce strain. But the time and effort needed to master the task and perform it well might reduce the ability to perform other tasks from the same or other roles. Then the individual might be motivated to perform the task poorly, reducing the rewards he gets from it in order to achieve greater rewards from other tasks. That is, role strain arises from the individual's total social obligations, not necessarily from tasks within a given role. In fact, the attempt to reduce role strain organizes the individual's efforts to set priorities among his diverse roles.

Goode points out that role strain can arise even in simple social structures. Even relatively pleasant, undemanding obligations will not always coincide with what one wants to do. But role strain is the normal state of affairs primarily because it is an invariable consequence of inter- and intrarole conflicts, which, as we have stressed, make conforming to the overall set of obligations impossible. Thus, the individual in a complex society characterized by role conflicts who is motivated to reduce the overall strain will be compelled to come to satisfactory terms with the particular set of contradictions and contingencies imposed on his conduct by his biographically particular set of social roles. If each individual finds, for example, that favoring the powerful people with whom he deals reduces strain and if power is characteristically associated with particular positions, then the individual reduction of role strain will also articulate role sets.

These basic assumptions of the theory of role strain have become so characteristic of sociological thinking that they are seldom explicitly associated with their source. It is worth reflecting on what was new in these assumptions: (1) The individual is responsive to normative obligations, but in a new more sophisticated model. She is still conceived as calculating the costs and benefits of each course of action within a given role but also capable of calculating costs and benefits across her biographically distinct package of roles. (2) To reduce strain, the individual must weigh very different kinds, as well as sources, of rewards and punishments against each other. For example, earning money generally takes time that is then not available for tasks that may bring other, nonmonetary rewards. The person must be able, for example, to weigh an increase in money earned in one role against time spent with family in another in order to reduce strain. A complex exchange ratio is implied. (3) If sanctions are properly arranged, the individual's participation in collective tasks need not assume shared values concerning the task, nor shared commitment to it. Personal motives can produce social coordination based on rewards, even if the members of that society differ in their values.

The Role Bargain

In the theory of role strain, although the individual internalizes a model of the social structure, its roles, and distribution of resources, he is not motivated to conform to the model. In fact, because the model includes dilemmas and contradictions that make conformity impossible, another orientation to social norms is necessary. Goode characterized that orientation as a *role bargain*. As seen by Goode, the individual consults his model of the social world as if it described a set of competing, sometimes contradictory offers for his participation. That is, the role obligations and the system of sanctions are treated as a set of contingencies something like this: If I do X, I will accomplish D and person A in position B will respond by doing Y; if I do XX, I will accomplish DD and person AA in position BB will respond by doing YY; if I do XXX, I will accomplish DDD and person AAA will respond by doing YYY; and so on. Based on this model, the individual can choose the set of accomplishments and responses that best suits his personal motivational needs, including the reduction of overall role strain. Based on this sort of reasoning, a person, such as myself—an employed, single parent—could decide to feed his children lunch rather than make them get their own, hoping to increase certain rewards from them while reducing the rewards from others who would have me write more pages of this chapter today. That person could also decide to insist that the children be relatively quiet, rendering his study habitable, at the cost of some negative response from them but allowing some work to be done. Another person might decide to leave certain tasks completely undone, accepting the consequences for that—it is December 20 and this person has not made or purchased any traditional holiday gifts.

The result of these considerations is a series of decisions concerning whether and how well to perform the tasks imposed by one's various roles. At any given moment, one's model of the prevailing contingencies enters the decision process as a set of parameters—fixed conditions, upon which the person can rely for the purpose of making a decision. However, it is also recognized that the model can be corrected in response to events or temporarily set aside. For example, the contingencies just indicated are not workday problems. Usually, the children are in school and in afterschool programs. Many plans and decisions are based on that model. But today, the schools are closed due to inclement weather. My model of the social structure does not need to be revised as it would if the programs closed indefinitely or the schools changed their hours of attendance on a continuing basis. Still, for today, the model must be set aside and a new set of decisions made.

Here we have a reminder that the role bargains are solutions to complex problems posed by contradictory contingencies. Even when they are stable, they can be revised as needed. This ability to revise solutions is decentralized and poses an interesting problem for all the parties to a complex set of interlocking decisions. For example, I could unilaterally decide to withhold lunch-making services based on an evaluation of my children's maturity and a felt need to work on other things. This is imposed on them, but their response, which I anticipate in my planning, may not be what I predict. In other words, they can unilaterally throw a snit. They can do that whether I feed them lunch or not. This will impact on those who would like to see some hurry-up on this writing, although they may not know the cause of the delay. Overall, then, the theory of role strain suggests a thinking, calculating person who internalizes models of the social structure which he uses as the basis for predictions, but which he is able to modify unilaterally. Each unilateral change may lead all those implicated in the decision to adjust their own conduct.

Goode's analysis of this decision-making process includes some consideration of how individuals structure their decisions. First, the individual has some control over whether she will enter role relationships and become subject to their contingencies. *Compartmentalization*, keeping contradictory activities separate, either by mental processes or by social arrangements that separate the contradictory activities in time or space, allows the individual to take on relationships that would otherwise cause strain. Sometimes, the individual can *delegate* specific duties to others, thus allowing her to sustain relationships that would otherwise cause strain. Sometimes, demanding *role relationships can be eliminated* and profitable ones begun voluntarily to reduce overall strain. Sometimes the individual can *prevent others from initiating contact* and making demands. These variables influence the person's ability to control her entry into and continuation of role relationships.

Second, once the individual has entered a role relationship, social conditions influence the degree to which parties are free to define the relationship on their own terms. These social conditions are imposed by and can be personified in terms of "third parties" to any given role bargain. Third parties are not directly implicated in the bargains, but they are affected by their consequences. For example, the bargain struck by me and my children over who will make lunch has the publisher of this book as a third party. There are other third parties, as well. The parents of my children's friends must explain why they do not make lunch when "all the kids' parents" do. And, reciprocally, I am a third party to the arrangements in other households that my children report, and so on. Even more indirectly, you, the reader, become a third party to my mundane household arrangements because they, and not something more lofty, are on my mind as I search for illustrative examples. In short, the entire social structure is implicated, but only by its imposition on bargains.

Goode suggests some structural patterns among these third party influences. Norms may set priorities among lower-level competing norms. (This idea was discussed in conjunction with Toby's work.) Some third party relationships are imposed by the role structure and are confronted typically by those in a role. This allows an entire role set to be implicated in each role relationship within it. The degree to which performance of one role is linked to performance of roles in other role sets varies. To the extent that linkage exists, one cannot reduce performance of one role to create or conserve resources for the other. For example, one cannot sacrifice work performance to make time for children to an extent that reduces one's employability or salary without hurting the children. Linkage makes some strategic choices counterproductive. Finally, ascriptive statuses impose role relationships on one, willy-nilly.[1] This is how auxiliary characteristics associated with roles enter the bargaining process.

Need to secure cooperation. As described by Goode, the process of setting a role bargain is essentially a decision-making process. The social structure and individuals holding other roles make demands and impose contingencies. The individual weighs these against his own motivational needs, treating them as parameters of choice, as a set of offers that are available at his own discretion. At the same time, the ability of all parties to unilaterally redefine the terms of their own participation and the ability of all parties to respond to changes in the environment are recognized. But Goode's theory does not extend to a crucial implication of these abilities—the need for parties to coordinate and recoordinate their decisions with one another. As an obvious case, one cannot reduce strain by delegating one's duties without getting another to take them, although one can decide to delegate on one's own. This omission is not a flaw in the theory, but rather one of its boundaries. The theory of role strain is concerned with the decision-making process, in which existing perceptions are employed as parameters. The communicative work that people do to coordinate their perceptions and conduct with one another, especially in social interaction, is the topic of other microsociological theories. We will return to that topic in subsequent chapters.

THE ECLIPSE OF STRUCTURAL ROLE THEORY

During the early part of the 1960s, there was extensive research on the topic of role conflict. The presence of role conflict was documented in a wide variety of roles and institutions, lending support to the view that conflict is a generic characteristic of role sets. But despite the extensive research supporting its basic premises, there was very little further development and refinement of conflict role theories, such as Merton's theory of the role set, which focused on the structural or social factual characteristics of roles. Interest in roles continued, but by the late 1960s it was focused almost exclusively on the process by which people holding various positions coordinate their activities in interaction.

Although the topics are closely related conceptually, the data required to address them are quite different, making it difficult for both topics to be pursued in the same research. The study of the process of coordination requires detailed knowledge of conduct in particular settings. Ethnographic observation, analysis of documents and how they are produced, interviews, and recently, detailed analysis of conversations are among the most common methodologies. The resulting studies attempt to identify processes in interaction that result in a particular resolution of particular local difficulties, often role conflicts. The processes identified may be quite commonly found in other settings. Some are thought to be characteristic of all interaction. However, the local outcomes depend on details of the local setting.

The structural theories deal with the statistical distribution of these outcomes across similar settings. They require knowledge of those outcomes in an appropriate sample of similar settings. Detailed knowledge of how the outcome is achieved in any given setting does not contribute to their topic. By the same token, neither the specification of role conflicts nor statistical evidence concerning their resolution contribute greatly to the study of the process of their resolution in particular settings.

Interest in the structural aspects of role was also diminished by two common misunderstandings of the implications of role sets and role conflict for structural role theory and of Merton's analysis of role sets in particular. As we have seen, recognition of role conflict as a characteristic of the system of roles requires a fundamentally different explanation of role-related behavior from Parsons's action theory. If a system of roles is characterized by role conflict, conformity to roles is disqualified as a summary of the social psychological processes and consensus is disqualified as an explanation for coordination of activities and stability. The transition of the form of explanation in structural role theories was simply overlooked by many theorists and sociologists who were only peripherally concerned with the topic of roles. Rejection of Parsons's theory of social roles became a rejection of social roles as a topic.

The second common misunderstanding is the classification of Merton's analysis of the role set as a social psychological theory rather than a social factual one. Merton's analysis concerns the statistical relationships among the many incumbents of the roles included in a role set. It is often understood, however, as applying to the relationships among a person and the other particular people he or she interacts with by virtue of their structural positions. Seen that way, role set analysis must be evaluated as an approach to behavioral decision making in competition with Goode's theory of role strain and other approaches to be discussed later and as an approach to how people coordinate their perception and conduct in competition with the interaction theories also to be discussed later. As the interaction theories developed, they were often seen as replacements for the structural ones.

In contrast, I am suggesting here that at least three different topics have emerged in the study of roles: social factual outcomes, behavioral decision making, and interaction processes. The emergent theories of these distinct topics should be regarded as supplementary work on related but different topics (Handel, 1979).

For these and other reasons, while the discipline concentrated on the interaction processes involved in role performance, study of structural aspects of role languished. The conceptual connection between the two aspects of role performance was not completely forgotten. Shibutani (1973), for example, showed that knowledge of interaction process allowed the prediction of outcomes on a societal scale under certain structural conditions. Specifically, he argued that sustained intergroup conflict restricts the flow of information about one's own and the opponent group. This restriction of information increasingly biases those outcomes of interaction that define the two groups relative to one another. The personification of the opponent group grows increasingly negative, biasing the interpretation of available evidence still further and justifying, in the extreme, wartime atrocities. Similarly, Farberman (1975) studied a few car dealerships in detail but focused on the resolution of financial pressures that were known to be generally experienced by car dealers. Thus, his detailed study achieved a high measure of generality.

But despite occasional exceptions, the study of structural roles and the study of the interaction processes involved in coordinating conduct had quite separate fates during the late 1960s and 1970s. The study of

interaction processes thrived while the study of role structure languished. The conceptual links between the two topics were increasingly
neglected so that by the late 1970s it was controversial to suggest that
the two concerns were compatible. Further discussion of this issue will
have to wait, however, until we have reviewed the process theories that
commanded sociological attention and temporarily eclipsed the study of
the structural characteristics of roles.

NETWORK ANALYSIS

During the 1980s, interest in the structural characteristics of roles re-
bounded. And with a vengeance! *Network analysis* is the collective term
for a family of statistical and methodological techniques for constructing
mathematical models of social structure. They are among the most sophisticated and mathematically rigorous techniques now in use by social
scientists. Burt (1982) has begun to apply these techniques to the study
of social action in role sets. At this time, the advances made by applying
network analytic techniques to role sets are methodological rather than
theoretical. New methodological approaches have been taken to the measurement of some crucial variables, and the promise of the approach
appears great. However, other variables cannot yet be rigorously measured. As a result, theories cannot yet be tested and the available analyses
are piecemeal.

It is not surprising that advances in structural role theory would
await major methodological developments. These theories propose that
people act in part from their own preferences and in part because of
sanctions imposed by others. To apply and test these theories, we must
be able to distinguish empirically between these two factors. This is not
an easy task. Blau (1960) was able to show that both of these factors did
indeed enter into behavioral decisions. Blau measured the attitudes of
caseworkers in public assistance agencies. He found that when the attitudes of others in an agency were statistically controlled, the caseworkers'
own attitudes were reflected in the distribution of their role-related decisions and when the caseworkers' own attitudes were controlled, the attitudes of their coworkers were reflected in the distribution of those
decisions. That is, in addition to the effect of internalized attitudes emphasized in Parsons's theory of action, there was a *structural effect* of
others' attitudes. Development of structural role theories requires some
technique for further analyzing these structural effects.

Enter network analysis. There has been a long tradition of constructing mathematical models of small groups and of relationships
among relatively small numbers of people. Many of these techniques are

called *sociometric*. For example, suppose we want to construct a model of a network of friends, centered around one person (ego). We determine how many friends ego has and what friendships exist among his friends. The network structure would include the number of people involved, the extent to which they are interconnected, and the pattern of connections. These structural variables can then be correlated with other interesting variables.

Burt observed the formal similarity between such empirically defined sociometric networks and the networks conceptually defined as role sets. Instead of a person as a center, there is a position. Instead of interpersonal relationships, there are interpositional ones. Instead of links between persons that must either be present or absent, there is a statistical link between positions, which is probabilistic. But with statistical manipulation to adjust for the probabilistic nature of the links, the underlying form is the same. Even though very many people can be involved, the number of positions is small. Role structures can therefore be modeled by applying modified sociometric techniques, and by analogy, the interpersonal consequences of sociometric structural variation can be applied to interpositional analyses. Eventually, perhaps, such substantive terms as *power* may be associated with or defined by microstructural form.

I hope this one example has conveyed the direction of applying network analysis to the problem of defining roles and action in them. For 30 years or more, the application of structural role theory has required complex statistical analysis of data concerning relationships. It is not easy conceptually, and it was unfeasible before powerful computers became available. Work on this topic has begun again and eventually will allow testing of existing theories or development of new theories based on empirical results. Integration of these mathematically sophisticated models with the substantive concerns of the discipline pose an interesting challenge.

NOTE

1. This expression meaning whether one wants to or not is derived from "will ye or nill ye" and is not used often enough, in my opinion.

REFERENCES

Blau, Peter. 1960. Structural Effects. *American Sociological Review* 25:178–193.
Burt, Ronald. 1982. Toward a Structural Theory of Action. New York: Academic Press.

Farberman, Harvey. 1975. A Criminogenic Market Structure: The Automobile Industry. *Sociological Quarterly* 16:438–457.

Goffman, Erving. 1959. The Presentation of Self in Everyday Life. Garden City, NY: Doubleday.

Goffman, Erving. 1961. Asylums. Garden City: Anchor.

Goffman, Erving. 1967. Interaction Ritual. Garden City: Anchor.

Goode, William. 1960. A Theory of Role Strain. *American Sociological Review* 25:483–496.

Handel, Warren. 1979. Normative Expectations and the Emergence of Meaning as Solutions to Problems. *American Journal of Sociology* 84:855–881.

Hughes, Everett. (1971/1945). Dilemmas and Contradictions of Status. Pp. 141–145 in The Sociological Eye. Chicago: Aldine.

Merton, Robert. 1957. The Role-Set: Problems in Sociological Theory. *British Journal of Sociology* 8 (June):106–120.

Merton, Robert, with Elinor Barber. 1976. Sociological Ambivalence. Pp. 3–32 in Robert Merton, Sociological Ambivalence and Other Essays. New York: Free Press.

Park, Robert. 1928. Human Migration and the Marginal Man. *American Journal of Sociology* 33:881–893.

Preiss, Jack and Howard Ehrlich. 1966. An Examination of Role Theory. Lincoln: University of Nebraska Press.

Schwartz, Barry. 1974. Waiting, Exchange and Power: The Distribution of Time in Social Systems. *American Journal of Sociology* 79:841–871.

Shibutani, Tamotsu. 1973. On the Personification of Adversaries. Pp. 223–233 in Tamotsu Shibutani (ed.), Human Nature and Collective Behavior: Papers in Honor of Herbert Blumer. New Brunswick, NJ: Transaction Press.

Stinchcombe, Arthur. 1975. Merton's Theory of Social Structure. Pp. 11–33 in Lewis Coser (ed.), The Idea of Social Structure. New York: Harcourt Brace Jovanovich.

Toby, Jackson. 1952. Some Variables in Role Conflict Analysis. *Social Forces* 30:323–327.

8

Symbolic Interaction

The study of symbolic interaction has a long history in American sociology. The term was coined by Herbert Blumer (1938), but this approach to social psychology had already been in use among Blumer's professors and colleagues at the University of Chicago as part of the broader "Chicago School" of sociology.[1] Although this approach predates Parsons's influential work, Blumer redefined it during the 1950s as part of the general critical response to structural functional thought and especially to Parsons's formulations of it.

Blumer's (1938) original statement of the symbolic interactionist position was developed primarily in critical contrast to psychological approaches to social psychology. But his later series of influential statements (1954, 1956, 1962) contrasted symbolic interaction with sociological theory and methodology. Blumer's basic criticism was the same in both cases. He argued that other approaches in psychology and sociology were too mechanistic and ignored the active process of interpretation involved in both individual and coordinated social conduct. He especially emphasized the importance of the self in human conduct. Blumer's work includes a program for developing a more adequate theory of social life, grounded in his critiques of other positions.

BLUMER'S CRITICAL PROGRAM:
PURPOSE IN HUMAN CONDUCT

Most of Blumer's (1938) early criticisms of competing approaches to social psychology were directed against views that have become out-moded. However, the contrast he draws between his own views and those of behaviorism remain instructive. Blumer (1938) accepted the idea that infants are equipped with a wide variety of complex, but unsystematized reflexes. Learning is required to adapt these reflexes to the environment by associating them with one another and by organizing them into mean-ingful conduct.

In Blumer's (1938:153) view, stimulus–response psychology and symbolic interaction are in agreement on this most general orientation, but they emphasize different attributes of behavior. Stimulus–response psychology, he argued, emphasizes how specific reflexes are chained together in response to environmental contingencies. In modern terms these contingencies result in classical and operant conditioning. As a result, the complex behavior comes under environmental control. The frequency of conduct and the order in which behavioral units occur are environmentally conditioned and can be described *mechanically* in terms of environmental regularities. Cognitive or mental processes were ig-nored and often regarded as either fictional, epiphenomenal, or irrele-vant by strict behaviorists.[2]

In contrast, symbolic interaction emphasizes the organization of complex conduct by purposes. We are able to mentally construct images of the future, to evaluate them in terms of purposes, and to choose from among available courses of action the one that is anticipated to result in the best approximation of the desired end or goal. In this process, our perception and evaluation of the environment are selective and are orga-nized by our goals or purposes. Different goals make different potential uses of things in the environment interesting and change our criteria for evaluation. Purposes create the environment in this sense and as our goals or purposes change, our perceptions and evaluations of the envi-ronment are reorganized.

Blumer was concerned with the process of interpreting the environ-ment and the potential for reinterpretation rather than the specific con-duct that resulted. At any time, the existing organization of the environment allows repetitive behavior. However, that repetition is orga-nized by an interpretation of the environment that should be included in theoretical accounts of conduct because (1) it is there even during periods of repetitious, predictable behavior, and (2) it can change even without changes in the external contingencies. The use of symbols to represent the environment is the human ability that makes this mental anticipation possible. Blumer's main point is that even repetitive conduct is not *mechanically* linked to the environment. A voluntaristic process, involving an active reflexive self occurs, and an adequate theory of conduct must include that process.[3]

In his later statements of the place of symbolic interaction with respect to sociology, Blumer (1954, 1956, 1962) turned his attention to the basis of coordinated action—action in which more than one person is involved and in which their *anticipated* individual lines of action are fit together. In social conduct, the anticipated success of one's own plans is contingent on the conduct of others. For example, my plan to send a message by placing it in a blue and red metal container by the roadside assumes a great deal about the conduct of others. We should not lose sight of the fact that it is *future* conduct that must be coordinated—thus far nonexistent conduct, conduct that exists only in mental images, plans, and intentions. The course of conduct into the future must be made public so that it can be coordinated. If others' plans could not be made public, we could only perceive and react to already occurring acts. This is often too late to avoid serious consequences.

The significant *symbol* is the vehicle by which humans communicate their plans, intentions, purposes, and thoughts—in short, their mental lives—to one another. Thus the symbol establishes a theoretical continuity between society and mind. Utilized in thought, the symbol allows individual planning and purposive conduct by formulating specific instances in a way that allows projections of the future to be made. By using symbols, the unique nature of each event becomes less important than its similarities with other events. By categorizing in terms of symbols, our knowledge of similar events can be applied to the specific case, whose unique characteristics remain and require adjustment of our plans and interpretations. Expressed in words or gestures so that others receive indications of our thought, the symbol allows coordination among thinking, communicating beings. This process of coordination through symbolic interpretation and communication, Blumer (1956) argues, must be included in sociological theory. His reasoning parallels his argument against a mechanistic behaviorism that excludes mental interpretive processes.

Variable analysis, or social factual reasoning, has a range of useful applications, Blumer argues. When the objects to which humans must respond remain relatively constant and when the meaning given those objects remains stable, conduct would be repetitive, and observed statistical relationships between selected independent and dependent variables would be reliable. Blumer (1956:687) observes that "The only necessary precaution would be not to assume that the stated relation between the variables was necessarily intrinsic and universal. Since anything that is defined may be redefined, the relation has no intrinsic fixity." Empirically, new events, discoveries, and ideas in a social group change the relationships among variables measured as indicators of group life. Theoretically, then, to account for both the stability and change in social life, theoretical analysis must give priority to the collective interpretive process that results in order when definitions and events are stable and change when they are not.

Stated negatively, Blumer's argument is that "social forces" or causes or environmental events do not operate mechanistically through people as mere vehicles for the causal relationships. Stated positively, there is a collective interpretive process, accomplished through the use of symbols, whose outcome creates both relative or temporary stability and change by developing definitions of events that are more or less shared in the social group and which change more or less quickly. As conceived by symbolic interactionists, the use of symbols, whether in thought or communication with others, involves the development of a self to which the individual can refer. Choosing, interpreting individuals are able to think, to coordinate their conduct, and to make themselves predictable to one another by utilizing symbols in an interpretive process requiring awareness of and reference to oneself. Symbolic interactionists attempt to study the process of symbol use and to explain social life in terms of that process.

SYMBOLS AND SELVES

Blumer and Mead before him were concerned with the symbolic basis of coordinated action—of collective, cooperative definitions and behavior. But for many years, the mainstream of symbolic interaction research and theorizing was greatly, perhaps primarily, concerned with deception and with adversarial processes of negotiation and bargaining. Oddly enough, these concerns are inherent in Mead's formulations of the concepts of *symbol* and *self*, two basic components of symbolic interactionist theory. We will try to understand the fundamental importance of deception as a phenomenon and the concern for adversarial processes in terms of the underlying concepts of self and symbol.

Self

In the first place, the *self* is an organized collection of attitudes, values, memories, purposes, and behavioral tendencies. This organization makes our conduct orderly, corresponding loosely to what we now call the "personality." But this cannot be all that is intended by the word *self*, because if it were, this organization would be a behavioral constant, and social forces would act mechanically and predictably on us once the self, or psychological organization, was taken into consideration. This constant could then be excluded from explanations of statistical regularities in conduct, or, at most, mentioned as a given condition.

Each self changes over time, in part as the result of learning. When we learn, in Mead's (1934; 1964) view, the self becomes reorganized (reintegrated). It does not simply add facts or accumulate responses. Change through learning still allows the environment to act mechanically through the self. Action of the environment over time could be taken into account along with the immediate situation. Previous experience, acting upon the self according to principles of learning, might predictably organize the self. Then, at any moment, environmental events might act mechanically through the self as it is currently organized and then alter it for future experience. Mead accepted the idea of self-change through learning, while incorporating additional elements, among them active consciousness and self-reference.

Active consciousness. By *active consciousness*, Mead meant more than awareness of events. He argued that as the nervous system evolved into more complex forms, a single event, acting as a stimulus, might activate more than one tendency to act. These conflicting possible actions interfere with one another. Consciousness, Mead argued, has emerged as a characteristic of the period during which our nervous system evaluates conflicting tendencies to act and decides among them.

Mead argued that we become conscious of generalizations or abstractions of which the conflicting tendencies are instances. Thinking is the manipulation of these generalizations or abstractions in consciousness, including our own anticipated courses of action and their consequences. In this way, we become conscious of the alternative futures suggested by the alternative courses of action, and we become capable of choosing a course of action on the basis of the future we anticipate it will produce. This provides us with a degree of voluntaristic choice within the parameters imposed by our experience, and it makes it possible for us to be ethical or moral agents, as well as to make and evaluate plans. In contrast to Parsons's approach, our learned values are conceived to enter into choices rather than to serve as mechanical criteria for rational thought.

In this view, other animals are aware of a stimulus, perhaps, but not of their own conduct until it occurs and not of the consequences of the conduct until they occur. Also, they are unable to formulate abstract relationships between conduct and consequences such as "a stitch in time saves nine," although they may act prudently anyway. (See Griffin [1976] for a modern discussion of animal awareness.)

Social origins. These abstractions and generalizations could conceivably be derived totally from one's own experience, and thinking could occur using private and personal indicators of the future. However, most of the abstractions we utilize are symbols, taught to us by other people through the regularities in their own conduct and their responses to our conduct. For example, we are aided in forming the abstraction "chair" by the regularity of other people's conduct toward chairs and their different but regular conduct toward tables. We are also aided by their making a characteristic noise to indicate chairs (a word) and different noises for other things. Finally, we are aided by their response to our treatment of things and noise making (speaking) and by their formulation of generalities such as "we don't sit on tables." In this sense, even our selves and private thoughts are social. Among the things we learn about the environment are the categories into which it should be divided, the proper use of things, proper noise making, and criteria for group membership.

It is possible to have an idea that is new to one's group, of course. In fact, that is the primary value of thinking. However, the adoption of the group's symbols predisposes one's thinking to utilize the terms, abstractions, and rules already existing in the group. Shibutani (1966) found that creative, unusual interpretations of the environment are only likely to be considered and applied when routine ones are an inadequate basis for behavior. The extremity of ideas considered, relative to cultural standards, varies with the extremity and duration of the failure of those cultural standards to guide conduct. He also found (1978) that conformity to prevailing sentiments is more stringently controlled in communication channels when group cohesion is valued highly, as it is during intergroup conflict.

Conforming to the categories and perceptions in the group, then, is a moral issue and is enforced. When we learn, for example, that we do not remove peanut butter from the jar on our fingers, we learn other things in addition to that fact (if it is a fact). We learn that our treatment by others in the group, our standing in the group, and sometimes our continued membership are contingent upon the appropriate conduct toward peanut butter. Although these social contingencies may alter the balance of pleasure and displeasure found in eating peanut butter on one's fingers by increasing its extrinsic displeasures, they do not diminish its intrinsic pleasures. This distinction is critical to the sociology of moral conduct. It provides an incentive to mislead others about our conduct in order to have its intrinsic pleasures without suffering disapproval.

Conflicting interests and preferences. Mead conceived the internal organization of the self as an integration of the various interests pressed upon a person by variously situated others. He suggested that the person learns each set of individual interests separately and then integrates them into a generalized model. If a person constructs such a model, and conducts himself or herself in terms of all of the diverse interests represented in the situation, conduct is moral. Sociologically, because all interests would be served, coordination and cooperation in the social relationship will be maximized as well as the probability of achieving the collective purpose.

It is critical to understand that the development of a truly generalized model and the organization of conduct in terms of all interests represented in a situation are ethical and normative ideals, not a workaday occurrence. In his classes, Mead (1934) illustrated this process using baseball, a team sport characterized by clearly defined common purposes, clearly defined division of responsibilities, clearly defined arbiters to enforce the rules, clearly defined chains of command to resolve disputes and select strategies when there are options, and excellent communication channels. These circumstances reduce cross-purposes on each team and provide an environment well suited to collectively pursue the common goals.

Comparable parameters do not characterize most situations. In fact, the circumstances described by Mead in learning to play a position in a team sport in a way that accommodates the needs of all the other positions resembles very closely the articulation of a role set at the positional level. This similarity was possibly intended by Merton (1935), who reviewed Mead's book, *Mind, Self and Society*, quite favorably upon its initial release. Merton's intention aside, in Mead's conception, the internal organization of the self, which is the basis for coordinated conduct, for cooperation, and for ethical conduct, is achieved by integrating contrary and competing interests in a generalized model, called the *generalized other*, and then by acting in a way that promotes the generalized, integrated interests of all those involved in a complex social relationship rather than the separate interests of some.

Reference groups as perspectives. When a fully generalized other, representing all interests in a complex social situation, is not formed, conduct is organized by partial perspectives, representing only some of those interests. The selection of interests to be represented often reflects ignorance that additional interests are affected. However, it may also reflect affiliation with one group and the desire to advance its interests, even at the expense of others. The persons associated with those interests may be real ones, as in the case of peer groups, or they may be imaginary. Dead parents, fictional characters in movies or on television, semifictional characters such as the manipulated public images of politicians or celebrities, and future evaluators such as one's posterity are instances of imaginary persons whom we try to accommodate. Shibutani (1978) calls these partial perspectives *reference groups.*

Reference groups and the conduct they legitimize are partly determined by conditions in the social group. Shibutani (1973) argued that intergroup conflict influences the operation of communication channels by constraining the messages that can be exchanged and the credibility of sources. Sanctions justified by the need for cohesion within the group are used to reduce negative communication about one's own group and positive communication about the other. Members of one's own group are regarded as credible, while members of the other are distrusted. Those within a group who are too positive about the other group and too negative about their own are discredited as well.

The effect of these restrictions of communication is to increasingly bias the images one holds of the conflicting groups. One's own group is increasingly portrayed as positive while the other or others are portrayed as negative. These images justify increasing negative conduct (ignoring their interests) toward the other group and increasing loyalty to one's own (pursuing its interests to the disadvantage of others), regardless of what the group does (self-righteousness). This differential conduct provides each group with evidence of the other's perfidy and its own right to retaliate. In extreme and/or long-lasting conflict situations, one's own group may come to appear almost divine while the other comes to appear less than human. Extreme contrast conceptions justify such conduct as torture and concentration camps. Milder ones justify discrimination based on race, religion, gender, age, ethnic group, or regional accent.

Shibutani (1978) emphasizes that the ethical, cooperative behavior resulting from utilizing a generalized other as a perspective and the brutal behavior of extreme conflict are poles of a continuum. This continuum is defined by the degree and length of conflict, which influences conduct by imposing itself on the communication channels through which the group interprets its environment. The definitions that result and the conduct they legitimize are influenced by the societal conditions, but only as they act through the interpretive process. Interpersonally, communication is distorted, and this, in turn, influences the operation of reference groups as perspectives upon which to base conduct. Shibutani

(1978) suggests that other social conditions may also impose characteristic patterns of social control and conduct through the interpretive process.

Self-reference or reflexivity. *Self-reference* means that the self can be taken as an object of conduct. The maintenance or alteration of the self can be adopted as a purpose among the other purposes of action. This implies more than being able to act in such ways as giving oneself a haircut. Here, the term *self* is not used in the technical sense we are developing, and this common usage makes it difficult to grasp fully the technical sense of acting on one's self. Try to think of your self, the organized pattern underlying your behavior, as a sort of a thing. It is not as concrete as your hair, which you can also act upon, but it is real nonetheless. One can perceive that organization and most importantly its organizing values and principles. One can think about one's self by reviewing what characteristics, for example, values, virtues, and faults, it has. One can adopt altering one's self-characteristics as a purpose to be achieved.

Self-reference provides a basis for altruistic and generally ethical conduct that does not require one to postulate altruistic drives or instincts. Suppose one adopts the value *kindness* as a desirable characteristic and undertakes action to make the self more consistent with that value by being intentionally kind. The action might favor others over one's self (nontechnical sense) with respect to money or convenience or other good things, but it still serves one's own rational interest by its consequences for one's self (technical sense). One can have a reasonable, self-serving interest in altruism. In theory, we can adopt such concepts as *utility-maximizing, reinforcement,* and *rational self-interest* when they are useful without relinquishing the idea of ethical or altruistic conduct. And we do not need to postulate specific drives or other circular explanations of conduct that is self-sacrificing with respect to various tangible rewards.

It is crucial to emphasize the social nature of self-reference. The character traits into which behavior is organized are provided by the society in the same way as other categories. In addition, the values placed on the various self-characteristics are imposed by the society in the same ways as other values. And, as with other values, our conduct is more or less reflective of all the interests involved. Sometimes we approximate the view of a generalized other and sometimes the view of a more limited reference group. Individual conduct is controlled to a great extent by the organized perspective of a social group and the approval of that group is an important motivating concern. In a society characterized by conflict, the desirability of traits, the priority among them, the degree to which various others are entitled to highly valued conduct, and so on will all be affected by the distortions of the channels of communication.

Role Making. This conception of an active interpretive process is fundamentally incompatible with Parsons's view that action is based on rational conformity to shared and relatively stable values. Symbolic interaction recognizes not only that purposive choices must be made, but also that the basis of the choice is variably guided by the complete set of interests and values in the society, that the degree of conflict within and between societies influences the application of values, and that the individual can intentionally reorganize his or her own principles of choice and action. As Turner (1962) puts it, the individual does not mechanically perform roles. He or she makes the roles by more or less creatively interpreting role requirements. Conformity is only one of many outcomes of this process.

Turner (1962) argues that the interpretive process organizes perception and conduct by grouping what one expects of others and what one perceives that others expect of him into roles. The external obligations for a role, expressed in rules of conduct and explicit sanctions, for examples vary in their degree of clearness, completeness, and consistency. But regardless of the amounts of ambiguity, discretion, and conflict with which the individual must cope, Turner argues that we attempt to define our roles clearly for our own purposes. The meaning of the action may be redefined, however, if the definition of the role changes.

Thus, role-organized conduct does not follow from role taking in the sense of internalizing existing rules and sanctions. Rather, it follows from role making—the interpretation of the situation and the creation of definitions, more or less constrained by the situation. When the environment is clearly, consistently, and completely defined by others, conformity results. But that is an ideal, not a description of this world. The process of role making occurs at all times, in this view, but the outcomes resemble conformity to varying degrees.

Turner (1962) argued that individual definitions of role will tend to develop toward clarity. The individual will define the interests and expectations of those with whom she has role relationships. Their perspectives and the organized perspective of the generalized other or reference group are taken to define one's own appropriate conduct. When inconsistencies must be resolved, Turner argues, a principle is developed to organize the inconsistent elements in a more abstract pattern within which they are made consistent. In Turner's (1952) own research, U.S. navy disbursing officers confronted occasional inconsistencies between the expectation that they follow navy regulations and the expectation that they obey commands from superior officers. The operation of a creative interpretive process is reflected in the presence of four typical patterns of response to the dilemma, each reflecting a different approach to reconciling regulations and orders that contradict them. Some follow regulations narrowly, ignoring contrary pressures; some assume they won't be punished and violate regulations freely; some fail to appreciate the reality of the conflicts and follow even illegal orders; some are realists, who see the contradictions and work the system for their own ends. The situations created by the navy as an organization do not determine the response. On the other hand, the choices made by the disbursing officers are not random, as if the situation did not matter at all. The constraint of the situation on definitions is reflected in the fact that only four typical responses develop, and even they are far from evenly chosen. The selection by most officers of the realistic approach to the conflict indicates both similarity of circumstance and similarity of values and other components of decision making. Finally, the constraint of the situation is reflected in the different career consequences of the different styles of response. One can choose to act as one wishes, but one cannot also choose the consequences that are to some extent entailed in the action. Just as the disbursing officers' choices are patterned by their common situation, the responses of others to them is also patterned. Only realism is compatible with a successful career.

In Turner's approach, we see the tension between the role as externally defined and as internally defined by the individual. Individuals tend to clarify and explicate their situations, producing principles of conduct to organize their choices. So, in conflict situations, individuals will still act from principle, even though the social environment does not provide unambiguous principles of conduct. We also see that the private principles of conduct are not necessarily shared. However the individual decides to act, others will differentially sanction that conduct. Neither the use of sanctions nor one's own principled conduct necessarily changes the mind of the other. After considering the nature of symbols, we will return to this dilemma: What does a person do who has resolved conflicts in the system to his own satisfaction and is acting from principle when others negatively sanction that conduct to various degrees?

Our concern with conflict situations may seem at odds with Blumer's and Mead's concerns with the basis of order, ethical conduct, and cooperation in social interaction. This shift of attention follows the transition from programmatic statements to empirically informed theoretical ones. An important aspect of sociological theory is the potential for improving social systems. Many programmatic statements are oriented to defining topics whose study would allow more desirable social conditions to be achieved. Thus, a program is not designed merely to understand the world as it exists, beginning with a conceptual scheme. Rather, the program also prominently includes arguments that the results of study and theoretical development will provide a basis for improvement of the social world.

But these bases for improvement must arise from studying the world as it is. So, although our goal may be to understand and promote equality, for example, our descriptive studies and theory will include descriptions of how inequality is produced, if inequality is the way of the world. The way to produce cooperation, for example, by utilizing symbols, must be inferred from the actual use of symbols in the world as it is now. The world as it is now suffers shortages of many desirable things. If the process underlying our conduct is interaction using symbols, then symbols provide a basis for what we have, for worse as well as for better. It is about time to consider what symbols are and then to review what we know about their use in this world.

Symbols

In Mead's view, the ability to use symbols is distinctively human, resulting from the application of active consciousness to the behavioral gestures that other animals utilize in communication. A *gesture* (Mead, 1934:14) is an observable part of conduct that indicates the future course of conduct and brings forth a response to that future conduct from others. For example, when a dog bares its teeth and snarls, other dogs respond in a very limited number of specific ways. Baring the teeth and snarling are gestures. The response to these gestures may act as a gesture itself. For example, if the response to the snarl is an aggressive posture, this posture calls out characteristic responses from the first dog. In many species, conversations of gestures allow complex ritual combat in which a series of gestures is exchanged and dominance established without actual fighting or injury. Although each animal responds to the gestures of the other, there is no indication that they are aware of the information contained in their own behavior for the other nor that they are able to control the gestures. The extent of this lack of control is highest, perhaps, in the response to chemical gestures or pheromones, such as those secreted by females in heat or by males marking a territory.

A gesture becomes significant, becomes a symbol, when the human is aware of the consequences of her own gesture for the response of others. That is, the person is able to take herself and her ongoing behavior as an object of consciousness, perceive it, and respond to it. When this is done, she can predict the consequences of her own conduct for the response of others before she acts. Prediction, of course, is not perfect, and accurate prediction exists as an ideal or possibility related to the completeness of the self. As the interests and perspectives informing self-awareness increase, the reference group approaches becoming a self, and gestures approach being shared symbols.

We humans are not uniformly aware of all of our communication, which, therefore, utilizes gestures and symbols that vary in the degree to which meanings are shared and intended. However, again as an ideal, there is no reason why any particular observable conduct that others respond to could not be made a symbol.[4] In the actual world, we are only sometimes aware, but the possibility of awareness makes it difficult, perhaps impossible, to tell whether or not the other person is aware. Is the other's conduct sending a message of which he is aware or not? If the person is aware of the messages being sent, is he also in control of them, or merely monitoring them as we are? Does my conduct include messages I am unaware of? Am I mistaken about the meaning of my intended messages to others?

Deception and strategy implied by core concepts. By distinguishing carefully between the ideals and potentials inherent in human conduct and the conduct we actually observe, we can understand the intense interest of symbolic interactionists in deception and strategy. In the case of conduct guided by reference groups as perspectives, the interests of some positions in society are not considered. In each interaction, then, participants cannot be certain that their interests and the interests of others in their own reference groups are being served by the other participants.

Each person, then, will have an incentive to discern the interests served by others and to conceal any failure to consider their interests.[5] This information must be obtained from the portions of conduct and results that are observable. Especially valuable, Goffman (1959) observes, is meaningful behavior that is not controlled by the individual and therefore carries an uncontrived message. And, as Goffman (1959) also observes, the use of intentionally misleading messages is best accomplished by making an intentional symbol of some behavior that is usually uncontrived. The incentive for strategy, then, is found in orientation of conduct to partial reference groups. And this, in turn, is constrained by social conditions, especially unresolved conflicts of interests and characteristics of the communication system.

The means of strategy derive from the nature of symbols. To the extent that we become aware of the meaning of our conduct and can control that conduct, we can lie. That is, we can send a message whose anticipated outcomes we prefer, even if that message is not true. Symbols have many advantages over gestures. However, reliability is not one of them. The flexibility to interpret and reinterpret events has great adaptive significance and can be utilized to coordinate conduct. However, it can also be used to communicate a basis for coordination—a set of definitions and intentions—to others manipulatively. By that I mean that the others can be convinced to follow a plan of action while the person proposing it does not.

Although lies that are merely self-serving (nontechnical sense) exist, they are not an important concern of symbolic interaction. Rather, the concern is for positional lies and positional strategic concerns. These are dilemmas imposed on many individuals by their common social circumstances and resolved in a small variety of typical ways by them: "Conflicts among individuals . . . are not mere conflicts among their primitive impulses but are conflicts among their respective selves . . . each with its definite social structure" (Mead, 1934:307). These conflicts cannot be resolved, Mead argued, without reconstruction of the society itself. Our active consciousness allows us to modify, reorganize, or reconstruct the social structure, which, in turn, would impose new conditions leading to the reconstruction of self (Mead, 1934:308–309).

This is not to suggest that one cannot redefine self first. However, if one redefines the mental basis of his or her social relationships without alteration of the real conditions in the society and the definitions of others, experience will weigh against the redefinition. The definition could be maintained at some personal cost (role strain), but that arrangement would not constitute a solution of any problem or a resolution of conflict. In modern terms, the negotiated order and role identities are intimately interrelated.

The crucial role of partially shared symbols in positional strategic responses to conflicts of interests is clearly shown in Daniels's (1970) study of deceptive practices in military psychiatry. At the time of the study, military regulations defined both alcoholism and homosexuality as disciplinary matters requiring punitive responses, including court martial, expulsion from the armed forces, and loss of various benefits. The medical profession, on the other hand, regarded both as psychiatric problems calling for treatment. The psychiatrists could not practice medicine according to the standards of their profession without violating military rules—a situation of role conflict.

The resolution of this conflict was complex, but an essential part was falsified paperwork. The psychiatrists submitted false diagnoses for alcoholic and homosexual patients. False diagnoses, such as depression, were selected because the treatment allowed for these conditions in the military regulations were the ones the medical community regarded as appropriate for alcoholism and homosexuality. In other words, the symbol was selected for its consequences in the response of others, rather than for its "truth." This was possible because the psychiatrists were aware of the responses that would follow their own symbolic conduct. The result was a genuine compromise, especially in the case of alcoholism, and not a case of upholding one set of standards by lying to those who tried to impose another. Treatment of alcoholism requires the patient to accept responsibility and acknowledge the problem. Conspiring with the patient to conceal the problem is not a good start.[6]

ERVING GOFFMAN: STRATEGIC CONCERNS
AND STRUCTURAL RESOURCES IN INTERACTION

Goffman's (1969:ix) explicit overall intention is to establish the study of face-to-face social interaction, per se, as a distinctive subarea of sociology. He argued (1964:136) that face-to-face interaction has its own rules, processes, and structure. Consequently, he does not approach interaction as a vehicle or medium in which other social relationships such as roles in the division of labor or placement in the system of stratification are expressed or enacted even though social interaction is usually just such a medium. Rather, Goffman attempts to abstract the distinctive form of relationship with its own reality, *sui generis* (1964:134), that characterizes interaction regardless of what other social relationships are implicated.

Our primary interest is the connection between social interaction and other social processes and institutions—that is, interaction as a medium for social relationships of other kinds. Goffman explicitly adopts the position that there are multiple principles of social organization. He accepts the relevance of a division of labor made up of systematically related roles with incomplete but real coercive force. His own (1961b) formulation of social role structure resembles Merton's, although his studies of the expression of roles in interaction led to modifications of Merton's model as well as different empirical concerns. Goffman was crucially concerned with the detailed analysis of stratification, especially attempts to enhance one's prestige and rights (e.g., 1959) and resistance to attempts to force conduct consistent with undesirable self-implications (1961a).

Hughes's view (discussed in Chapter 7) that each social role carries with it an auxiliary stereotypic self rooted in the traditions and history of the society is the crucial conceptual link between Goffman's study of interaction process and broader sociological issues. Because of these implicit auxiliary characteristics, when people enter interactions, the symbolic categorization of one's self and others defines the social relationships of the society as a whole and everyone's place in it, even if the categories refer explicitly only to the immediate situation. It is in this sense that people who interact do not so much create a definition as find one that has been prefabricated by their society (Goffman, 1974).

But at best, the prefabricated or culturally given definitions define an *appropriate* set of symbolic interpretations, what the situation *ought* to be (Goffman, 1974). What it *is* is another matter. Role conflicts are to be expected and considered options rather than prescriptions. The exercise of these options must be coordinated by participants. Roles vary in their degree of specificity, allowing variance in the details of performance without deviance. This discretionary conduct may tend to define participants and must be coordinated. People may simply reject aspects of their role or its auxiliary implications and negotiate a revision of terms within the interaction.

Interaction requires each person to assess the degree to which each other person fits the cultural expectation. Knowing that one will be scrutinized in this way provides an incentive to present an appearance that, although not necessarily truthful, will support categorization leading to the desired treatment. Knowing that others have the same incentive provides an additional incentive to scrutinize others skeptically. Looked at in this way, Goffman's approach justifies Blumer's doctrine that symbolic interpretation must be included in sociological accounts, even in the routinized instances. In addition it casts the interpretive process in strategic terms, appropriate to the distribution of an ambiguous and conflicting set of values and interests among participants in interaction.

Identity as a Generic Strategic Concern

Preferred role identities. The term *self*, as defined by Mead and Blumer, refers to the regularities and processes of the individual's organization of behavior. It is internal to the individual and primarily mental. But to Goffman, treatment in interaction depends not so much on the person's real self as on the interpretation of that self by others. Goffman uses the terms *identity* or *situated identity* to refer to this image of the person that arises in interaction but includes auxiliary characteristics that may be quite extensive and may approach broadly defining a whole person rather than focusing on the specific narrow concerns of the interaction. In this sense, an identity is a reputation or an image embedded in group life and is a collective interpretation of the person.

As McCall and Simmons (1978) formulate it, the individual imagines himself as he would like to be and act in each social role. They call the preferred images *role identities* and argue that the role-specific identities are loosely coherent, allowing variation of the traits the individual prefers in his diverse roles and also a sense of an underlying ideal self. The ideal self as well as the role identities guide conduct in interaction. This formulation provides a possible basis for applying symbolic interaction to the trade-off among rewards from different roles suggested in Goode's theory of role strain.

Suppose the following is true: Each person is obligated, at any moment to fulfill the terms of some roles. She is entitled to perform others at the same time if she likes. She is entitled to treatment according to the assortment of roles that are performed, and how well they are performed. Others will not be certain what to expect or how to treat that person unless some symbolic representation is made of all of this. Whatever the person does will be treated as a symbolic representation of intentions. Because of structural and idiosyncratic factors, disagreement, at least on details, will be common so that the initial symbolic representation of the person's preferred role identity will often receive corrective feedback and require modification of both the symbolic representation and the intended course of action.

In this context, establishing, defending, and maintaining the preferred identity is a generic concern in two senses. It is extremely common, perhaps intrinsic to all interaction. It remains an issue regardless of the particular identities at stake and the particular role relationships involved. The concern is strategic because the incentive is not necessarily to make an accurate symbolic representation of one's self. Rather, the incentive is to make a symbolic representation that will influence others to accept the preferred role identity. There is a reciprocal incentive, then, not to be taken in. If I act upon and commit my resources based upon the image you project, and you have misled me, my plans will not work out. (I, of course, would never project a false image, so you do not have to be concerned.) This process could be cooperative, but in social systems characterized by role conflict, it will be strategic and somewhat adversarial, even if no conflict is present in a particular interaction.

The most obvious sort of identity manipulation involves making false positive claims about one's commitment, competence, and so on in order to maximize the rewards one receives from others. But the preferred role identity is not necessarily favorable in a straightforward way. For example, for a variety of reasons, both men and women "play dumb"—men more at work, women more in their personal relationships (Gove, Hughes, and Geerken, 1980) Second, even an attractive role identity in a central role may be sacrificed to more crucial concerns. Goffman (1961) reports that surgeons forgo some deference and status to reduce tensions and improve the surgical team's instrumental performance during surgery. Third, even when the penalties are severe, as they are in mental hospitals for example, personal identity can be sacrificed spitefully in order to sabotage the efforts of others who depend on them. Goffman (1961a) reports that mental patients utilize timely outbursts to discipline lower-level staff by embarrassing them when guests or superiors are present. The threat of such outbursts is a factor in negotiating arrangements with the staff. Finally, people sometimes choose to express distaste for their current role as a way to claim the higher status associated with their other roles. Zurcher, Sonenschein, and Metzner (1973), for example, found that male college students used a variety of ways to express their attitude that their jobs as "hashers" in sorority house kitchens were beneath them and reaffirm the higher status of their student role.

In addition, role conflicts in a situation may make identity expression very difficult, even in good faith. Emerson's (1970a, b) studies of gynecological examinations by male physicians is a striking case. The same conduct by the doctor that expresses warmth and caring could be extremely threatening sexually in that context. However, cold and mechanical conduct makes the examination unpleasant as well. Thus, the physician must avoid these two very salient and undesirable identity messages, and patients experience some degree of confusion.

Limits to identity games. Although social incentives encourage an adversarial approach to interaction, the manipulative expression of one's own identity and the detailed attention to the meaning of others' identities apparently do not escalate into unmanageable distrust and conflict. First, it is important to remember that the other business of the interaction may be of greater concern. Other sorts of work are being accomplished, and often the details of role identity are of minor concern. We have already noted that identity claims may be reduced in favor of various other concerns. To that extent, people will not tend unduly to the identity implications of their own conduct, nor challenge others' treatment of them, even if they could demand better for themselves and offer less to others.

Perhaps the greater importance of other matters accounts for Goffman's (1959) observation that people tend to allow one another to control the definitions that concern them. No true belief in others' claims is implied, just a willingness to accept identity claims for the purpose of the situation at hand. For whatever reason, the mutual willingness to accept others' claims within reason without detailed consideration prevents escalation of the gamelike aspects of communication.

This acceptance of claims without true belief has an interesting implication for attempts to transform the stereotypes associated with a role, as women, blacks, and other minorities have tried to do as they enter previously closed occupations. Considerable success can be achieved in being treated by new definitions without corresponding success in changing attitudes about the accuracy of the definitions. This makes it very difficult to assess progress in transforming the underlying attitudes and implies that whenever it becomes convenient to do so, others may cease honoring new claims with which they do not agree but which they have tacitly accepted to expedite more pressing concerns. The current anti-smoking climate, for example, has revealed a considerable reservoir of resentment against smoke, stale smoke odors, and ashes that was not expressed earlier. If this reasoning is sound, we can expect the gay community, for example, to lose much of its recent acceptance if AIDS impoverishes the community and otherwise reduces its political influence.

There are limits to the degree to which individuals can control their conduct and its identity implications. First, we must keep in mind that the symbols are imperfectly shared. As a result, even absolute behavioral control would communicate the intended meaning imperfectly. In addition, behavioral control is also incomplete. Slips are made that indicate contrivance, attempts to control expression, and sometimes, the reality that one is attempting to conceal with a contrived message. Finally, there are limits to the ability to coordinate the messages expressed by various participants who contribute to a collective definition. These limits prevent escalation of manipulation and control, regardless of intent. In effect, they guarantee that although some people will be more manipulative than others, the manipulation cannot exceed limits that are beyond intentional control. This may tend to reduce observer attention to detail by promoting confidence and curtailing attempts to uncover secrets, which, in turn, limits the need to work at covering them.

Thus far, we have seen that the practical concern of pursuing more important business and limits of capability tend to limit deception, manipulation, and game playing in identity expression. There is moral constraint as well. Goffman (1969:123–130) asserts the general presence of moral constraints on conduct in interaction. He cites an internalized value against cheating and a degree of shame linked to being caught. In part, these are rational concerns, because the reputation as a cheater may disqualify one from further interaction. However, the concern for reputation and for adhering to rules seems to survive even when the gains from cheating exceed the practical consequences of diminished reputation. This indicates a value placed on the reputation apart from other practical considerations.

But Goffman does not ground moral concern in individual or group life. For him, it is simply there as an observed fact of interaction. It is best to reiterate in this context that the symbols themselves have a moral character. Also, following McCall and Simmons's (1978) approach, we must remember the concern for self that transcends the individual role identities. This concern for self is an integrative force that brings each person's diverse institutional connections to bear on each interaction. The incentives to achieve the best role identity possible remain, but the constraints are expanded beyond the sanctions of the particular situation to include consistency with one's moral standing (reputation) and practical circumstances in all aspects of life.

A note on method. Goffman developed a distinctive method for analyzing interaction in everyday life, which provides insight into the strengths and limits of his approach. The same role is enacted or performed in a number of situations and in the company of different combinations of others. The transformation of expressive behavior as one passes from one physical setting or group of participants to another *in the context of the same role* exposes the characteristic influences of interaction. For example, restaurant workers change behavior when passing from the kitchen to dining areas. Goffman's work was distinctive for its attention to boundaries. Sometimes these were physical boundaries such as walls or other barriers that tended to make it clear when people became or ceased to be observable to one another, establishing the beginning and end of interaction. Sometimes the boundaries were codes, such as slang, which allowed communication to occur among some while excluding others. Sometimes the boundaries were changes in the personnel present.

Observing on both sides of the boundary allowed Goffman to assess the identity expression in both situations, specify behavioral and equipment differences by which different meanings were expressed, and specify the process by which discrepancies among the various meanings were managed. In addition, he was concerned with the systemic consequences of people expressing different identities *within a given role,* especially when the duplicity was apparent and confrontation threatened.

Confidence that one could assess the true intentions, character, and competence of another person is a casualty of this concentration on transformations. How can we observe the real, underlying self if relatively complete, but contradictory identities are expressed and defended in the routine course of events?

To his credit, Goffman did not fall into the methodological trap of assuming that the less attractive set of implications was the more accurate. It is a tempting rule of thumb. On one side of the boundary a person expresses respect and deference to his customers; on the other, in an employee's lounge for example, he makes rude comments about them. Perhaps the rude comments are true expressions of feelings that are concealed while the customers are present.

However, there are two shortcomings to any such blanket rule of interpretation. First, the unattractive or undesirable expressions may be required in their setting as fully as the polite ones are required in theirs. Zurcher et al. (1973), for example, found that disrespectful behavior toward the sorority was *required and sanctioned* among male student sorority house kitchen workers. Second, the two bounded situations are not the only ones in which the role is relevant. What are we to make of a person who complains about customers to coworkers, about coworkers to a spouse, about the spouse to friends? Perhaps all of these complaints reflect true attitudes. Or perhaps the complaints are all institutionalized parts of separate routines and reflect more about the situation than about the attitudes of the person.

If Goffman is to be commended for not assuming he could identify the truth among the many meanings expressed, he is also to be chided for not pursuing how it might be identified. His solution was to suspend interest in the truth and intention of expressions and concentrate on their conventional meaning. He projects this methodological dilemma onto his subjects.

> To uncover fully the factual nature of the situation, it would be necessary for the individual to know all the relevant social data about the others. . . . Full information of this order is rarely available; in its absence the individual tends to employ substitutes—cues, tests, hints . . . etc.—as predictive devices. . . . And, paradoxically, the more the individual is concerned with the reality that is not available in perception, the more he must concentrate on appearances. . . . Instead of attempting to achieve certain ends by acceptable means, they can attempt to achieve the impression that they are achieving certain ends by acceptable means (1954: 160–162).

Just as people need a great deal of social data to uncover the factual nature of situations, so does the researcher. The information is simply not available. Our knowledge of situations has the methodological implication that we cannot assume that behavior occurring in one setting is consistent with behavior in another. This makes questionnaires administered in one situation dubious sources of information about other situations (Deutscher, 1973), and we are not usually able to observe people as they move from setting to setting in their daily lives. Goffman's solution is to turn away from the factual nature of the situation and concentrate on how impressions are managed and constrained by circumstances as far as they can be determined, and how they impact on circumstances.

There is no denial of the existence or significance of the matters he does not discuss. He acknowledges a basic dialectic between the moral concern of people for their reputations and products on the one hand, and the amoral technique of managing the appropriate *impressions* on the other (1954:162). His analysis displays the characteristic incompleteness of middle-range theories. Therefore the value of the analysis is determined by the degree to which the remaining issues are addressed elsewhere, as well as by its own merits. Others, for example McCall and Simmons, have attempted to combine situational analysis similar to

Goffman's with consideration of the self, which, in turn, allows consideration of the moral element in conduct and implicates the broader system of real social relationships. Considerable methodological work remains to be done, however, before convincing data are available for this task.

Structural Resources

Before considering the type of order that emerges from and constrains these interactions, we should briefly consider how position in a social system, a role for example, provides resources to incumbents for their own purposes. First, of course, the rewards earned in a position are expendable elsewhere in systemically unrelated exchanges. This is obviously true of using such material rewards as salary and also for receiving such nontangible benefits as prestige in one setting that is earned in another. This expenditure of resources earned in one setting in other settings is a primary means of integrating various situations in society. Much identity expression consists of communicating that one deserves treatment as a result of positions that are enacted elsewhere and beyond perception.

Second, the resources of the position can be appropriated for personal use to the extent that supervision is imperfect and values such as commitment to the role allow that to occur. As we have seen, military psychiatrists can exploit their situational control of diagnosis to use military treatment opportunities in forbidden ways. Anyone with control over the flow of goods or services can do favors with respect to who receives them and how they are scheduled. This same control allows coercion by withdrawing or threatening to withdraw goods and services to which others are entitled unless they perform personal favors. The worst kinds of sexual harassment are examples of this kind of coercion. All of these appropriations of resources for personal ends have identity implications as well as the material benefits of using and exchanging resources.

Finally, the position provides reputational and cognitive resources within the interaction. The incumbent of a position has a stereotyped identity that requires only routine maintenance. She need not construct an image from scratch. Ordinarily, the incumbent will also want to personalize that identity consistent with her other positions and attitudes. The expressive routine associated with a position is a crucial resource in modifying it. To the extent that the expressive behavior is routinized, an individual can personalize the expression by slight modifications of the routine. The meaning of the conduct is visible in discrepancies between the actual and routine performance. Without the routine, expression of meaning contrary to stereotype would be much more difficult.

The availability of routine and stereotype also makes interpreting the conduct of others simpler. Conduct can be analyzed by comparison with a preexisting model, an easier process than building a cognitive model.

NEGOTIATED ORDER

Individuals' role identities or reputations emerge in interaction as a result of a negotiating process in which mutually agreeable adjustments are made to the stereotypical auxiliary characteristics attached to roles and to the details of role expectations themselves. Goffman intentionally restricts attention to the interaction process per se, and pays little attention to the broader systems in which the interactions are embedded. Other interactionists, however, are concerned with the way in which negotiations in interaction contribute to the operation of social systems, for good or ill. The two topics, identity and system, are closely related. Much of the role identity consists of obligations and rights within the system of roles and many of the auxiliary characteristics relate to position in the system and the quality of role performance. In addition, mutual acceptability of identities is judged by, among other criteria, whether the system of roles will meet participants' needs if the identity definitions are accepted.

Use of the term *negotiation* evokes a specific image of one process that occurs in interaction and in social systems more generally. People enter interaction with divergent views about what each should do, how each should be treated, and what the interaction should produce. When the divergence is recognized as a result of identity expressions or instrumental role performance, the participants communicate among themselves until a satisfactory working arrangement is defined. The imagery is economic, but more nearly barter than cash economy because all kinds of rights and obligations are exchanged for one another without benefit of a standard medium of exchange such as money. In the classic bargain "I will gladly pay you Tuesday for a hamburger today," gladness is an important part of the offer, but one with no readily calculable cash value. The reputation that results from not paying on Tuesday is also crucial to the bargain, but that value is difficult to specify, too.

Strauss (1978) argues that negotiating is just one of the processes by which activities are coordinated, but one that is found in all social systems. He chooses the most repressive dictatorship imaginable as the potential limiting case and observes that even in those circumstances, command through force and threat of force could not always be used. Some issues and activities would have to be negotiated. Note that in this imagery, the negotiations coordinate conduct among choosing people who disagree initially about the proper course of conduct. This approach to social life is similar to that of role theory. Although Strauss does not attempt to specify the various ways in which the initial disagreements may arise, role conflict is one source that is compatible with his formulation.

In his summary of negotiation processes, Strauss (1978) emphasizes that the character and outcome of negotiations are embedded in and influenced by structural properties of the organization in which they occur. These structural properties or contexts are relatively stable aspects of the organization and include rules, policies, the relative prevalance of legitimacy and conflict, the stakes of participants in the system, and the distribution of power and other resources. The structure of the organization may also dictate some features of the negotiations themselves, such as the number of parties, publicity of arrangements, whether negotiations are one time or ongoing, and the number and clarity of negotiable issues. These matters may themselves be the result of negotiations that have settled issues for a relatively long period or they may have arisen by other processes.

Structural contexts do not determine behavior within the organization, nor do they stabilize other conduct uniformly. There is considerable variation in the stability of different patterns of conduct within a stable organizational structure. If one examines behavior within a system in enough detail, certain arrangements will be found to be settled daily, or perhaps more frequently, while others remain fixed for longer periods.

Strauss's concern is with developing a theory of negotiations. Although the details of the theory are not developed, the general form is. The structural context is reflected in the nature of the negotiations and the degree to which negotiation rather than some other process such as coercion occurs. Note that the direction of inference is from structure to interaction process. Then, different types of negotiations and different distributions of negotiation and other processes are conceived to have different consequences for the organization. In this aspect of the theory, the inference is from interaction process to structure. Maines (1977, 1983) and Hall (1987) stress that institutional structure beyond the particular organization and historical factors also impact on the interaction process. The identity-claiming aspects of interaction also reflect these broad constraints. The auxiliary characteristics associated with certain roles, such as gender and race, make historically developed stereotypes relevant in even fleeting interactions with few systemic consequences.

Weinstein and Tanur (1978) help formulate the relationship between the conduct within interaction and broader social concerns. First, they observe that the course of interaction depends, in part, on the aggregated consequences of other interactions. For example, if the same people interact repeatedly, the definitions developed in prior interactions become expectations in each new instance. In addition, the promises made by individuals in organizational roles are often fulfilled by other people in other settings. Sales personnel typically make promises to be filled by manufacturing service, and delivery personnel. Rates of occurrence of the outcomes of interactions of the same type may also act as expectations, even if the particular people were not involved. Second, they observe that the resources available in an interaction are potential and must be made actual in the interaction. The course of the interaction, the identities established, and the operation of the system are all contingent upon the coordinated choice among available resources.

The negotiated order, then, is characterized by voluntary compliance as a result of bargaining or negotiating in interaction. The conceptual imagery is that of economy, especially barter economy, not normative consensus. Norms are but one structural constraint on whether and how to bargain. In fact, the occasion for bargaining includes initial divergence concerning the proper division of tasks in social systems and the distribution of role identities. The agreements vary greatly in duration—from moods that must be accommodated for a day to settled issues functioning as structural context. The organizational and broader structures are analyzed from the actors' point of view as potential resources and constraints. Each interaction is viewed as being constrained by structural context and as feeding back into the structure. But, of course, the effect of each particular interaction on structure can be very small unless it is aggregated with others. It is interesting that the same processes occur in interactions that because of their place in the system have considerable impact. Among these are selecting and formulating the news (Fishman, 1978; Gans, 1979; Molotch and Lester, 1974, 1975; Tuchman, 1978) and image making by politicians as a tool of governing (Hall, 1972, 1979).

Just as a negotiated order has a different dynamic than one based on conformity to consensual norms, it also differs from the exercise of power. Symbolic interactionist studies concentrate on negotiation as a means to coordinate conduct. The studies reflect the initial differences of interest and values that necessitate negotiating. The use of power and the threat of using power are a different approach to coordinating conduct in a population that does not agree with nor spontaneously conform to systemic norms. The use of power is a potential strategy in centrally coordinated systems. This raises a crucial social psychological question: Under what conditions does the potential for using power become salient so that people stop behaving as if they accept the conditions within which they bargain and begin to act as if they have been threatened? The distinguishing condition is called the *legitimacy* of norms, and the ability to coordinate that accompanies it is called *authority*. The degree of legitimacy of the system is a parameter of negotiating. Conceptualizing and measuring legitimacy as a condition of situations, not a moral judgment of the researcher, will be necessary to formulate when our knowledge of negotiations as opposed to our knowledge of power, conformity, or other coordinating processes applies, and how the various processes relate to one another.

SUMMARY

Symbolic interaction is a social psychological approach to the coordination of conduct and accepts the premises that people are active and purposive interpreters of the environment and that they respond to the environment on the basis of those interpretations. Real conditions in the environment are not denied, but they are conceived to influence conduct through the interpretation process rather than mechanically or automatically. The interpretive process has a private component in thought, and a public, collective component in the use of symbols.

The symbols are learned and have their basis in participation in group life. As an ideal, they might be perfectly shared and reflect the interests of all. However, in this world, they are imperfectly shared and used manipulatively to some extent. Within interaction, the identities of the participants are negotiated from a stereotypic base of auxiliary characteristics associated with roles. These identities define a complete person but are characterized by discrepancies from situation to situation even within the single role. The underlying self is closely related to the person's integration in group life and is a basis of moral concern beyond situational expediency. The discrepancies among expressed images of that self, role identities, raise serious methodological challenges.

When considered from the systemic, rather than individual, point of view, the negotiations are crucial to coordinated conduct. As with identities, some coordinated system activities are quite ephemeral and, in effect, under continuous negotiation. Others are more settled and serve as parameters or contexts of ongoing negotiations. Negotiations vary in a variety of ways, depending upon context, and differences among negotiations have systemic consequences. Negotiations are distinguished from other techniques of coordination such as the exercise of power and the conformity to consensual norms. Legitimacy, conceived as a variable condition of situations, influences the nature of the coordinating process.

NOTES

1. There were many influences upon Blumer's thought within the Chicago School, but the two most directly reflected in Blumer's approach were G. H. Mead (cf., 1934, 1964) and W. I. Thomas (cf., 1927, 1928 [with D. S. Thomas]).

2. B. F. Skinner's behavioristic arguments were developed later than Blumer's and are anachronistic in this context. Still, his views are the most widely associated with a thorough behavioristic perspective and are an excellent statement of the position that Blumer contrasted with his own. See, for example, Skinner 1969, 1971, 1974.

3. Although Blumer is concerned only with human behavior, the distinction between rote stimulus–response learning and purposive learning also was developed among animal behaviorists. Because the examples are so simple and uncluttered, their work is useful in defining this distinction clearly. Watson's early work attempted to show strict mechanical linkages between the stimulus and specifically defined behavioral responses. He taught rats a sequence of turns in a maze, which he conceived to be memorized motor responses—an exact number of steps of a specific size, for example. Later, the legs of the maze were lengthened or shortened. In shortened passages, the rats ran headlong into the wall, attempting to take their accustomed number of steps. In lengthened passages they attempted to turn too soon and ran into the maze side. They had learned an exact series of behaviors.

   Later, though, Tolman and others showed that this was not necessarily typical of rat learning. For example, when rats received food in a maze at a point under a lighted window, they would run to that place, even if the maze were reoriented so that a different sequence of turns was required. Other researchers flooded mazes so that rats could not run at all. They swam. The rats made their way through the mazes but were not performing the same behavior. These and other experiments indicate that even rats can learn a purpose and adapt their conduct as needed to achieve it (Gleitman, 1967).

4. There is evidence, for an extreme example, that even the rate of firing of a single neuron can be brought under control with appropriate biofeedback. There is no reason to assume that our postures, the discharge of chemicals that carry scents, the dilation of our pupils, the steadiness of voice, or any other behavior that might carry information to another person could not be brought under control and made symbolic.

5. The degree to which this sharing and neglect of interests is a product of definition and interpretation is indicated by LaPiere's (1973/1934) classic study of actual and reported racism in business transactions. A Chinese couple was able to register at a number of hotels and receive service at restaurants on a cross-country trip. However, an attitude survey sent to the same establishments indicated that Orientals would not be served. Lying about racism is not alien to modern sensibilities. However, the overwhelming expression of *more* racism than was actually practiced reminds us that the symbolic expression of our attitudes, and perhaps the attitudes themselves, are subject to redefinition, even if other factors stabilize practices.

6. For straightforward examples of face-to-face positional strategy involving intentional manipulation of symbols, see Berk's (1977) description of characteristic face-saving lies exchanged at singles dances and Emerson's (1970a,b) study of the effort required to sustain nonthreatening definitions of the doctor–patient relationship during gynecological examinations.

REFERENCES

Blumer, Herbert. 1938. Social Psychology. Pp. 144–198 in Emerson R. Schmidt (ed.), Man and Society. Englewood Cliffs, NJ: Prentice Hall.

Blumer, Herbert. 1954. What Is Wrong with Social Theory? *American Sociological Review* 19:3–10.

Blumer, Herbert. 1956. Sociological Analysis and the Variable. *American Sociological Review* 21:683–690.

Blumer, Herbert. 1962. Society as Symbolic Interaction. Pp. 179–192 in Arnold Rose (ed.), Human Behavior and Social Processes. Boston: Houghton Mifflin.

Daniels, Arlene. 1970. The Social Construction of Military Psychiatric Diagnosis. Pp. 181–208 in Hans Dreitzel (ed.), Recent Sociology no. 2. New York: Macmillan.

Deutscher, Irwin. 1973. What We Say/What We Do. Glenview, IL: Scott Foresman.

Emerson, Joan. 1970a. Nothing Unusual Is Happening. Pp. 208–220 in Tamotsu Shibutani (ed.), Human Nature and Collective Behavior. Englewood Cliffs, NJ: Prentice Hall.

Emerson, Joan. 1970b. Behavior in Private Places. Pp. 73–100 in Hans Dreitzel (ed.), Recent Sociology no. 2. New York: Macmillan.

Fishman, Mark. 1978. Crime Waves as Ideology. *Social Problems* 25:531–543.

Gans, Herbert. 1979. Deciding What's News. New York: Pantheon.

Gleitman, Henry. 1967. Place-Learning. Pp. 120–125 in Psychobiology: Readings from Scientific American. San Francisco: Freeman.

Goffman, Erving. 1954. The Presentation of Self in Everyday Life. Edinburgh: University of Edinburgh Social Sciences Research Center.

Goffman, Erving. 1959. The Presentation of Self in Everyday Life. Garden City: Anchor.

Goffman, Erving. 1961a. The Underlife of a Public Institution. Pp. 171–320 in Asylums. Garden City, NY: Doubleday.

Goffman, Erving. 1961b. Role Distance. Pp. 85–152 in Encounters. Indianapolis: Bobbs-Merrill.

Goffman, Erving. 1964. The Neglected Situation. *American Anthropologist* 66 (6 Part 2):133–137.

Goffman, Erving. 1969. Strategic Interaction. Philadelphia: University of Pennsylvania Press.

Goffman, Erving. 1974. Frame Analysis. Cambridge: Harvard University Press.

Gove, W., M. Hughes, and M. Geerken. 1980. Playing Dumb: A Form of Impression Management with Undesirable Side Effects. *Social Psychology Quarterly* 43:89–102.

Griffin, Donald. 1976. The Question of Animal Awareness. New York: Rockefeller University Press.

Hall, Peter. 1972. A Symbolic Interactionist Analysis of Politics. *Sociological Inquiry* 42:35–75.

Hall, Peter. 1979. The Presidency and Impression Management. In Norman K. Denzin (ed.), Studies in Symbolic Interaction, Volume 2. Greenwich, CT: JAI Press.

Hall, Peter. 1987. Interactionism and the Study of Social Organization. *Sociological Quarterly* 28:1–22.

LaPiere, Richard. 1973/1934. Attitudes vs. Actions. Pp. 14–21 in Irwin Deutscher (ed.), What We Say/What We Do. Glenview IL: Scott Foresman.

Maines, David. 1977. Social Organization and Structure in Symbolic Interactionist Thought. Pp. 235–259 in A. Inkeles, J. Coleman, and N. Smelser (eds.), *Annual Review of Sociology* 3. Palo Alto: Annual Reviews.

Maines, David. 1983. In Search of Mesostructure. *Urban Life* 11:267–279.

McCall, George, and J. L. Simmons. 1978. Identities and Interactions, rev. ed. New York: Free Press.

Mead, George Herbert. 1934. Mind, Self and Society. Chicago: University of Chicago Press.

Mead, George Herbert. 1964. In Andrew Reck (ed.), Selected Writings. Indianapolis: Bobbs-Merrill.

Merton, Robert. 1935. Review of *Mind, Self and Society. Isis* 24:189–191.

Molotch, Harvey, and Marilyn Lester. 1974. News as Purposive Behavior. *American Sociological Review* 39:101–112.

Molotch, Harvey, and Marilyn Lester. 1975. Accidental News. *American Journal of Sociology* 81:235–260.

Shibutani, Tamotsu. 1962. Reference Groups and Social Control. Pp. 128–147 in A. Rose (ed.), Human Behavior and Social Processes. Boston: Houghton Mifflin.

Shibutani, Tamotsu. 1966. Improvised News. Indianapolis: Bobbs-Merrill.

Shibutani, Tamotsu. 1973. The Personification of Adversaries. Pp. 223–233 in T. Shibutani (ed.), Human Nature and Collective Behavior. New Brunswick, NJ: Transaction.

Shibutani, Tamotsu. 1978. Reference Groups as Perspectives. Pp. 108–115 in J. Manis and B. Meltzer (eds.), Symbolic Interaction. Boston: Allyn and Bacon.

Skinner, B. F. 1969. Contingencies of Reinforcement. New York: Appleton Century Crofts.

Skinner, B. F. 1971. Beyond Freedom and Dignity. New York: Knopf.

Skinner, B. F. 1974. About Behaviorism. New York: Knopf.

Strauss, Anselm. 1978. Negotiations. San Francisco: Josey Bass.

Thomas, W. I. 1927. The Behavior Pattern and the Situation. *American Sociological Association Publications* 22:1–13.

Thomas, W. I., and D. S. Thomas. 1928. The Child in America. New York: Knopf.

Tuchman, Gaye. 1978. Making News: A Study in the Construction of Reality. New York: Free Press.

Turner, Ralph. 1962. Role-Taking: Process Versus Conformity. Pp. 20–40 in A. Rose (ed.), Human Behavior and Social Processes. Boston: Houghton Mifflin.

Weinstein, Eugene, and Judith Tanur. 1978. Meanings, Purposes and Structural Resources in Social Interaction. Pp. 138–146 in J. Manis and B. Meltzer (eds.), Symbolic Interaction. Boston: Allyn and Bacon.

Zurcher, Louis, David Sonenschein, and Eric Metzner. 1973. The Hasher. Pp. 25–37 in Billy Franklin and Frank Kohout (eds.), Social Psychology and Everyday Life. New York: McKay.

9

Exchange Theories

The social exchange theories address social behavior as the exchange of goods. Some of the goods are material and some, such as the identities studied by symbolic interactionists, are symbolic or affective. The conduct of each participant is conceived to have consequences for the others that can be considered as supplied benefits (rewards) or imposed costs (punishments). The balance of rewards and costs a person has received in the past or anticipates for the future predicts his or her conduct. Sometimes the rewards and punishments are conceived to act as reinforcers in theoretical arguments grounded in operant behaviorist psychology. Sometimes they are conceived to be the basis for choice in arguments grounded in rational choice economic theories. In both cases, the exchange of rewards and punishments is the fundamental principle controlling individual behavior and defining relationships.

HOMANS'S THEORY OF ELEMENTARY FORMS
OF SOCIAL BEHAVIOR

Relationship Between Conditioning and Choice

George Homans (e.g., 1958, 1969) regards social exchange theory as a formalization of one of our oldest theories of social behavior. In its commonsense form, the theory holds that people choose to behave in ways that they anticipate will be the most rewarding. Because these antici- pations are based upon prior experience, people tend to repeat behavior that has been rewarding in the past and avoid behavior that has been punishing in the past. His theory is an attempt to state this ancient insight in propositional form that supports predictive deductions when the con- ditions of choice are stated. When people choose separately and take the response of others as a condition of the choice, exchange occurs. Each acts in a way that will lead the other to provide rewards. To do so, each must provide the other with rewards as well.

Homans's theory incorporates elements of two separate bodies of work that attempt to address how human beings adjust their behavior to its consequences. The model of the person as choosing among lines of conduct by considering their anticipated rewards is a core idea of economics. Technically, Homans bases his argument on a "rational man" or "utility-maximizing" model of human conduct. Economists do not typically address how the person learns to anticipate the consequences of his action, nor how values develop over time. Homans observed that the core empirical findings of operant behavioral psychology are consis- tent with the utility-maximizing approach and, in addition, address these important topics. Homan's strategy was to derive principles underlying the conditioning of behavior from the empirical findings of operant behavioral psychology and then express them as principles of choice.[1] This treats conditioning, which adjusts behavior to environmental conse- quences in all species without intention necessarily being present, as the way in which humans learn to choose rationally as well.

Homans (1969) argued that behavioral psychology is more general than economic theory because it addresses learning and value develop- ment and because it is more amenable to incorporating emotional behav- ior. However, when emotion is not an important factor, the predictions of the two theories would be identical. In effect, Homans regards economic theory as a special case of the more general behavioral theory. Although he does not mention it, behavioral theory has the further advantage of being based on empirical research. Although sociologists are primarily interested in using established behavioral principles for the purposes of deduction in their own theories, behaviorists continue to challenge and test them. Thus, even the parts of sociological theories that are taken for granted as basic propositions need not be assumed, but rather can be subjected to continuing scientific scrutiny.

The Basic Propositions

The propositions that follow and the brief discussion of each are based on the revised (1974) edition of *Social Behavior: Its Elementary Forms*, the book in which Homans presents his theory in its most general form.

1. Success Proposition. *For all actions taken by persons, the more often a particular action of a person is rewarded, the more likely the person is to perform that action.* The success proposition defines the fundamental link between experience and future conduct. When behavior is rewarded in a situation, the person becomes more likely to repeat that behavior when similar situations arise. This temporal element avoids teleological reasoning because the conduct is not caused by its own consequences but by the learned consequences of similar conduct in the past (pp. 16–17).

The success proposition defines a relationship between any given act and its reinforcement contingencies. However, as Homans recognizes (p. 21), alternative courses of action are typically available to people. As a result, the behavior in a situation does not reflect the frequency of success of any one of the options, but rather their success relative to one another. The issue of choice among alternative courses of action has already been discussed at length in the context of role conflict and the resolution of role strain.

2. Stimulus Proposition. *If in the past the occurrence of a particular stimulus, or set of stimuli, has been the occasion on which a person's action has been rewarded, then the more similar the present stimuli are to the past ones, the more likely the person is to perform the action, or some similar action, now.* A successful action is only successful in a limited range of circumstances. Eating chili is a successful action if one is hungry, but not if one wants to soothe an upset stomach. Shouting pleasantries in someone's ear is successful in discos and machine shops, but not in a library or symphony hall. The similarity of a new situation to ones previously experienced, then, is a variable in the resultant behavior. It links the situation to an appropriate set of estimates of the success of various behaviors. Because situations are similar in some ways, but different in others, the person must identify the relevant dimensions of similarity if he or she is to estimate correctly.

3. Value Proposition. *The more valuable to a person is the result of her action, the more likely she is to perform the action.* The value proposition introduces the size of the reward as a variable in causing behavior. In

Homans's treatment, although punishment and reward are defined as negative and positive values of a single variable, the inefficiency of punishment in controlling behavior is recognized. Animal behaviorists sometimes go further and treat reward and punishment as different processes (cf., Rachlin, 1976:130–135).

Homans conceives of values as partly acquired by being linked to success in obtaining more primordial values (p. 27). Some values, he argues, are probably innate—for example, a child receiving a hug from its mother.[2] Verbal reinforcement, such as compliments, become valuable in themselves by prior association with these innate values in increasingly longer and complex chains. This allows certain generalized values, like money or social approval, to be very commonly held in a society because they are associated with fulfilling so many different more basic needs. Despite the possibility of generalized values, Homans regards acquired values as numerous and diverse. He argues that we can make no generalized statements about values apart from the "past history and present circumstances of particular men" (p. 28). Despite the individualistic phrasing, Homans does not seem to mean that values must be ascertained one person at a time in order to apply exchange propositions. Rather, in his own analyses, he refers to classes of people in like circumstances as having values that are relatively alike when compared to the historic and social possibilities. In empirical applications, the term *current circumstances* refers to something very much like one's role in a social system at a moment in history.

The behavior required to receive a reward will impose costs on the individual: effort and other resources and other available rewards forgone by choosing one behavior rather than others. When these costs are held constant, the behavior would be controlled by the value of the reward. In real situations, however, the costs are not constant, and behavior is controlled by consideration of both reward and cost, computed as a profit.

4. Deprivation–Satiation Proposition. *The more often in the recent past a person has received a particular reward, the less valuable any further unit of the reward becomes for him.* The concept of satiation applies best to rewards that satisfy organismic needs and are associated with drive states. For example, when one has eaten recently, he will not value food as highly as when he is hungry. The tendency to satiation is very general, Homans argues, and the temporal dimension varies with the nature of the reward. In addition, as rewards become more generalized, they become less subject to satiation because they are linked to so many more basic needs. Because each reward has its own level of satiation at any moment, the priorities among them on any occasion must be determined empirically.

5. Aggression–Approval Propositions. (a) *When a person's action does*

not receive the reward she expected or receives punishment she did not expect, she will be angry; she becomes more likely to perform aggressive behavior, and the results of such behavior become more valuable to her. (b) *When a person's action receives reward she expected, especially a greater reward than she expected, or does not receive punishment she expected, she will be pleased; she becomes more likely to perform approving behavior, and the results of such behavior become more valuable to her.* These propositions link behavior to a comparison between one's expectations and actual rewards, rather than to the absolute value of the rewards. The recognition of these emotional reactions is very important. First, it coincides with Dahrendorf's discussion of the effects of relative deprivation in conflict. Second, it reminds us to predict variation in behavior based on individual variation in expectations. Third, this proposition provides a link with the role theoretic and symbolic interaction discussions of appropriate treatment for roles and identities.

AN ILLUSTRATIVE EXCHANGE ARGUMENT

Homans's (1964) presidential address to the American Sociological Association includes a theoretical analysis explicitly intended to demonstrate the utility of exchange theoretic analysis applied to large-scale sociological phenomena. In addition, his analysis is offered in the context of a critique of functionalism as a school that concludes that functionalism never produced theory worthy of the name. For our purposes, this context guarantees that this, of all Homans's empirical analyses, can stand as an example of how he thinks theoretical analysis should be done.

First, Homans argues that two crucial sociological concepts—values and rules or norms—cannot be taken as given but must be explained by theoretical analysis of the behavior of individuals. With respect to norms, Homans adopts Coleman's (1964) earlier argument that norms emerge from the pursuit of self-interest by individuals acting in their own interests in a context of other individuals acting in their own interests. Adopting a norm and arranging to apply sanctions collectively allow a coalition to enforce conduct that its members could not enforce separately. Such a coalition is an interest group in Dahrendorf's sense. The type of norm that emerges will depend on circumstances and will tend to stabilize exchange relations, among other functions.

Even when norms develop to stabilize existing exchange relations, conformity to them cannot be assumed. As Coleman (1964) puts it, people do not submit to rules, but adapt rules to life. Thus, for Homans, both the presence of rules in a society and the degree of conformity to them are to be explained in psychological terms. By taking the values and norms observed in social systems as given, and assuming conformity to them in explanations, Homans argues, the functionalists truncated their analyses, losing much explanatory power.

Homans finds the evidence of this truncation in discrepancies between the form of theoretical analysis proposed in theory and the actual arguments that carry the explanatory burden in particular applications. He turns to Neil Smelser's (1959) explanation of social change during the industrial revolution. He recommends this analysis as good sociology in its own right because it makes sound arguments, even though they contradict the functional theoretical starting point. Smelser argues that industrialization proceeds through seven steps. Homans observes that these steps begin with dissatisfaction with productive achievements in portions of the industry and a sense of opportunity to achieve higher productivity through technology. This leads to emotional reactions in some segments of the population. That is, Homans observes, when analyzing cases, functionalists argue psychologically. In this case, people involved in the textile industry are motivated by the potential for increased profit and see the opportunity to reap large profits through labor saving machinery. The state of technology made the successful invention of such machinery seem plausible. This led to experimentation with the invention and use of labor-saving machinery in the textile industry.

Homans then formalizes this explanation by expressing the profit-seeking and willingness to experiment at that time in history in terms of his own theoretical propositions. The enormous profits anticipated increase experimentation because the *value proposition* applies. The high probability of success, due to existing technology, leads to experimentation because the *success proposition* applies. The actual successes of some innovators led to the rapid spread of technological innovation because both propositions apply. Thus, Homans argues, the actual explanations offered of large-scale social change conform to the basic propositions of exchange theory.

Homans does not regard his own explanation as complete. It takes for granted the presence of technology, the dominance of the textile industry, and a host of other social conditions. However, he does claim that any of these conditions could also be explained in the same way and that the basic propositions of exchange theory could be applied until a satisfactorily complete explanation was available. In its present form, though, the explanation is no more complete than those offered by middle-range exchange arguments. The differences lie not in the substance or quality of current explanations, but rather in (1) the a priori commitment to explanation using an integrated theory with a few basic propositions and (2) the recommendation that the basic propositions are known. We now turn briefly to consideration of Homans's propositions to assess whether they are a potential set of sound fundamental principles for a deductive theory in their current form.

SOUNDNESS OF THE BASIC PROPOSITIONS

Schedules

Homans has variously characterized his own propositions as vulgar forms of propositions of behavioral psychology (1969), as admitting exceptions, and as being in crude form (1974). We begin with his own qualifications of the success proposition and then consider some empirical results that suggest further qualifications of the basic propositions. The issue, of course, is not whether the exchange approach has utility. That has been established by success in several disciplines. Rather, we are concerned with whether current knowledge supports a general theory using propositions approximately like Homans's.

In discussing the success proposition, Homans acknowledges that the scheduling of reinforcement influences the resulting behavior, as well as its absolute frequency. However, he argues, this does not invalidate the success proposition, which applies even in this crude form to a wide range of behavior (1974, p. 18). The success proposition states a unidirectional linear relationship between frequency of reward and repetition of the behavior. As the number of successful experiences increases, the likelihood of repeating the behavior increases as well. But as Homans notes, this is not strictly true. First, it has been known since the 1930s that a fixed interval schedule, one in which the rewards are delivered for appropriate behavior but only after the designated period of time has elapsed, actually results in more repetitions of the behavior than one in which the behavior is rewarded every time. It is also known (Skinner (1972/1948) that if the intervals are too long, the organism does not learn the behavior efficiently; rather, it develops superstitious behavior, unrelated to reward. Finally, we know that once a behavior is learned, considerably less reinforcement is needed to sustain it than is needed to learn it in the first place.

Taking these facts together, the relationship between frequency of reward and behavior is this: As frequency of reward increases, repetition of behavior increases but only until the frequency reaches a good learning interval. Further increases in the frequency of reward slow down the increase in behavior repetition. Once a high rate of behavior repetition is established, increases in reward will not improve performance and, in fact, reward may be reduced without decrement of performance until it is reduced so much that extinction occurs. After extinction, prior learning experiences become a crucial variable because two organisms with the same overt behavior but different past experiences will respond differently to reward. An extinguished behavior is relearned with far less reward than the same behavior is learned the first time. This is a somewhat more refined expression of the reality Homans attempts to codify in the success proposition. When fixed ratio schedules, in which rewards are given on a fixed proportion of behaviors, and mixed schedules are considered, the situation becomes even more complex.

Drift Toward Species Behavior

Breland and Breland (1961) report a persistent breakdown in conditioning and the replacement of learned behavior with an approximation of behavior characteristic of the species. Their reports were based on experience with trained animals that were used in promotional displays. For example, raccoons were trained to put coins through the slot into a piggy bank for displays in bank windows. With many species, after the trick had been mastered and successfully performed for a period of time, and with no change in the reinforcement, the animals would abandon the trick in favor of unrewarded behavior that resembled a naturally common, perhaps instinctual, behavior of that species. For example, the raccoons would stop putting the coins in the bank. Instead, they would take the shiny coins and manipulate them in a way similar to the way they wash their food. This is another type of limit on the effectiveness of rewards, whether frequency or size is considered. If the species has a characteristic behavior, this behavior or an approximation of it, tends to intrude on conditioning and override the effects of reward, even if the instinctual behavior is not rewarding in the circumstance.

Value Disturbances Near Neutrality

Most outcomes of behavior include both negative and positive aspects—costs or punishments and rewards. Behavior is controlled by the overall value of these complex outcomes. When the overall value of the outcomes is nearly neutral, however, the usual relationships between the reward and a variety of outcomes do not apply. The best documented effects are the family of attitudinal changes produced by cognitive dissonance. These attitude changes occur when a person has performed a behavior for a small reward or avoided it under a mild punishment. The person's attitudes subsequently change to be more in line with the behavior, as if a better reason for the behavior were being sought. This is accompanied by behavioral disturbances in the response to rewards and punishments.

First, the dissonance studies indicate that when the rewards are relatively small, performance of experimental tasks is not changed by slight increases in reward. For example in Festinger and Carlsmith's (1959) classic study, both the smaller and larger of the two promised rewards induced subjects to lie about the attractiveness of the task to the next subject. Once a threshold of adequacy is reached, then, increases of the anticipated reward had no observable behavioral effect. The smaller reward, however, does tend to produce an attitude change and, paradoxically, greater willingness to do the initial task than the larger reward as measured by questionnaires during the study. Mild punishments (Aronson and Carlsmith, 1963) are more effective in changing behavior than larger ones. Both children anticipating severe punishments and those anticipating mild ones for playing with an attractive toy avoided the toy when the control agent was present. However, those mildly threatened continued to avoid the toy in her absence while those more severely threatened played with the toy as soon as surveillance was reduced. We know that these are not artifacts of the verbal expression of attitude because analogous behavioral effects were also found in a variety of infrahuman species (Lawrence and Festinger, 1962).

Commitment to Failing Courses of Action

Homans proposes a straightforward relationship between the failure to be rewarded as expected and conduct. When rewards are not forthcoming, he proposes that anger and aggressive behavior will follow. However, under some circumstances, the failure of reward is followed by escalating commitment to the failed course of action. Festinger, Riecken and Schachter (1956) have documented a case in which an apocalyptic prophecy failed. The followers of the prophecy revised their beliefs and continued to follow the prophet. Staw (1981) shows the everyday relevance of this dynamic. He observed that under certain conditions, more and more resources were committed to failed business decisions.

Detrimental Effects of Reward on Performance

McCullers (1978) and McGraw (1978) review theories and empirical evidence that establish a detrimental effect of rewards on performance in some circumstances. McCullers cites the Yerkes-Dodson Law, formulated in 1908, as one of the earliest formulations of the relationship between motivation and performance. The Yerkes-Dodson Law proposes that increasing reward levels for difficult tasks will enhance performance up to a point, after which increased reward levels will reduce performance. No such effect is proposed for simple tasks, for which increased rewards seem to enhance behavior at any reward level. Although tested primarily on animals, the Yerkes-Dodson Law has been applied to people by a wide variety of theorists.

Later, McCullers reports, the Hull-Spence theory made similar predictions about the enhancement of rewards upon complex behavioral tasks. The Hull-Spence reasoning was that in simple tasks, the already learned dominant response to a stimulus is more likely to be correct. Therefore, increasing the reward, which increases the tendency to try the already conditioned response, works well for simple tasks, enhancing performance. In complex problem solving, existing solutions are less likely to succeed, so increasing the tendency to try them by enhancing reward tends to reduce correct response.

McGraw (1978) reviews empirical evidence that establishes a detrimental effect of reward on performance in concept attainment, discrimination tasks, incidental learning, and tasks involving insight and creativity. He proposes that two characteristics of the task determine when the detrimental effect of reward will occur. Reward will have a detrimental effect when the task is (1) attractive to subjects and (2) sufficiently complex that the solution is not immediately obvious, requiring a heuristic approach.

On both theoretical and empirical grounds, then, we are led to expect an inverted U-shaped relationship between reward and conduct for a wide variety of tasks. These effects are not the result of satiation or unexpected levels of reward, but rather are intrinsic to the relationship between reward and performance of certain kinds of tasks.

Implications

Although Homans's basic propositions apply in a great many situations, there are also many disconfirming exceptions. Both reward size and scheduling have effects contrary to the simple principles proposed by Homans. In addition, as Homans recognizes, generalized reinforcers do not become satiated in the same way as more basic ones. Thus, although the basic propositions have been and continue to be useful in a variety of applications, they clearly have a delimited range of application and cannot be taken as a general theory of human behavior.

This evaluation suggests remarkably few substantive correctives for social exchange theory. As noted earlier, social exchange theorists already utilize formalized models of rationality in middle-range theorizing.

In some instances, apparent contradictions of these general principles becomes topics for empirical study. Often, as in Coleman's discussion of zealots and free riders (discussed later), further specifications of the rewards operating in a situation eliminate the contradictions. In other cases, such as the analyses of power or the emergence of norms (both also discussed later), the social conditions disturbing purely rational exchange are identified. In any event, exchange theory has been more concerned with the emergence and consequences of social structures than with individual behavior.

The metatheoretical rhetoric claiming to have proposed a general theory, however, is severely discredited. There is not much dispute concerning the desirability of a general theory. However, the first requirement of a theory is to explain the available empirical findings. This means not only those findings gathered by proponents to illustrate and support the theory, but also those findings gathered by others. The theory must stand up to empirical tests. I suppose that what we all want is the most general theory that is empirically sound.

Exchange theory is not unique within sociology for controversial claims to general theoretical status. It is unique, however, in the availability of extensive empirical evidence with which to assess the claims. The evidence is available because of the close link between exchange theories and work in other disciplines that addresses related questions. For that reason, exchange theory is a convenient case with which to illustrate how any theory should be tested by empirical data. The case analysis also suggests caution in accepting claims to explain a great deal of human social life, or all of it, utilizing a few variables or propositions.

NETWORKS

"An exchange network is a set of two or more connected exchange relations" (Cook and Emerson, 1978). Connections exist between exchange relations to the extent that one exchange relationship is contingent upon the activity in the others. The connection is positive when exchange in one relationship is contingent upon exchange occurring in the others, and negative when the exchange in one relationship is contingent upon exchange not occurring in the others. For example, my exchange with the supermarket is positively connected to my exchange with my employer and the supermarket's exchange with its suppliers. It is negatively connected to my exchange with roadside vegetable stands, butchers, and the quick shop.

Networks differ in their size, of course, and also in their internal structure. When an exchange relationship exists between person *A* and person *B* contingent upon another exchange relationship between *B* and *C*, a network exists between the two relationships. There may or may not be a direct relationship between *A* and *C*. These alternatives define two different network structures. For example, if *B* exchanges secrets about *C* to *A* for some favor and gets the secrets from *C* in exchange for promises of confidentiality, the stability of this network is altered dramatically by direct conversations between *A* and *C*. The internal structure of the network—the resources available to each position and the pattern of direct and indirect links—is regarded as a causal factor in the exchanges that will occur in the network.

But perhaps the most important aspect of network analysis of exchange relationships is the methodological compatibility with network analyses of roles. The similarity of positions in role structures and positions in exchange networks is established in the same way—by the pattern of connections among participants. At least with respect to formal or normatively defined reward systems, every system of roles is also an exchange network. In addition, those in similar roles will have similar positions in the exchange network.

But neither the formal reward system defined in organizations nor the normative reward systems known to exist in relationships are descriptively perfect. In fact, they are far from it, as documented by the extensive symbolic interaction literature on deception in obtaining identity-linked rewards. Role theory and exchange theory converge on the proposition that people in similar positions behave similarly. However, empirically, there is considerable diversity of actual behavior among occupants of similar roles. By analyzing exchange-relevant differences between similar role systems, exchange theory can isolate variables that influence conduct but are not captured in the initial role description. For example, similar role systems, normatively defined, can differ in the extent of secondary rewards provided through interaction.

Exchange analysis of normative conflict would be especially appropriate, considering the current conception of the structure of role systems. Blau (1960) has already shown that the distribution of work-related attitudes in a workplace influences work performance independently of the worker's own attitude. And Schwartz (1975b) has found that when a client is required to wait for his appointment with mortgage company executives, implying a diminished identity, compensatory deferential acts were performed, such as offers to serve the client coffee or tea. These compensatory offers varied with the length of wait, an index of damage or insult to client identity, and with the position of the person causing the wait. There findings require integration of role theoretic, exchange, and symbolic interaction concepts. But such instances do not comprise a general analysis and do not systematically incorporate the variables that influence the nature and extent of conflict.

Coleman's (1990) discussion of rights is a beginning step in an exchange analysis of conflict. Coleman (1990:49) conceives of rights as intrinsically involving more than one person. A person has the right to perform a given act when she and others agree that the right exists, allowing the conduct to be performed without interference or retaliation. Intrinsic to this formulation is the idea that a person may think she has a right but may be mistaken because others do not agree and respond negatively. A person may also have a right in the opinion of others but mistakenly think they will oppose her conduct and therefore may refrain from it. When the relevant parties disagree about whether a right exists, the right is in dispute. This situation is equivalent to role conflict.

Coleman observes that each person has her own model of the distribution of rights. Conduct is constrained in specific situations by the distribution of opinions among the relevant participants and, of course, by their ability to work out their differences in a variety of ways. This formulation, terminology aside, is identical to the symbolic interaction view of what occurs in interaction. And, as in the other perspectives on interaction, the scope of one's rights and the response to one's conduct are contingent upon the acquiescence of others. Coleman puts the matter bluntly: The prevailing rights are those that can be enforced by those who hold that view of the distribution of rights. The source of rights is power (Coleman, 1990:58). The distribution of prevailing rights is, in Merton's terms, the regularity of an articulated role set. Merton, however, recognizes other resources in addition to power that establish prevailing rights.

POWER

Power, in the technical sense of the term, is a different form of social relationship from exchange, and the presence of power relations is a boundary condition for applying exchange theory. In power relationships, one party has the ability to control the conduct of another against that party's will. Force, threat of force, and the denial of essential goods and services are important instruments of power. In a sense, we could say that a person who follows orders at the point of a gun is still choosing to do so, rather than die. But this extends the idea of choice, especially free choice, past its useful meaning. In such situations, we say the person acts against his or her will.[3] Exchange relationships, on the other hand, are defined, in part, by voluntary participation.

Coleman (1990) maintains the classical distinction between power and authority relationships. In authority relationships, people voluntarily comply with commands for a variety of reasons. Although their conduct is no longer purely governed by rational exchange considerations, it remains voluntary and can be considered within the exchange framework as a special case. In addition, Coleman observes, submission to authority, including giving up certain rights, may be what one offers in exchange for products, services, or compensatory surrender of rights. In those cases, the establishment of authority, if not its operation once in place, can be treated in a straightforward exchange theory.

Although exchange and power are different kinds of relationships, exchange theorists have added to our understanding of power in two ways. First, they show that one way in which power arises is through characteristics of exchange relationships. Second, there are many real-world relationships that are neither purely voluntary exchange nor purely controlled by power.[4] The exercise of power within such relationships has been shown to be contingent on the structure of exchange networks. It is expressed in the setting of inequitable terms of exchange.

Emergence of Power

Blau (1967) built his analysis of how power differentials emerge from exchange relationships on Emerson's (1962) earlier discussion of power-dependence relations. Power differentials emerge from exchange relationships when four conditions are met. To generate power, the source must have desirable goods or services that are (1) not available from other sources. Those who want the service must (2) not have goods or services to exchange, (3) not have enough power to force the source to provide the goods or services, and (4) be unwilling or unable to forgo the goods or services. Under these conditions, the supplier can demand compliance with commands from those who want his or her services. That is, control of the commodity becomes a degree of power over those who want it. The power need not be restricted to topics directly related to the commodity. In 1991, for example, the United Nations went to war against Iraq, largely to prevent shifts in the balance of power generated by control of oil.

In Blau's analysis then, power may arise from control over any desired commodity or service, as well as from control over the means of force and destruction. As in other analyses of power, the economic and political are intimately connected. The political system, in controlling the use of coercion, preserves the power of those with economic control over commodities as well as its own monopoly on the use of force. This abstract analysis is compatible with Chambliss's account of the historical development of the law of vagrancy (discussed in Chapter 4). Control of wages or market structure or other means of preventing others from buying goods and services in a market system not only enhances economic advantage, but also the power in other areas derived from it.

To the extent that suppliers of goods and services cooperate with one another to their mutual advantage, they will constitute a social class. This class will be defined by its participation in the exploitation of its consumers in the sense that economic advantage is transformed into political power that preserves both itself and economic control.

Exercise of Power in Exchange Networks

Cook and Emerson (1978) conducted an experimental test of the influence of network structure on the exercise of power within the context of exchange. Each subject could make or accept offers from three others, but each transaction was between two subjects. Each subject received a list of possible exchanges of points he or she could make. Between some pairs of subjects (balanced), the schedules were arranged so that both could maximize their profits. Between others (unbalanced), the schedules were arranged so that if each party pursued his or her own profit, one would profit more than the other. If both did not profit in the exchanges, they would not enter transactions at all. But uneven profit is conceived as the exercise of structurally given power even in those experimental conditions in which the subjects were unaware of the imbalance.

As anticipated, in balanced pairs the offers stabilized at the point where each was receiving the same benefit. In unbalanced ones, the routinized transaction gave a bigger profit to one of the partners. When partners were made aware of the other's profits, however, the unbalanced relationships stabilized at a more equal profit level. This shows the operation of a standard of equity that counterbalanced power when information was available.

Some partners were more committed to ongoing relationships than others. They tended to repeat transactions with the same partner rather than to enter exchanges with all of them. Commitment did not have a significant effect on the exercise of power, but even in the small sample there was a measurable difference with committed partners utilizing power less. There were no significant gender differences in power use.

The conception that norms, in this case standards of equity, constrain the exercise of power and the selfish pursuit of power is not a new one. It is important, however, that this study provides a limited experimental test of that idea. We must now consider the exchange theorists' account of the origin of norms in exchange relationships.

NORMS

Blau (1967) and Coleman (1990) offer two distinctive approaches to the origin of norms in exchange relationships. Blau's (1967) argument does not articulate well with recent sociological theory because it relies on functional imperatives and value consensus. Blau (1967:255) argues that norms are essential for social life because they prevent antisocial practices that interfere with self-regulating exchange. The pursuit of self-interest without normative restraints, he argues, defeats the pursuit of self-interest. Norms, he argues, prevent the exploitation of others, reduce the use of force and fraud when they might be useful in selfish pursuit of ends, and promote the trust necessary for indirect exchange. This closely resembles Parsons's analysis of the relationship between rationality and norms. These consequences of norms result from their expression of commonly held values (1964:280).

Coleman (1990) takes rational pursuit of one's interests as a constant in human behavior. He argues that specific social structural conditions create a demand for social norms that can be satisfied under additional social structural conditions. Thus, in his argument, the characteristics of human beings are made explicit as an intervening step in an essentially structural argument. The demand for norms arises when people are affected by others' behavior over which they cannot achieve control through direct exchange. For Coleman (1990:266) the critical factor in establishing a norm is arranging for the norm to be backed by sanctions. Because the demand for norms arises from inadequate sanctions, the condition for creating a norm is the pooling of resources among those interested in having norms. Each person uses his own resources to the benefit of others by sanctioning matters in which he may have little stake, while they sanction matters important to him. Norms may be held by a limited coalition rather than the entire social group. One may be aware of norms and orient to them because of the attendant sanctions without internalizing them as personal values.

Coleman recognizes that human action cannot be reduced to single well-defined exchanges. Rather, he sees the self as divided and requiring choice among and integration of its components. He explicitly recognizes reference group behavior and key aspects of Mead's model of the self (1990:503–507). Although he is concerned with psychological mechanisms, his analysis is compatible with structural determinants, such as role, and with determining choice among components of the self (identities). But to analyze complex choices within an exchange framework, knowledge of the relationships among the values of various reinforcers and their sources, an exchange rate is needed.

EMERSON'S THEORY OF VALUE

Prior to his death, Emerson's effort to develop a theoretical basis for establishing exchange rates, among other things, was circulating among friends and colleagues for about four years (Friedman, 1987). The paper was incomplete but was published posthumously (Emerson, 1987). Friedman (1987), in discussing the paper, reports the difficulties experienced by her colleagues in understanding the incomplete argument and implies by her analysis the incomplete links of the ideas to broader issues. After very briefly reviewing some points raised by Emerson, I will try to indicate important substantive problems that would be addressed by the development of theory along those lines.

First, Emerson (1987) links the theory of values to a theory of the actor. In the laboratory, experimenters are able to severely restrict the relevant behavioral alternatives, control the stimuli and other information received, and manipulate need levels. In animal studies, selective breeding adds additional control to the nature of the subjects. In human studies, the subjects are selected by role, age, gender, and so on. These controls hold constant a great many factors that vary in the natural environment. In so doing, they isolate specific contingencies from other variations common in natural settings.

To generalize the experimental results to naturally occurring behavior, the complexities must be restored. In addition to knowing the principles underlying the response to each set of specific contingencies, we must also know how the person integrates those contingencies with the others in a natural environment that has not been impoverished to achieve control. In Emerson's terms, we must understand the whole person. This is a variation of the integrative issues raised in the context of role conflict and identity management.

Second, Emerson (1987) indicates the importance of value domains: "Any two valued things are in the same *value domain* if acquisition of one reduces the unit value of the other" (p. 15). In ordinary language, items in a value domain can substitute for one another or satisfy the person's desires for one another. In the laboratory, very few different rewards are used. For animals, food pellets, and for people, credit or points in classes and money are the most common. But in the real world, people have a variety of courses of action open to them that are expected to produce different rewards. In their choices, which rewards will they regard as fitting the same need? In addressing complex reward situations, what needs (domains) are addressed by the outcome? What needs remain to be served, influencing subsequent choices?

Emerson proposes that need/satiation operates in domains, not necessarily particular rewards. Individual choices among concrete possibilities, whether consciously made or habitual, compare the possible outcomes and choose the package that addresses the most salient needs or value domains. This proposal is quite similar to Goode's discussion of role strain reduction.

Past this, Emerson's paper becomes confusing. The most important cause of the confusion, in my view, is the absence of concrete empirical evidence to address these problems. At this point, I should like to turn to a more formal account of the problems caused by not knowing exchange rates and how they enter decisions.

Circularity

To apply the abstract principles of rationality, the underlying values must be known apart from the particular choice to be explained. Suppose I suggest that people do favors because they value the expressions of gratitude that result. How do I know they value gratitude? I infer it from the fact that people expend effort (cost) for no reward except the expressions of gratitude. This is a circular argument. It has many problems. One is that the claim that some behavior expresses gratitude is always a debatable interpretation of what is rewarding about it. One could also see that behavior as acknowledging dominance. But suppose I suggest that people back their cars into drainage ditches after parties because they like wrecking their cars and trying to get tow trucks at 3:00 A.M. My evidence? They do it. As values are less widely shared, their status as values becomes less convincing. In the extreme, we regard the behavior as irrational rather than acknowledge the uncommon value. This is better moralizing than it is science.

In animal behavioral experiments, circularity is avoided by empirical test. Measured units of food are used almost exclusively. Not only is the food biologically necessary, but the satiation level of the animals is kept low by forced weight reduction. Biological need gives the food great credibility as a reward. But in addition, the food has been established as a reinforcer that works to control behavior in a great many circumstances and for a great many tasks. Thus, when a new task is considered, if food does not work to reinforce the task, the weight of evidence leads us to believe that the task or stimulus was not properly designed or not within the capabilities of the organism. The value of the food is not questioned.

This is not absolute or philosophical certainty. Logically, a biological need could exist that could not work as a reward. However, willingness to accept the weight of evidence as more definitive than a priori considerations and logical possibility is one of the divisions between science and philosophy.

Many of the large variety of rewards to which we think humans respond have neither biological necessity nor the weight of evidence to justify considering them as rewards: Improved reputation or role identity? Gratitude? Prestige? Control of scheduling? Also, the particulars that we believe satisfy these needs are not fixed. Until some way is found to order the rewards or value domains, the application of exchange theory or other theories that assume rational pursuit of purpose will be technically circular.

In addition, without a theory of value there must be a gap in any explanation linking the exchange principles to concrete cases. In effect, we might do just as well without the theory, substituting a naked claim that people use "common sense" or act "reasonably." This implication is not generous, but it is identical to the reasoning behind Homans's claim that functionalists produced no theory.

The very large ethnographic literature includes already gathered evidence of patterned choices in situations with reasonably well-known contingencies. A factor analysis or other ordering of that evidence might provide a good first approximation of relevant value domains.

Ecological Validity

Results observed in a laboratory are sometimes not replicated in natural settings. When this mismatch occurs, the experimental results are said to lack *ecological validity*. Sometimes the results are artifacts of the experimental situation. This means that they occur naturally only when the variables not controlled in the experiment are at the same values in the natural environment. For example, experimenters have expectancies for how subjects in different experimental conditions will perform and may accidentally communicate them to the subjects. This has been shown to influence experimental results in a variety of tasks. Subjects' behavior, then, does not reflect the intended experimental variables, but rather, responses to uncontrolled cues. In natural settings, when the cues are not present, the experimental results do not hold (cf., Rosenthal, 1964). However, if people unintentionally cue one another in natural settings with similar power and authority relations to the experiment, the relationship will reappear.

Experimental results may also be an artifact of the peculiar authority structure of the experimental setting. Subjects may act in ways that they would not repeat in other settings because they trust the experimenter or because they submit to the high authority of science (cf., Milgram, 1972; Orne and Holland, 1972). In response to these problems, many experiments utilize double-blind designs in which the experimenter does not know which condition each subject is in. The administration of look-alike placebos in medical experiments is an example. Other experiments standardize experimenter performance by using videotapes or written messages.

Usually, variation that is controlled in the experiment complicates the relationships among the experimental variables in natural settings. For example, Cook and Emerson (1978) found that information about unequal distribution of rewards led to behavioral changes that reduced the differences. However, Schwartz (1975a) reports that in a variety of settings, including courts and doctors' offices, the schedule of one position, that of the judge or doctor, is made efficient by having everyone else wait. This reduces their efficiency. Value of time is not necessarily the deciding issue, because many lawyers earn more than the judges for whom they wait. All involved are aware of the wait and its costs. This does not mean that the relationship between information and reducing inequities is invalid. It does mean, however, that other factors can override the simple relationship observed in the laboratory. A theory of value would include the relationships among the factors involved.

The Done Deal Problem

Although most experimentation on animals is concerned with the factors leading to changes in behavior, very little human research traces the effects of rewards on behavior over time (cf., Burgess and Huston, 1979, for studies of changing exchange relationships). Most studies that apply exchange principles to natural settings attempt to identify the rewards obtained by people in already routinized behavior—done deals.

We know from extensive experimentation that more frequent rewards are needed to condition a behavior pattern than to maintain it after it has been conditioned. We also know that there is a lag between the reduction of rewards below the level necessary to maintain a behavior pattern and the extinction of the behavior. In existing patterns of behavior, even if we correctly and completely identify the reward structure, we cannot be sure whether the reward structure would produce the same behavior patterns if introduced elsewhere. The rewards might be adequate to maintain but not to condition the behavior. They may even have fallen below the level necessary to sustain it, but not yet resulted in extinction. The time frame for extinction in the natural world is not well known.

In general, even if we could identify reward-bearing events without a theory of value, we could not estimate their effectiveness in conditioning or maintaining behavior without experimental manipulation in each case. This has more than academic interest and illustrates the importance of Coleman's (1990) suggestion that intervention is the test of theoretical completeness. Without a theory of value, we can describe cases, but we cannot predict what the rewards will accomplish in new settings. That is not a good basis for planning.

ISSUES: INDIVIDUALISM AND THE SCOPE OF THEORY

Individualism versus Collectivism

Ekeh (1974) argues that fundamentally incompatible exchange theories have developed in two great sociological traditions—individualism and collectivism. Ekeh discusses Durkheim[5] as the chief representative of the collectivistic tradition, which is characterized by concern with social structure and aggregate regularities, rather than the behavior of individual people. He traces individualistic thought to the British Utilitarian philosophers. It is characterized by consideration of how the activities of separate individuals, each with his or her own motives, perceptions, and values are coordinated in systems.

Claude Levi-Strauss (e.g., 1963, 1969), the French anthropologist, developed a collectivist treatment of exchange and reciprocity in social systems. Levi-Strauss distinguished between *mutual reciprocity* between two persons who directly exchange goods with one another and *univocal reciprocity* involving several participants, as when person *A* buys popcorn for person *B* because person *B* gave person *C* a ride to the theater and person *C* bought person *A* a ticket.

Univocal reciprocity is most sociologically interesting when it becomes institutionalized in positional exchanges, as when all families in a kinship category reserve their daughters for marriage to members of a particular other kinship category while the daughters in a third kinship category are reserved for their sons. In these positional exchanges, the relationship being analyzed is between the positions or groups that have a regular exchange relationship rather than between the individuals involved. Any division of labor requires generalized exchange in which many participants are involved and in which the benefits and costs are not exchanged directly with particular other people.

Such systems of reciprocity are sustained by their consequences for the positions involved and for the systems in which they are implicated, rather than by the benefits and costs to particular people. For example, a family with several daughters and no sons will give their daughters in marriage while receiving none. Depending upon the customs in the society, the particular family may suffer or prosper disproportionately by that accident of birth. Levi-Strauss (1963) argued that direct exchange between individuals and generalized exchange support different types of social control. Following Durkheim, systems of generalized exchange, with univocal reciprocity, are conceived as social facts, relatively independent of the particular people in each social category.

George Casper Homans (e.g., 1950, 1958, 1961, 1964), the American sociologist most readily associated with social exchange theory, argues consistently for a strictly individualistic approach. He has argued that there are no general sociological propositions and that all explanation in the social sciences rests ultimately on propositions about individual behavior. Early in his career (Homans and Schneider, 1955), Homans criticized Levi-Strauss's approach to exchange and reciprocity on the fundamental ground that collectivist explanations, in general, were impossible and that explanation in the social sciences must ultimately rest on individualistic principles. In fact, Ekeh (1974) argues, Homans's own approach to exchange was first expressed in polemic attacks on Levi-Strauss.

In Homans's view, although the word *exchange* is used in both cases, the generalized and direct forms of exchange are fundamentally different phenomena. Ekeh (1974) argues similarly that the collectivist and individualistic traditions in sociology are fundamentally incompatible. Each benefits the other, but not by combination of ideas. Rather, the ongoing polemic leads each side to sharpen its own arguments and thinking under attack from the other.

But the view that individualistic and collectivistic or sociological principles are fundamentally incompatible is not shared by most exchange theorists. With Homans, Peter Blau, Richard Emerson, and James Coleman are three major pioneers of exchange theory in American sociology. All three place great emphasis on individual choices and behavior, but all three also incorporate collectivistic or sociological arguments.

Coleman (1990) accepts the explanation of and intervention in system-level events as the goal of sociological theory. System-level regularities, he argues, result from the actions of lower-level components. Explanations that include individual decision making are more likely to be useful than those excluding them. He suggests that multilevel arguments are appropriate in which system-level events and conditions create distributions of individual-level conditions such as values. These values lead to characteristic behavior, whose distribution is a new set of structural conditions. Thus, his form of argument begins and ends with system-level events. Some of the steps in the argument, however, are at the individual level that is both consequence and cause of system-level ones. His approach allows movement from system level to individual level by regarding the system as both analyzable into the actions of its components, ultimately people, and as a corporate acting unit in its own right. The distribution of individual actions is the corporate action (1975).

Blau (1960, 1967) has been concerned with social exchange in the context of structural considerations, especially social norms and power relations. He argues that social exchange occurs in the context of social norms and values that set broad limits within which people are free to enter exchange relationships. Blau (1960) demonstrated empirically that the distribution of norms and values (a social fact) in a work setting influenced the thinking and acting of workers independently of their own values. In a social service agency, caseworkers were more oriented toward casework services if the predominant value in their agency was pro-client. Blau calls the influence of the distribution of values on think-ing and acting *structural effects*. He also argues that power emerges from exchange relationships under specifiable conditions and is fundamen-tally different from voluntary exchange.

Richard Emerson (1969, 1981) proposes the most comprehensive program for integrating sociological and psychological arguments. He begins from the position that as propositions such as the basic proposi-tions derived from operant behavioral analysis or from economic models of rationality become more general, they explain "less and less about more and more" (1969:382). Emerson concludes that to apply the gen-eral propositions to concrete situations in the development of exchange theory, additional propositions will be needed. Some of these proposi-tions will be sociological, he argues. He suggests, as examples, the opera-tion of norms and the necessity for multiple independent people to act in concert to be effective in controlling anyone's behavior.[6] Thus, Emerson argues that the development of exchange theory must involve the incor-poration of additional propositions not derivable from the basic princi-ples of operant behavior as well as deduction from those principles.

In his own work, Emerson (cf., 1981) recognizes a wide variety of sociological phenomena along with the basic behavioral principles. He recognizes that patterns of conduct become institutionalized, and that institutionalized relationships have emergent social characteristics. Insti-tutionalized exchange relationships, he argues, may reveal fundamental sociological principles of exchange, relating to the institutionalized form. He conceives of the form of relationships in terms of networks, or sets of exchange connections among various participants. The participants may be individuals or role positions or corporate agents. He accepts the concept of generalized exchanges, both among networks of individuals and among networks of corporate agents. Generalized exchange networks can be institutionalized. Much of his work has been concerned with power relations. Emerson utilizes a wide variety of sociological principles and takes the network, which is a social structure, as his basic unit of analysis, rather than the individual person.

Scope of Theory

Throughout his career, Homans (cf., 1961, 1964, 1969) has taken a strong position on the nature of theory. First, a theory is an asymmetrical deductive system. Its lowest-level propositions are the facts or regularities to be explained. Higher-level propositions state regularities in more general form. The lower-level propositions can be deduced, using rules of logic, from given conditions and the higher-level propositions. However, the higher-level propositions cannot be deduced from the lower-level ones. They must be induced. Although the rules governing deduction are extensive and detailed, there are no rules governing induction, which involves an element of creative insight or inspiration.

Homans also insists that a theory, and theoretical explanations, must always begin with general propositions. These general propositions cannot themselves be explained at the current state of scientific knowledge (1969:3). In his polemic criticisms of functionalism (1964, 1969), Homans took functionalists to task for not extending their deductive reasoning to incorporate general propositions. He argues, in fact, that they never produced a theoretical explanation (1964:818). His individualistic approach is expressed in this context by the criticism that if the functionalists, and other collectivists, had completed their arguments, they would have found that their explanations were based on implicit psychological principles.

Although exchange theorists have accepted the concept of explanation as deduction, Homans view that all theoretical explanations must be deduced from general propositions is not shared. Coleman (1990) partially evades the issue by subordinating the evaluation of theoretical explanation to the purpose of the explanation. Generally, he argues, explanations of system-level events consider the interaction of components internal to the system. In the case of human society, the individual person is the most basic component, but there are corporate units, such as families, companies, governmental agencies, that are also subordinate to the social system as a whole. Thus, the most general explanations in the social sciences will begin their deductive reasoning at the level of individual behavior. However, for many purposes, explanation can stop well short of analysis to general principles of individual conduct. Coleman's basic rule is that "an explanation is sufficiently fundamental . . . if it provides a basis for knowledgeable intervention which can change system behavior" (1990:4).

Emerson (1969, 1981) conceives of social exchange theory as an explicitly middle-range theory. We have already noted that Emerson expects emergent sociological concepts to be added to the elementary psychological principles in which exchange theory is grounded. In addition, he argues, the principles themselves are drawn from too narrow a base. There are other theoretical and methodological approaches that have generated knowledge that should be incorporated in exchange theoretical arguments. His strategy is to "draw upon reliable and relevant principles wherever they can be found" (1969:404). This approach runs directly against the formation of a tightly integrated theory deduced from a few principles. He also portrays social exchange as one of many phenomena abstracted for explanation from social interaction (1981:33). Social exchange theory is focused on the flow of benefits through social interaction, he argues, while symbolic interaction is focused on the flow of information. He sees these two theories as supplementary ways of organizing the same events. This approach to other theories also runs counter to the attempt to explain all social behavior using one general theory.

SOCIAL EXCHANGE: A CASE OF MIDDLE-RANGE DEDUCTIVE THEORIZING

Homans remains an important figure for his promotion of operant conditioning principles in sociology and for his part in the development of social exchange theory. However, the development of exchange theory has not taken the path he proposed. His reductionism, or denial of emergent sociological regularities, has been rejected by the other contributors to exchange theory. All utilize both sociological and individualistic propositions in their theories. Although they recognize that the *elementary* propositions of *individual* behavior may be psychological, all also recognize that sociological propositions emerge as more complex behavior is considered. Emerson has even argued that exchange goes beyond the elementary level to *require* sociological analysis.

In addition, excepting Coleman's (1990) general theoretical statement, exchange theorists have engaged in a relatively eclectic form of middle-range theorizing. Theorizing has consistently taken the deductive form, although mathematical models are at least as common as syllogistic reasoning. Humans and corporate agents are regarded as essentially rational in their choices, but whether this doctrine is a set of elementary propositions in Homans's sense, or just a convenient model, is seldom at issue. Additional propositions are added—some are empirical observations, some are theoretical principles about group life or individual psychology. The deductive arguments are typically short and leave a great many questions to be answered in separate arguments and by other theories.

Coleman's (1987) discussion of zealots and free riders is substantively interesting because of its relationship to symbolic interaction.[7] It is empirically quite narrow, but its deductive chain is typical in length and complexity. The empirical observations to be explained are the presence of two types of individual contributions to group projects that do not conform to a straightforward exchange of effort for rewards. He calls one *zealotry*, making an effort that is disproportionally large for the benefits received as one's share of the group effort. The other, *free riding*, is taking one's share of the benefits of group effort without doing one's share of the work.

Coleman introduces a sociological variable to explain these types of participation. Organizations vary in the degree to which secondary rewards are available to participants through interaction, along with the share of the manifest benefits. When secondary rewards are high and added to the benefits, they make increased zealotry rational. When they are limited, free riding increases. Both sociological and psychological propositions are employed. Neither has a clear claim to be more fundamental than the other.

Several important questions are not answered. Why do organizations vary along this dimension? Can the secondary rewards be increased by intervention? How? Why do people free ride when they can? Is it possible to promote altruism? Is the narrowly self-interested base of rational choice a characteristic of our species or a sociological variable?[8] It is crucial to this kind of theorizing that the limited explanation remains sound under many answers to those questions. To make a more complete theoretical explanation, the answers to these and other questions would have to be added. The answers to these questions might require explanations that are not exchange theoretic.

The resulting combined explanations, when attempted, are not elegant. Facts and reasoning are borrowed from research traditions that develop separately and, as a result, produce their own jargon and methods. The combined explanation includes all the jargon and depends on the validity and reliability of all the methods. There is also no single vision uniting the separate pieces as there is in a more general theory. These are aesthetic considerations. Personally, I like patchwork quilts better than designer blankets, and I like arguments that draw their principles from empirical research rather than doctrine, even at the expense of theoretical elegance. Suit yourself.

There is one substantive advantage to this form of theorizing. If a mistake is made, only a limited portion of the overall explanation must be altered. To switch metaphors, each argument acts in the overall explanation like a prewired circuit board or module in an electrical appliance or computer. If one is defective, it can be removed and replaced or altered. In a more integrated deductive model, the consequence of errors depends on where they occur in the deductive chain. If the basic propositions are incomplete or inaccurate in some way, then the entire theoretical chain is affected. This is not an argument against general theorizing, but only against premature general theorizing, uncertain or unclear with respect to basic matters. As Minsky (1986:39) puts it, "It often does more harm than good to force definitions on things we don't understand. . . . Especially when it comes to understanding minds, we still know so little that we can't be sure our ideas about psychology are even aimed in the right directions. In any case, one must not mistake defining things for knowing what they are."

The issue of how integrated and general a theory ought to be is a doctrinal matter in the philosophy of science more than a matter of substantive sociological interest. I have raised it in this context because it has two substantive implications in this case. First, it is imperative in understanding Homans's importance to also understand that his views do not represent those of exchange theorists on these issues. This is especially crucial because Homans is often presented as the authoritative spokesperson for exchange theory. If one requires that one such person represent the group, Richard Emerson would probably be the better choice. Second, as we have seen in evaluating Homans's basic propositions, they are not empirically sound in detail.

NOTES

1. The creativity involved in this task of derivation should not be underestimated. Operant behavioral research results are not typically codified in propositional form. For the most part, even textbooks concentrate on detailed discriminations among different conditioning schedules and do not abstract general principles.

2. Baldwin and Baldwin (1981) review the argument that certain unconditioned reinforcers have been selected in the evolutionary process and are innate. Among the commonly effective unconditioned reinforcers, they include food; water; normal body temperature; optimal levels of sensory stimulation; sleep; caresses; genital simulation; nipple and breast stimulation; and nicotine, alcohol, and various other drugs. Among innate punishers, they include extreme temperatures, cuts, sharp blows, shocks, stings, burns, overly full stomach or bladder, effortful work, certain odors and tastes, loud noise, lack of air, water in the lungs, and causes of nausea.

3. At milder levels of sanctions, we have already seen that options exist that neither defy others, accepting sanctions for misconduct, nor conform to their wishes. Deception plays a large part. It is interesting to note that as sanctions become more extreme, there are still alternatives to the choice between compliance and defiance. The Nazi work camp at Auschwitz, for example, worked 25,000 of the 300,000 inmates to death, and absorbed 900 million Reichsmarks. Nonetheless it produced none of the artificial rubber and only a little synthetic fuel, which it was designed to produce (Borkin, 1978). Apparently there are ways to neither defy power nor acquiesce to it, even when the sanctions are severe.

4. One could argue along Durkheimian lines that any situation in which coercive social facts are implicated has an element of power. One could also argue along Marxist lines that any situation within a stratified society has an element of power. Either line of reasoning implies that all social situations in a society include some element of power.

5. Durkheim (1938:2) argued that social facts existed that exerted a power of coercion over an individual "by which they impose themselves upon him, independent of his individual will." The coercion, he proposes, is found in sanctions for violating the social factual customs. The sanctions may take the form of direct punishment, as when the law is violated, public scorn and ridicule, or total failure of all plans based on contrary behavior, such as if one tried to talk a language other than the locally understood one or attempted to ignore available technology in business. The coercion may be so indirect that it is not recognized. Each society can be identified and differentiated from the others on the basis of this coerced behavior.

   In his most famous application of this approach, Durkheim (1951) showed that the rate of suicide in societies varied with other social structural conditions in the society. These conditions, related to social norms, are plausibly interpreted as part of the mechanism of coercion. No individual suicide is explained, nor any individual's reasons or motives for committing suicide discussed. Only the rates of suicide are considered.

   Although the suicide rate is quite small, the study of suicide is not methodologically different from the study of instances of seeming unanimity, such as all members of the society speaking the same language. There are differences in vocabulary and slang employed, in correctness of grammar, in accent, and so on. "Speaking the same language" is best considered a loose summary of a great deal of variation—a statistical and probabilistic situation, not one involving uniformity of behavior. To be consistent, we would have to assume that the absolute level of the rates, higher for language speaking than for suicide, reflect differences in the patterns of coercion controlling different behavior within a society.

6. Emerson argues that if the sanctions imposed on a person from various sources are contradictory, none of them, considered singly, will have the effect predicted on the basis of laboratory findings. In the laboratory, all reinforcers are controlled by a single source and administered on a known schedule. This issue has been raised in evaluating the general propositions derived from operant behavioral experiments and in discussing Emerson's work in more detail. This same issue has also appeared in the context of role theory, especially the theory of role strain, and symbolic interaction.

7. Much of the identity negotiation discussed by symbolic interactionists can be construed, in Coleman's terms, as the attempt to deal with free riding in the context of the vulnerability of communication.
8. Note that this is one of C. Wright Mills's basic questions about society: What sorts of people does society produce?

REFERENCES

Aronson, Elliot and J. M. Carlsmith. 1963. Effect of Severity of Threat on the Devaluation of Forbidden Behavior. *Journal of Abnormal and Social Psychology* 66: 584–588.

Baldwin, John and Janice Baldwin. 1981. Behavior Principles in Everyday Life. Englewood Cliffs: Prentice Hall.

Blau, Peter. 1960. Structural Effects. *American Sociological Review* 25:178–193.

Blau, Peter. 1967. Exchange and Power in Social Life. New York: Wiley.

Borkin, Joseph. 1978. The Crime and Punishment of I. G. Farben. New York: Free Press.

Breland, K. and M. Breland. 1961. The Misbehavior of Organisms. *American Psychologist* 16:681–684.

Burgess, Robert and Ted Huston (eds). 1979. Social Exchange in Developing Relationships. New York: Academic Press.

Coleman, James. 1964. Collective Decisions. *Sociological Inquiry* 34:166–181.

Coleman, James. 1975. Social Structure and a Theory of Action. Pp. 76–94 in Peter Blau (ed.), Approaches to the Study of Social Structure. New York: Free Press.

Coleman, James. 1987. Free Riders and Zealots. Pp. 59–82 in Karen Cook (ed.), Social Exchange Theory. Beverly Hills: Sage.

Coleman, James. 1990. Foundations of Social Theory. Cambridge, MA: Belknap Press.

Cook, Karen and Richard Emerson. 1978. Power, Equity, Commitment in Exchange Networks. *American Sociological Review* 43:721–739.

Durkheim, Emile. 1951. Suicide. Glencoe: Free Press.

Durkheim, Emile. 1966/1938. The Rules of the Sociological Method. New York: Free Press.

Ekeh, Peter. 1974. Social Exchange Theory. Cambridge, MA: Harvard University Press.

Emerson, Richard. 1962. Power-Dependence Relations. *American Sociological Review* 27:31–41.

Emerson, Richard. 1969. Operant Psychology and Exchange Theory. Pp. 379–406 in Robert Burgess and Don Bushell (eds.), Behavioral Sociology. New York: Columbia University Press.

Emerson, Richard. 1981. Social Exchange Theory. Pp. 30–66 in Morris Rosenberg and Ralph Turner (eds.), Social Psychology. New York: Basic Books.

Emerson, Richard. 1987. Toward a Theory of Value in Social Exchange. Pp. 11–46 in Karen Cook (ed.), Social Exchange Theory. Beverly Hills: Sage.

Festinger, Leon and J. M. Carlsmith. 1959. The Cognitive Consequences of Forced Compliance. *Journal of Abnormal and Social Psychology* 58:203–210.

Festinger, Leon, Henry Riecken, and Stanley Schachter. 1956. When Prophecy Fails. New York: Harper.

Friedman, Debra. 1987. Notes on "Toward a Theory of Value in Social Exchange." Pp. 47–58 in Karen Cook (ed.), Social Exchange Theory. Beverly Hills: Sage.

Heath, Anthony. 1976. Rational Choice and Social Exchange. New York: Cambridge University Press.

Homans, George. 1950. The Human Group. New York: Harcourt Brace Jovanovich.

Homans, George. 1958. Social Behavior as Exchange. *American Journal of Sociology* 62:597–606.

Homans, George. 1961. Social Behavior: Its Elementary Forms. New York: Harcourt, Brace and World.

Homans, George. 1964. Bringing Men Back In. *American Sociological Review* 29:809–819.

Homans, George. 1969. The Sociological Relevance of Behaviorism. Pp. 1–26 in Robert Burgess and Don Bushell (eds.), Behavioral Sociology. New York: Columbia University Press.

Homans, George. 1974. Social Behavior: Its Elementary Forms, rev. ed. New York: Harcourt Brace Jovanovich.

Homans, George. 1975. What Do We Mean by Social "Structure"? Pp. 53–65 in Peter Blau (ed.), Approaches to the Study of Social Structure. New York: Free Press.

Homans, George and David Schneider. 1955. Marriage Authority and Final Causes. New York: Free Press.

Lawrence, Douglas and Leon Festinger. 1962. Deterrents and Reinforcement. Stanford: Stanford University Press.

Levi-Strauss, Claude. 1963. Structural Anthropology. New York: Harper.

Levi-Strauss, Claude. 1969. Elementary Structures of Kinship. Boston: Beacon Press.

McCullers, John. 1978. Issues in Learning and Motivation. Pp. 5–18 in Mark Lepper and David Greene (eds.), The Hidden Costs of Reward. New York: Wiley.

McGraw, Kenneth. 1978. The Detrimental Effects of Reward on Performance. Pp. 33–60 in Mark Lepper and David Greene (eds.), The Hidden Costs of Reward. New York: Wiley.

Milgram, Stanley. 1972. Some Conditions of Obedience and Disobedience to Authority. Pp. 82–105 in Arthur Miller (ed.), The Social Psychology of Psychological Research. New York: Free Press.

Minsky, Marvin. 1986. The Society of Mind. New York: Simon & Schuster.

Orne, Martin. 1972. On the Social Psychology of the Psychological Experiment. Pp. 233–246 in Arthur Miller (ed.), The Social Psychology of Psychological Research. New York: Free Press.

Orne, Martin and Charles Holland. 1972. On the Ecological Validity of Laboratory Research. Pp. 122–137 in Arthur Miller (ed.), The Social Psychology of Psychological Research. New York: Free Press.

Rachlin, Howard. 1976. Modern Behaviorism, 2nd ed. San Francisco: Freeman.

Rosenthal, Robert. 1964. The Effects of the Experimenter on the Results of Psychological Research. Pp. 79–114 in B. Maher (ed.), Progress in Experimental Personality Research, Vol 1. New York: Academic Press.

Schwartz, Barry. 1975a. Waiting, Exchange and Power. Pp. 13–46 in Queuing and Waiting. Chicago: University of Chicago Press.

Schwartz, Barry. 1975b. Waiting, Deference and Distributive Justice. Pp. 135–152 in Queuing and Waiting. Chicago: University of Chicago Press.

Skinner, B. F. 1972/1948. "Superstition" in the Pigeon. Pp. 524–528 in The Cumulative Record. New York: Appleton Century Crofts.

Smelser, Neil. 1959. Social Change in the Industrial Revolution. Chicago: University of Chicago Press.

Staw, Barry. 1981. The Escalation of Commitment to a Course of Action. *Academy of Management Review* 6: 577–587.

10 ───────────────────────

Ethnomethodology

───────────────────────

Harold Garfinkel coined the term *ethnomethodology* to refer to the study of folk (ethno) methods for making sense of the environment, especially the social environment. Ethnomethodologists draw a parallel between the methods that people use to reach an understanding of events and the methods used by scientists. For them, the crucial problem in understanding social conduct is not cataloging the values, ideas, cognitive maps, and perceptions that are implicated in conduct, but rather determining *how* they are assembled, communicated, manipulated, and in general *used* in interaction. That is, they study the methods of understanding, not the specific understandings achieved.

One of the most persistent themes in social conduct is the belief among participants that outcomes are contingent upon the nature of a real world that is an objective condition of their action. Ethnomethodology is a study of how people convince themselves and one another that there is a stable order in society and of the nature of that order during, and as a basis for, interaction. People's development and use of ideas about the broader social world during interaction are addressed by all of the microsociological theories. And all of the microsociological approaches carefully express their radical (paradigmatic) differences from

Parsons's analytic theory of action. But some early, programmatic ethno-methodological work also seems to claim radical differences from the other post-Parsons approaches. In fact, for a while, this claim itself was the topic of considerable debate within the discipline.[1]

For our purposes, it is necessary to distinguish ethnomethodology from Parson's analytic theory of action in two ways. First, although Parsons emphasized the voluntaristic nature of action, the view that people simply conform to socially given values once they are learned renders conduct basically mechanical. Voluntarism is, in effect, negated by the internalization of norms and knowledge, which makes people reliable as interchangeable system parts. Each socialized individual, having internalized the knowledge and values of his or her society, will perceive situations, including the right course of action, identically with others in the society. In Garfinkel's view, there is considerable judgmental work overlooked in this imagery, which he rejects for conceiving of people as "judgmental dopes" (Garfinkel, 1967).[2]

Second, Garfinkel rejects Parsons's approach to the social reality external to interaction. In Garfinkel's view, Parsons accepts the existence of that reality as prior to and constraining conduct. This implies that people believe in this reality because it is there. They may be wrong in their appraisals of the world and act ineffectively, but the world is there, independent of their beliefs. In fact, ineffective action can be regarded as the best evidence of the world's constraining presence. Action is ineffective because there are contingencies that impose themselves on conduct whether they are recognized or not. Theorists who share belief in an objective order use that prior belief as a theoretical resource in various ways. It eliminates several philosophical issues about the nature of reality and the basis of belief in it. Moreover, it allows scientific appraisals of reality to be used in evaluating folk knowledge and explaining the outcomes of conduct. Finally, it suggests an invidious comparison between scientific procedures and knowledge and those found in everyday use. Folk knowledge is often found inadequate compared to scientific method and logic. So is the way the knowledge is used and developed.

For Garfinkel (1967), the sense of order and of external reality is accomplished by judgmental work. People have to convince themselves of the presence of order as well as its substantive details. His rejection of the assumption of an external reality as a theoretical resource differentiates Garfinkel from other microsociologists as well as from Parsons. An important element in all of the other microsociological theories is the adjustment of individual ideas about the social world to the realities of the social world. Adjustment is motivated by the consequences of the degree to which one's perceptions and models of the social world are accurate. This process of adjustment, in fact, is among the core concerns of role theory, symbolic interaction, and social exchange theory. Defining the intellectual relationship between ethnomethodology and other specialties in sociology requires clarification of this issue. Especially, we must develop some idea of what one studies and what one does not study when the objective reality of society is forgone as a resource.

The philosophical bases of ethnomethodology can be quite daunting, but substantively it can be understood as an important supplement to the other theories. We can begin defining the ethnomethodological position by considering how interaction proceeds when the ideas about society on which it is based are not grounded in real social conditions. For example, an interaction can be organized by reference groups that include imaginary people such as one's future descendants or people who have died. One can participate in an exchange network ignorant of the true distribution of rewards in it and the degree of equity. Or one might participate in interaction in which structural barriers to perception preclude relevant knowledge about others' conduct. *The ideas about the social world beyond the interaction, developed in such circumstances, would be developed and used within the interaction just as if they had a greater external basis.* That is, at least some processes of interaction operate regardless of the accuracy of participants' ideas, and they are sufficient to sustain the interaction.

Ethnomethodologists, then, are concerned with those processes in interaction that occur regardless of whether the ideas developed and used in the interaction contradict information developed elsewhere, regardless of whether the outcomes are desirable, and regardless of whether the interaction is coordinated with other events in a larger social system. *To isolate these processes, belief in the larger system is suspended.* Instead of focusing on the content of ideas and the impact of practicalities on that content over time, ethnomethodologists focus on the *form* of the ideas.

The term *form* is not understood in a static way. By the form of ideas, or formal structure (Garfinkel and Sacks, 1970), ethnomethodologists mean rules governing knowledge and its use. These rules are conceived to organize knowledge in everyday life parallel to the way in which scientific method and logic organize science. However, the rules are different from those upheld as a normative standard for scientific methodology. Among the concerns are how ideas are organized and how contradictions are expressed and kept from disrupting the sense of order. What ethnomethodologists do will be developed later in this chapter. What they do not do is stop when they encounter an idea expressed in interaction to consider whether it is correct or valid or practical when compared to some external standard. Instead, they consider how it is used, with the goal, in part, to establish the rules of everyday logic by empirical investigation.

"Suspending belief" in objective realities can be interpreted as a theoretical commitment or as a methodological procedure. If it is taken theoretically, it amounts to denying the existence of those structures, to denying the existence of an external world. In that interpretation, ethnomethodology is fundamentally different from the rest of sociology and incompatible with it. Sociology, because it accepts belief in those realities, as do we all in everyday life, becomes just another folk belief to be analyzed by ethnomethodology for its actual rules of procedure (as opposed to the normative rules found in methods texts). However, taken methodologically, there is no contradiction—there is simply a procedure that makes certain processes available for study. Other processes, such as learning in response to consequences, cannot be studied in this way because they transcend single interactions and require acceptance of the objectivity of external realities.

There is good reason to regard the suspension of belief in external realities methodologically. Granted, a theoretical interpretation was probably intended in the philosophical analyses that ground ethnomethodology and in some early statements of the ethnomethodological program, as well. But the ethnomethodological studies and substantive statements are very loosely connected to their philosophical base and program. They are driven by the data and by other aspects of the research methods employed, as well as by belief suspension. Whatever the original intent, the theoretical implications of the studies and the subsequent theoretical arguments must be considered in their own right. In short, theories beginning from fundamentally different philosophical traditions may not be incompatible. Moreover, recent studies have unambiguously adopted such sociological concerns as the mobilization of political resources and gender discrimination and used sociological concepts such as role. Thus, rather than belaboring the early ambiguous intent, I recommend taking the literature as a consistent whole by interpreting the ambiguities methodologically.

A crucial difference does remain between ethnomethodology and the other microsociological theories. It can be summed up in this imagined dialogue:

> *E:* How do people define social reality during interaction?
> *S:* They begin with ideas about social reality and revise them in response to the consequences of the actions based on those ideas. Subsequently, in similar situations, they act on the basis of the revised ideas.
> *E:* No, No, No, No, No, O best beloved! Not why, *how!*

Ethnomethodology answers *how*, but not *why*, about social interaction, while the other microsociological theories answer *why*, but not *how*. Ethnomethodologists cannot study social processes that transcend interaction while the other microsociological theories cannot address the formal structure of practical knowledge within interaction. This is a very important difference, but it poses no contradiction unless we assume that there is only one social process.

PHILOSOPHY AND FORMAL STRUCTURES

Multiple Realities

Alfred Schutz, a phenomenologically oriented philosopher, whose work originally appeared during the 1940s and 1950s, was a major influence on the development of ethnomethodology. Schutz (1967) argued that there are many realities, each with its own "attitude" or "style of existence." Each style of existence is a way of selecting facts for attention and assembling them into a coherent perception. For example, in the theater, the actions on the stage are interpreted differently from those in the audience. We distinguish between the actor and the character he plays, for instance, and understand that the character displays emotions that are not the actor's own, that we may see traces of the actor in the character, that the actor will not be changed by the events that happen to the character, and so on.

The most important contrasting realities considered by Schutz were the attitude of scientific theorizing and the attitude of everyday life. The attitude of pure scientific theorizing is not practical. It does not "gear into" (Schutz, 1967) the world nor does it have an immediate intent to manipulate or alter it. In scientific theorizing, one employs well-defined concepts and rigorous logic to understand the relationships among the concepts clearly. Only the concepts are manipulated and the only product is argument or explanation. When empirical application is attempted either in engineering or research, generating new information about the concepts, the pure theoretical attitude must be abandoned. That is, the entire edifice of scientific theorizing has its foundation in another way of assembling a world. There are multiple realities, but they are not equally fundamental. The most fundamental reality, the one that gears into the real world, Schutz called the reality of everyday life.

The main features of the attitude of everyday life are an unquestioning belief in the objective existence of a world beyond our experience upon which action is contingent and a practical concern for consequences. Our knowledge is consulted and evaluated as it relates to our ability to successfully achieve our ends. Logic, in the rigorous sense, is not applied systematically. We attend, and think, and act only carefully enough to accomplish the purpose at hand. The rules for assembling a commonsense world are not visible within the attitude of common sense.

Largely, the suspension of belief in reality discussed earlier is an attempt to see the rules or formal structure of the commonsense attitude from a theoretic point of view.

Indexicality

Logicians also consider the fundamental difference between the clarity of theorizing and the problems of applying concepts to the empirical world. Black (1970) referred to empirical terms and concepts as *loose*. By this, he meant that it is not always clear whether things or events fit a definition and whether they belong in or out of the defined category. This kind of precision or clarity or tightness is crucial to theorizing and the application of logic.

To clarify the issue, Black proposed a word game. Consider the word *short*. We can agree that any adult human, 4 feet tall or less is short. How about an adult human 4.0001 feet tall? 4.0002? If we continue, eventually we will have to make a choice that is nonsensical. Either we will have to continue calling everyone short or we will have to arbitrarily say that a person at some height is short, while a person 0.0001 feet taller, an imperceptible difference to the naked eye, is not. This demonstrates that the meaning of empirical terms such as *short* does not support strict logical manipulation.

Black was concerned to allow philosophical and theoretical reasoning to apply to empirical matters. Of course, science is involved, but also, and maybe more important, the relevance of philosophical reasoning to practical and ethical questions, which necessarily gear into the world. Black argued that empirical terms have a range of applicability. Sometimes we are confident that the term has been applied carefully to the empirical event. Then, if we apply logic to the terms our conclusions will be empirically accurate. Other times, we are not confident about the fit between the definition of the term and the event it has been applied to. Then, if we apply logic, we could not expect the deductions to match the empirical events. Instances of this sort of reasoning are familiar to us all. We know that manufactured items only approximate their specifications and that the instructions for assembly and use will work only if the approximations are within acceptable "tolerances." Black argues that all empirical descriptions must be taken that way, whether in science or in everyday life.[3]

Bar-Hillel's (1954) discussion of these indexical (loose) expressions was extremely influential in Garfinkel's work. Bar-Hillel argued that the indexical expression often seems clear in its meaning, but that the meaning is derived partly from an interpretation of context, not from the indexical statement itself. Among the contextual features that can impart meaning are the identity of the speaker, the purposes of the hearer, the time and situation of the statement, and the purposes imputed to the speaker. In Black's terms, these are the things that affect our level of confidence that we know whether the definitional meaning of the term fits the empirical case to which it is applied.

Garfinkel and Sacks (1970) formulate their empirical concerns in terms of these philosophical issues. If we identify a meaningful particular item, whether it is a word or other symbolic expression, what is the relationship among that item (the indexical particular), its meaning, and the context in which the particular appears? That is the core empirical concern of ethnomethodology. Put in an active way, how are the indexical particulars, taken as context for each other, made meaningful?

A simple example may help. Zimmerman (1970) studied how a receptionist assigned clients to intake workers in a welfare agency. In order to assign clients to available intake workers on a "first come, first served" basis, a checkerboard chart was used. The names of the intake workers were placed in a column down the left side. Then, by putting clients' names into the checkerboard from top to bottom, and left to right, a queue was approximated. Each client was assigned by this procedure to the worker whose last assigned client arrived before the last assigned clients of all the other workers.

If each case took the same amount of time, the clients would be served in the same order in which they arrived and were placed on the chart. But sometimes, a worker's case took an unusually long time. Then, clients assigned to that worker might have to wait while later arriving clients were taken by other workers. In those cases, the receptionist reassigned clients and erased and revised the chart. Thus, the purpose of the rule was served by violating the rule when necessary. The rule was loose. It has exceptions that cannot be listed in advance but can be recognized when they occur. These exceptions reveal that the meaning of the rule must be interpreted in light of the waiting clients who serve as its context. The chart is loose. After revision, it no longer reflects initial assignments. When the logic of the rule gears into the world, some precision is lost. Having observed this looseness, ethnomethdologists want to know, for example, how problems are recognized, how revised procedures are reconciled with the rules, and how a sense of rule-governed orderliness is sustained.

Documentary Method of Interpretation

Mannheim's (1964) discussion of the documentary method of interpretation in social and historical studies has many similarities to the logicians' discussion of indexical or loose concepts and serves to link the concerns of ethnomethodology to the larger-scale issues in sociology. Mannheim argued that social or historical knowledge, which he called *documentary*, is different in kind from that of the natural sciences and is achieved in a fundamentally different way. Documentary knowledge is an underlying pattern apprehended or induced from examination of a large number of particular items. The pattern gives meaning to the diverse items. Once one has grasped a pattern, the selection and interpretation of items is altered. Thus, the pattern and its elementary parts give meaning to one another.[4]

Formally, then, the documentary meaning of items in a culture is similar to the relationship among indexical particulars acting as context for one another. For example, the various paintings (documents/indexical particulars) of an artist allow themes and patterns (meanings) to be seen in his or her work. Then the themes or patterns provide a context for perceiving each separate piece. But substantively, Mannheim's interests are quite different. When a large number of items from diverse aspects of a society are considered, such as art, culture, politics, religious belief, technology and science, and patterns of social inequality, a global intuitive grasp of the sociohistorical period is attained. This Weltanschauung, or worldview, is to an entire historical epoch what a theme is to a single artist's work. Mannheim, then, reminds us that the structure of a society, its institutions, its inequalities, its particular place in history, and the particular place of a person within that society are among the items that influence the selection and interpretation of particular events. In the welfare office, for instance, in addition to the local difficulties of maintaining a fair queue, a society with welfare clients and offices is revealed. The natures of the clients and workers and the society that produces them are also part of the meaning of that office.

It is in this enlarged spirit that Molotch (1973) and Molotch and Lester (1974) apply ethnomethodology to a politically significant event, an oil spill off the coast of Santa Barbara, by California. By suspending belief in the content of the news stories, the process of assembling the story as a thematic, meaningful whole becomes visible. The practical concerns of the newspapers result in reporting the story one way, rather than another. That is, the story is not a literal account of what really happened but a loose collection of indexical items. But beyond that, the influence of oil companies and political figures is also documented in the patterns of newspaper choice. Accommodating these powerful interests is among the practical concerns of the newspaper. In this way, a detailed account can be given of how powerful interests in a society are able to exercise their influence by controlling the meaning given to events.

Reflexivity of Accounts

A reflexive relationship is one that something has with itself and, by extension, a reflexive action is an action the acting agent takes upon itself. For example, when I shave myself, the action is reflexive. All accounts are reflexive, take some action upon themselves, because an account is an indexical particular or document. Each account, by being added to the body of accounts, somewhat alters the pattern perceived in the body of accounts. In turn, this change influences the meaning of the account itself.

It is crucial to note that the reflexivity of accounts is a relationship among accounts and not between accounts and an objective world. This reflexivity is only interesting within the attitude of scientific theorizing. Within that attitude the "truth" of accounts is put aside by suspending belief and interest is refocused on how meaning is developed. When the scientific attitude is taken, then, the world consists entirely of accounts, of indexical displays serving as context for one another. Questions of truth do not arise, only questions of how these accounts are assembled into a choherent theme one can believe to be true in the commonsense attitude.

PRACTICALITIES OF SCIENTIFIC RESEARCH

Cicourel's (1964, 1968, 1974) work reflects ethnomethodology's interest in science as a special case of reflexivity. Science is a social activity and has the same characteristics as other social activities. Empirical science is grounded in, and accepts the reality of, the objective world. In Schutz's (1967) terms, the empirical application of scientific concepts is grounded in the attitude of everyday life. Of course, as logicians point out, this means that scientific concepts, however rigorously they are defined within a theory, are loose in application. That is, science is not objective in a philosophical sense, but only in the practical sense supported by the attitude of everyday life.

Cicourel (1968, 1974) developed and applied a method to demonstrate the looseness of scientific measurement. He conducted his own social scientific studies. One was an ethnographic study of the juvenile justice system in two communities. The other was a demographic study of fertility in Argentina. Both studies employed methods that were competent by prevailing social scientific standards. And both reported findings that were legitimate in their own right. Simultaneously, Cicourel took the conduct of his own research as a topic and studied how measurement was done or, in other words, how his study gave meaning to the particulars of its data.

Cicourel found two fundamental points of entry for commonsense reasoning into his empirical research. First, the subjects being studied become, in effect, confederates in the research. If the answers to a questionnaire are accepted as scientific data, then however the subjects arrive at the answers becomes part of the research method. So, for example, if subjects are not truthful in answering embarrassing questions, the norms and assumptions governing their embarrassment are part of the research method. In addition, subjects may not understand the questions in the way they are intended. In ethnographic study, formal questionnaires may not be used, but the subjects are still asked to interpret events, tell the researcher about occurrences the researcher has not seen firsthand, and elaborate on the meaning of events. The practicalities of the subjects' lives are implicated in the gathering of data.

Second, Cicourel found that he and his research team were also forced to engage in practical reasoning during the empirical study. His interviewers in the fertility study were required to make complex judgments concerning the probes. Standardized questionnaire items are supplemented by probes to encourage more detailed responses. However, there is always the risk that subjects would terminate the interview if the probes were too personal. Thus, the interviewers made character and mood assessments and adjusted the extent of probing to gather as much information as they could without angering the subject. These judgments were all of the practical sort and influenced the data and, in fact, the exact questions asked. Complete standardization of the questionnaire was not achieved.

Cicourel reports his own use of practical reasoning primarily in the ethnographic study. First, he was unable to observe all the relevant events firsthand. Consequently, he relied on hearsay evidence from participants, which he interpreted in terms of his own practical understandings of local politics, the motives of the reporter, and so on. The written files posed similar difficulties. These tended to be cryptic and incomplete and were designed to be filled in from the background knowledge of those involved in the case. In order to learn "what happened" from the files, Cicourel relied on his own background knowledge.

Thus, Cicourel's studies establish that practicing science is not an exception to the looseness of empirical concepts. Even trained researchers employ commonsense reasoning, as opposed to the logic of theory, in the process of gathering data and applying conceptual categories to empirical cases. His recommendation is that these aspects of method should regularly be reported so that judgments can be made concerning their implications for the results.

Sense In Senseless Situations

Garfinkel (1963, 1964) attempted to demonstrate that sense could be made in a senseless environment and that when subjects abandoned belief in the sense of the environment, they were able to perceive how the environment was given sense in the first place. To demonstrate that sense could be made in a senseless environment, Garfinkel produced a partly senseless environment in the laboratory. Ten volunteer subjects, all undergraduate students, were recruited for a study of a new psychiatric technique. Subjects were to think aloud about an important personal situation until they arrived at a question that could be answered "yes" or "no" by the therapist. After each answer, they were to continue reflecting aloud, beginning with an interpretation of the answer, until they formulated another question. Each subject produced 10 questions in this way. The therapist was in another room, communicating by intercom.

The senselessness consisted in this: The sequence of yes/no answers to the questions was selected by consulting a table of random numbers and was not in any way selected to fit the subjects' questions or problems. Despite this randomness, all subjects were able to find a thematic thread to the "advice," even in cases in which the answers were plainly contradictory. None doubted that there was a therapist who was responding to his or her questions.

However, this is far from a totally senseless environment. There is no theme, except an accidental one, to the sequence of answers. That much of the environment is senseless. As long as the subjects continue to believe that there is a real therapist who is listening and responding to them, and whatever else they may believe about therapists, they can make sense of whatever is said.

Adopting the attitude of scientific theorizing is one way to make the sense-making process observable. But Garfinkel (1964) developed another way to breach or get people to abandon the commonsense attitude, at least in part. Subjects, students again, were instructed to act in unusual ways and then to resist efforts by others to normalize their conduct. In the responses of the others to them, students and Garfinkel were able to see how their ordinary behavior is sensible. In one demonstration, students were to refuse to understand colloquial expressions. To a question such as "How are you?," they would reply, "What do you mean? Physically? Emotionally?" As the students continued to press for a literal expression, the others become angry. This demonstrates that the right to use indexical expressions is defended as a moral right, and that others are expected to understand when things are "clear enough" or suffer the consequences. That is, the looseness of the everyday world is defended by norms.

In another demonstration, (Garfinkel, 1964) students were told to act as "boarders" in their own homes. They were to be polite and not participate in their usual intimacies. This produced anger and suspicion about the boarders' motives and feelings. When the boarders revealed the reasons for their behavior, the anger was not dissipated. Their families defended their moral right to be treated in their habitual and expected way. That is, the obligation to believe and adhere to the "real" relationships is defended by norms. Note that adherence to habit is enforced as well as the particular habit. This practice produces stability, rather than being derived from a preexisting stability.

Garfinkel (1964) assigned students to bargain for relatively low-priced items with posted prices. This is fairly common practice for high-priced items such as cars and major appliances, but the students experienced anxiety in anticipation of bargaining when it was uncustomary. Some refused to do it. However, shopkeepers engaged in the bargaining without crisis and in some cases lowered the prices. Here, we see an instance in which the morality of the rule, reflected in anxiety, protects the students from the discovery that the rule is flexible.

Taken together, these demonstrations indicate that sense can be achieved, even in a partially senseless environment. Further, they show that the belief in a firm reality is protected from test by anxiety experienced when one anticipates violating "the rules" and by the response of others when they become uncomfortable with unusual conduct. In Garfinkel's demonstrations, the conduct was specifically arranged to contradict the normal sense of things.

Agnes

But what about real life? To what extent can we generalize from the ability to make sense of events that are senseless in limited and partial ways to the general features of social life? Could we not argue that the angry families in the "boarder" demonstration were simply continuing to socialize an ill-mannered adolescent and that despite their intention to act as boarders, the students were only successful in acting out one more variation on adolescent unreliability? Could we not argue that in the "therapy" demonstration, the personal problems the students were discussing were so confusing to them that the inconsistencies of the responses could not be noticed in only 10 tries? When the problem is complex and confusing, both "yes" and "no" are reasonable. That is the problem. Inconsistencies were only noticed when the student asked two very closely related questions and happened to receive contrary answers.

Garfinkel's (1967) study of Agnes, a hermaphrodite, establishes that even one of the most basic judgments of social life, gender, is not based on the biological facts, but rather on a complicated set of assumptions and moral expectations about gender and ways of observing events. Among the assumptions are these: There are two genders. Everyone fits in one or the other. Gender is a biological given, not an option. Even though there are many social consequences to gender, the judgment that a person is a male or female is basically a biological one. Before reviewing some of the facts of Agnes's case, we should remember that most of the time we are not able to observe the biological features that define gender. We make the judgment based on a variety of conventional gender markers and the assumption that gender is unambiguous is important in the judgment.

The account of Agnes's situation was based on extensive interviews conducted when she applied for a sex-change operation. Agnes had primary male sex characteristics, a penis, and was identified as a male on her birth certificate. She was raised as a male child. However, at puberty she developed secondary female sex characteristics—enlarged breasts, female hip shape, and female hair distribution. She finished high school as a boy, wearing loose-fitting clothes to disguise her body shape. She was somewhat vague about gym classes.

Upon graduation, Agnes moved to another city, changed her clothes, had her hair cut, and began to live as a woman. Our first observation, then, is that gender differences in behavior patterns that result from our childhood socialization are not so compelling that a boy cannot quickly behave as a woman. The behavior differences may appear greater than they are because we assume gender differences. Also, the assumption of unambiguous gender may be so strong that even though problems are noted in behavior, they are never attributed to ambiguity of gender.

Agnes encountered a number of problems in living as a woman. They related to the terrible penalties she anticipated if the details of her anatomy became known and also to not fitting in socially because she lacked the experiences and skills women learn as girls. She had a female roommate. Agnes always locked the bathroom door and insisted on privacy when dressing. When she went to the beach, Agnes wore bathing suits with skirts. She would excuse herself from changing into a swimsuit if the locker rooms were not private enough, saying she changed her mind. She listened to other women's childhood stories, borrowed some, and told them as her own. Through instruction in cooking particular recipes, she managed to learn to cook without acknowledging her general lack of skill. If a job called for a physical examination, she prepared to leave in a hurry if there was a gynecological component. She resisted her boyfriend's sexual advances, allowing petting only above the waist.

From these various practical concealment techniques, a picture emerges. Agnes was a bit prudish, perhaps, even by the standards of her time. She was a bit unskilled. She changed her mind quite a bit. However, none of these behaviors was seen as a problem of ambiguous gender. There is no implication that Agnes's problems are common. However, the way we establish and utilize gender does not preclude that. When the biological facts are ambiguous (senseless), it becomes clear that we make the judgment in another way and that we do not examine people closely enough to uncover discrepancies. The assumption of unambiguous gender discourages interpreting peculiarities as signs of ambiguity. Apparently, that judgment or theme informs how we deal with all the facts with the effect that the assumption is difficult to challenge.

Members' Practices

Early ethnomethodological studies attempted to formulate members' practices for accounting or making sense of the world. In logicians' terms, these were practices for dealing with loose or indexical particulars. The specific practices were visible against a global background of trust or unquestioned belief in the objective existence of the world and the inflexibility of its routines. Themes in the meaning of events serve as context for particular events and give them meaning as parts of the pattern. Belief in these patterns and the routine behavior they justify is defended as a normative right not only against deviant behavior, but also against the inability to see the meaning and the unwillingness to accept routinely vague messages. But it is the nature of loose expressions to fit empirical cases only with difficulty on some occasions. The specific practices identified in early statements were formulations of how the fit was accomplished when these global processes did not go smoothly.

One such practice is called *etc.* Definitions and rules are understood to include possibilities that have not been listed, no matter how fully the rule is expressed.[5] When a previously unanticipated particular appears, it is understood to fit the rule as part of the etc. and always to have fit. That is, the rule or category is seen to have intended this sort of thing all along and to have been adequate. For example, when children list the breakfast cereals they like, the list can be understood to include any additional cereal advertised on television with marshmallows in it, sugar on it, cartoon heroes on the box, prizes inside, etc., even though neither the specific cereal nor the criteria are named in advance.

Another practice is *let it pass*. People allow discrepancies to pass without remark or response if they are not detrimental to achieving the task at hand. In the demonstrations, we saw that when one refused to let things pass, people became angry and defended this latitude (slack) as a right. Another practice is *ceteris paribus*, understanding rules to apply "all things being equal." When one of the conditions is not met, even if the exception had not been anticipated, the rule is suspended. This does not constitute violating the rule; rather, it invokes a boundary. For example, one should drive with both hands on the steering wheel *unless* one is holding a cup of coffee in one hand, or reaching for the lighter, or replacing a tape, or holding hands. Doing these things is following the rule in the spirit of *ceteris paribus* by applying the rule *mutatis mutandis*, another practice, which is to alter the conduct to accommodate exceptional conditions while still following the rule in this qualified sense. Thus, the alteration of the client–assignment chart in Zimmerman's study is seen as following the *mutatis mutandis* rule, not violating it.

Two things are apparent in these practices. First, we begin to see how things mean. They do not have literal or objective meaning in the logical sense, but rather, a meaning defined by these practices. Second, we can see that these practices are located as exceptions to literal or objective meaning. If the research had proceeded for a long time in this direction, the practices would not form a coherent positive statement, but rather a series of differences between the practices underlying folk knowledge and the rules of logical argument and scientific measurement. In fact, research and theorizing did not continue along these lines.

CONVERSATION ANALYSIS

By the early 1970s ethnomethodological interest had shifted to a line of research called *conversation analysis*. In some respects, the shift represented a departure from earlier lines of thought within ethnomethodology. The detailed ethnographic attention to context was abandoned and data were restricted almost completely to speech, excluding nonverbal conduct. However, the underlying concern is quite the same. In conversation analysis, all talk is addressed as competent folk description or argumentation with no use of formal logic as a standard of comparison. Then the talk is analyzed in detail to determine how meaning is accomplished, or how a point is made. The issue of correctness is not raised. However, points are made is how points are made. By not using logic or objective standards for categorizing as a point of departure, an attempt is made to offer a positive statement of how meaning is done.

General Rules of Conversation

Conversational analysts argue that conversation exhibits regularities of form regardless of variation in content and context. Insofar as that is true, regularities exhibited in any type of conversation can be generalized. Care is required to avoid confusing regularities peculiar to one type of conversation with regularities common to all. Also, types of behavior may be absent in some types of conversation. These qualifications suggest a sampling problem, but one that is solvable in principle.

Schegloff (1968) used the openings of telephone conversations to formulate rules for opening conversations. Conversation openings, often by an exchange of greetings, accomplish at least two objectives for speakers. By the exchange, each speaker indicates willingness to engage in conversation. The first greeting is a summons to conversation; the returned greeting responds to the summons. The response also establishes who the first speaker will be after the exchange of greetings and who, therefore, will have initial control of the conversation. Thus the exchange of greetings ritually acknowledges willingness to converse with a particular person and also to abide by the rules governing conversation.

Sacks, Schegloff, and Jefferson (1978) identify taking turns as the most fundamental gross behavioral regularity in conversation. Although it is common for two speakers to speak simultaneously in conversation, the overlaps are typically very brief. Generally, the transition from one speaker to another occurs with only slight overlaps or gaps in the flow of talk, or none at all. The order and length of turns at talk vary and so do the number of parties and overall length of conversations. None of these factors can regulate turn taking in a mechanical way. The regulation of turns and the transitions from one speaker to another are coordinated during conversation by practices contained in the conversation. In addition, when these transitions are not smooth, additional practices correct the errors and sustain the conversation.

Sacks, Schegloff, and Jefferson (1978) propose normative rules of conversation as practices that produce turn-taking regularities. The next turn, they argue, can be either assigned by the current speaker or claimed by the next for him- or herself. Turns at talk include transitional points, such as asking a question, at which it is appropriate to change speakers. At these points, the current speaker can indicate the next speaker by, for instance, directing a question to him or her, thereby imposing an obligation to speak. If the speaker does not indicate whose turn is next, another conversant can claim a turn by starting to speak first. Another set of practices marking transitional points is implied and would be studied in the same way.

Schegloff and Sacks (1974) studied the termination of conversations. The final step, of course, is an exchange of ritual acknowledgments that indicate termination of conversation with the particular person or group and of the applicability of conversational norms. That is, they ritually mark the end of the conversation as greetings mark the beginning. Examples of such markers are "good-bye," "later," "catch you on the flip-flop," and "I'm outta here." The collection of closings is loose. The researchers also found that practices in the conversation created opportunities to close, just as they created opportunities to change speakers. They called these *preclosing* remarks. Some, such as "so," "well," or "okay," spoken with correct inflection simply signal that the conversation can be ended with no elaboration of reason. Others express pressing priorities: "I've got to go," "Supper's ready," and "I'll let you go" are examples.

This sketchy specification of practices indicates that conversation analysts views the flow of conversation as sustained by a large family of contingent rules. If you want to start a conversation, use a ritual greeting. If you want to accept the summons to converse, acknowledge the greeting. If you want a turn, create a turn transition point and take it. If you want to end the conversation, preclose and then ritually sign off. Each of these instructions refers to an open-ended category of particular utterances that are functionally equivalent in achieving their main objective, but they may vary in their other consequences. For example, if you want to terminate the conversation and simultaneously offend the others, you would say different things than if you wanted to avoid giving offense. We must consider, then, how more specific meanings are communicated, as well as how the flow of conversation is controlled.

Conversational Opportunities

Sacks and Schegloff (1979) studied how conversational reference is made to people who are not present. They begin with the premise, consistent with the holding of multiple roles, that a person could be identified by mentioning any of a large number of facts about him or her. They found two norms operating in the process of identification. First, there is a normative preference to establish identity using one reference form or identifying fact rather than several. Second, there is a normative preference to achieve clear recognition once the identifying process has begun. These two norms produce a regularity in conversation. People are identified by reference to one fact and then, if recognition is not signaled, another single fact, and so on, until recognition is signaled or a signal indicates that establishing recognition is not worth further effort.

These normative preferences provide resources in conversation in several ways. First, by failing to recognize the first identifying fact, the hearer obligates the speaker to tell more. Although the facts come one at a time, the hearer can use the identity process to find out such things as new facts about the identified person, what the speaker knows, how the speaker thinks about the person, and the extent of the relationship between speaker and identified person. In short, the identifying process is a proper occasion for gossip, although in a highly ritualized form. Second, the selection of which identifying facts one uses communicates a great deal besides the individual fact and the identity of the person. For example, selection of a private or compromising fact can indicate intimacy and trust. Also, the fact selected may have implications known to only some of the people in the conversation. As a result, although all learn who is being discussed and one fact, some may be able to draw additional inferences.

Goodwin (1979) identified two norms that allow remarks to be directed at a particular person by patterns of gaze direction and eye contact. First, directing the gaze at a person signals that the remarks are directed to that person as well. Second, there is a preference for eye contact while remarks are being directed in this manner. Eye contact has many other implications, including establishing intimacy. By directing remarks at a person, using eye contact is justified and may be exploited for purposes having nothing to do with the remarks.

Heritage and Watson (1979) found that people sometimes formulate or sum up the conversation within the conversation itself. For example, if a sequence of events is described, the time might be formulated: "All this happened last weekend?" The obvious and straightforward use of formulation is to clarify what has been said. However, the formulation sequence includes an acknowledgment of the formulation's accuracy. Thus, formulating may publicly bind others to a version of events, a purpose, or a future course of action. In effect, by formulating, the person makes a promise ritually obligatory.

Content through Form

The manner of speaking can sometimes communicate the content or the nature of a relationship independent of the specific topics discussed. Some preliminary work has shown how male dominance, a specific theme in gender relationships, is produced by practices in interaction that are not linked to gender as an explicit topic.

Fishman (1978) gathered her data by placing tape recorders in the apartments of three couples. The couples controlled the recording schedule, making tapes of household conversation for periods ranging from one to four hours. Women asked questions approximately three times as often as men. Twice as often as men, they initiated conversation with openings such as "Guess what?," which oblige the other to answer, as questions do, but do not introduce the topic. In these instances, two or three turns at talk are required before the topic is introduced. Men tended to begin conversations with direct statements more than women. Women responded to men's openings more reliably than men responded to women's openings. In addition, women tended to encourage men to continue speaking by supportive remarks during the conversation. Men were less encouraging and tended to discourage continued talk by women.

Fishman (1978) interprets these regularities in terms of a division of labor based on gender. Women, she argues, take a supportive role, doing the greater share of the work to start conversations and keep them going. Also, they must do more work to have their topics discussed because the men do not respond as favorably to them. In Fishman's view, the interpretation of these regularities in terms of subordination/dominance receives support from studies indicating that the techniques used by children while talking to adults are similar to those used by women while talking to men.

West and Zimmerman (1977) studied conversational interruptions. In conversations between two people of the same gender, each speaker interrupted the other approximately the same number of times. Of 48 interruptions in conversations between a man and a woman, however, 46 were interruptions of women by men. Interruptions are important with respect to subordination/dominance because they violate the strong turn-taking norms and deny the right of the interrupted person to finish the turn. Assuming that no signals were present that indicated that a change of speaker was appropriate, interruptions are a direct and aggressive form of conversational control.

West (1979) pursued this issue by studying the responses to interruption in conversations between men and women. About 75 percent of the interruptions observed were by men. Once interrupted, the immediate responses of men and women were similar. Fourteen percent of the interrupted people continued to talk simultaneously with the interruptor. About 43 percent of men and 38 percent of women continued briefly after being interrupted and then stopped. Forty-eight percent of the women and 43 percent of the men stopped without finishing their statements.

The difference between the men's and women's responses to interruptions occurs later. Fourteen percent of the men and 10 percent of the women reintroduce their own topic later. But 43 percent of the women reintroduced the man's topic after interrupting him while only 19 percent of the men reintroduced the women's topic they interrupted. As a result, after an interruption, the women's topics were dropped, without reintroduction 71 percent of the time to only 43 percent of the men's topics. This supports the theme observed by Fishman (1978). Women appear to be more supportive of men in conversations than men are supportive of women.

WHOSE MEANING?

In order to understand the direction in which recent ethnomethodological work has gone, it is necessary to consider whose thematic meaning the observed conversational or other practices are claimed to accomplish. In the case of subordination/dominance, for example, to see *how* that theme has been accomplished one must see *that* the theme has been accomplished. If the dominance/subordination theme is replaced with another, the same talk must be seen as practices achieving the new theme. That is, recognizing practices requires the recognition of thematic patterns.

The thematic patterns to which practices are linked are not necessarily recognized by the participants. For example, the couples in Fishman's (1978) study do not necessarily regard their household conversations as exercises of male dominance. This point was made explicit by Zimmerman and Wieder (1977) in a study of casual drug use in a student community. The norms of the community stress spontaneity, and the perceptions of community members stress that marijuana use is a casual, spontaneous event. However, the organized routines of the community make smoking regular and predictable. In addition, the habitual "dropping in" on one another within the community and the routine of spending the day dropping in on one person after another are consistent with the interpretation that the subjects gather briefly and then move on until they are offered marijuana somewhere. Finding marijuana may be an important goal. What is clear here is that the researchers' thematic understanding is the crucial one in identifying practices. It could not be otherwise.

THEMATIC CONVERSATIONAL ANALYSIS

In recent studies, conversational analysts have abstracted the conversations from thematically significant conversations and turned to how the themes particular to those conversations were achieved. Clayman (1989) studied how interviews are terminated within the temporal limits established in advance and imposed on the interaction by the scheduling constraints of broadcasting. But in recognizing prior structural constraints of scheduling, the contribution of the talk to the termination of the interview is muddled. We could argue strongly that the talk does not accomplish the termination. That is accomplished by structural constraints. The talk only gives a ritually polite appearance to the termination, covering the operation of power. More reasonably, we could argue that the practices in the talk coordinate the details of closing to the extent that the participants all accept the relevance of the constraints. In either case, we are confronted with a theme established by other means.

This ambiguity suggests a proper linkage between ethnomethodological studies, conducted with methodologically suspended belief in external reality, and sociological studies conducted without suspended belief. The identification of themes ought to be done carefully in the manner of sociological research, rather than casually in the manner of offhand observations. That is, within the attitude of everyday life, some accounts are considered better than others. So long as we are to begin with thematic patterns established within that attitude, we should, I think, subject them to appropriate standards of evaluation. Once a theme is established as real and important, belief can be suspended and the assembly of the theme addressed.

One reason for taking the establishment of themes seriously is to avoid detailed study of practices on unacceptable premises about what they accomplish. Another reason is to take advantage of practical knowledge in assembling data. In Clayman's (1989) study, for example, the interviews were recorded from the TV transmission. That means that any conversation in the studio over earphones was not included, nor was conversation off camera between on-screen and off-screen people in the studio. Off-camera gestures and cue cards were not observable. Depending on what is included in those portions of the conversation that are not transmitted, we would alter our interpretation of what the on-screen talk accomplished. Did it coordinate the interview or did it accomplish a polite appearance to coordination accomplished by other means? We might also want to know the contractual arrangements among the on-screen participants and the television producers.

Halkowski (1990) uses transcriptions of the Iran-contra congressional hearings as data. His major focus is how a witness refers to Attorney General Meese, and especially the difficulties of selecting the appropriate reference. The difficulties were indicated by a series of correct references that were nonetheless replaced with other correct references. Consistently, the issue was whether to refer to Edwin Meese as Mr. Meese or as the Attorney General. Halkowski's paper concerns what is accomplished by the various references and corrections. Most important, he observes that the reference is equivalent to assigning a role to Mr. Meese and, of course, implying the structure of obligations of that role. Acts under consideration in the testimony become proper or improper depending on the role assigned to Mr. Meese. This concern for propriety and precision among participants is inferred in the context of knowledge that the two speakers are properly labeled "committee counsel" and "witness" and more generally of the Iran-contra hearings. In the detailed analysis, the strategies and intentions of the participants in the hearing are linked by Halkowski (1990) to their specific roles. For example, the counsel's remarks are seen as preparatory to making an accusation, a role-related goal.

In these two studies, the technical interests of conversational analysis in conversation closings and identifying people are pursued. But their contribution is not to identify new practices, but rather to apply existing knowledge and procedures to case studies. The case studies are important for thematic content, and not especially for theoretical reasons. The specific themes analyzed are narrowly defined, and so it may seem like a quibble to observe that the themes are not carefully elaborated. However, if conversation analysis is to be brought to bear in discovering how broader and more important themes in social life are organized, the themes will need more careful definition. For example, how is the fairness or legitimacy of the Iran-contra hearings embodied in the talk? How is the journalistic integrity of news interviews embodied in them? But first, are those themes achieved? Preliminary elaboration of themes through sound sociological analysis seems to be an essential step.

SUMMARY

Ethnomethodology, grounded in phenomenological philosophy, is often construed to be fundamentally different from other approaches to sociology. The difference is related to the practice of "suspending belief" in the objective reality of the observed world in order to refocus attention from *what* is observed to *how* it is observed. Early studies attempted to demonstrate the utility of ethnomethodology's basic premises. They showed that sense could be made of an environment that was senseless in specific and limited ways. They also showed that our fundamental empirical judgments were based on a complex set of assumptions and routines of observation. Interaction could proceed on the basis of judgments that would not be sustained if additional facts were known.

Practical knowledge, knowledge assembled under the assumption of reality that characterizes everyday life, was identified as indexical and reflexive. Indexicality refers to context dependence or looseness in empirical statements or expressions. Reflexivity refers to the self-containment of the body of accounts when their connection to an external reality is not assumed. A variety of studies showed how people used context and a variety of practices to establish the meaning of indexical particulars.

Subsequently, attention shifted to a research procedure called conversation analysis. Conversation analysis can be taken as an attempt to describe how people make sense in conversation without reference to logic or other normative standards as a standard. Conversation analysis proposes that contingent rules, followed as norms, organize conversation from within and allow a variety of purposes to be achieved by the form of talk as well as by the explicit content.

Conversational practices are used to accomplish some particular meaning that is identified by the researcher, who then is able to determine how it was done. This meaning need not be shared with the participants in the conversation. Recent studies have examined cases of conversation made interesting by their practical significance. In these studies, we can see clearly that the themes are identified by some form of practical reasoning as a preliminary to the analysis of practices. Methodologically, I suggested using the best available sociological methods to identify such themes, rather than a more casual approach to that step.

NOTES

1. For representative arguments see Wilson (1970), Denzin (1970), Zimmerman and Wieder (1970), and Coser (1975).
2. Dennis Wrong (1961) also recognized that Parsons's model of human conduct was "oversocialized." Whereas Garfinkel addressed the judgmental work of perceiving the situation and the appropriate course of action in it, Wrong stressed motivational considerations.
3. For extended discussions of how tolerances operate in everyday life, see the discussion of identities by symbolic interactionists as well as the ethnomethodological discussions later in the chapter.
4. Mannheim's discussion of this complex relationship between the specific items that are assembled into a pattern and the pattern itself is also similar to that discussed by Gestalt psychologists. For an excellent summary of the Gestalt approach, see Kohler (1969).
5. This is similar to Durkheim's (1933) idea of noncontractual elements in contracts.

REFERENCES

Bar-Hillel, Yehoshua. 1954. Indexical Expressions. *Mind* 63:359–379.

Black, Max. 1970. Reasoning with Loose Concepts. Pp. 14–22 in Margins of Precision. Ithaca, NY: Cornell University Press.

Cicourel, Aaron. 1964. Method and Measurement in Sociology. New York: Free Press.

Cicourel, Aaron. 1968. The Social Organization of Juvenile Justice. New York: Wiley.

Cicourel, Aaron. 1974. Theory and Method in a Study of Argentine Fertility. New York: Wiley.

Clayman, Steven. 1989. The Production of Punctuality. *American Journal of Sociology* 95:659–691.

Coser, Lewis. 1975. Presidential Address: Two Methods in Search of a Substance. *American Sociological Review* 40:691–700.

Denzin, Norman. 1970. Symbolic Interaction and Ethnomethodology. Pp. 261–287 in Jack Douglas (ed.), Understanding Everyday Life. Chicago: Aldine.

Durkheim, Emile. 1933. The Division of Labor in Society. New York: Macmillan.

Fishman, Pamela. 1978. Interaction: The Work Women Do. *Social Problems* 25:397–406.

Garfinkel, Harold. 1963. A Conception of and Experiments with "Trust" as a Condition of Stable Concerted Actions. Pp. 187–238 in O. J. Harvey (ed.), Motivation and Social Interaction. New York: Ronald Press.

Garfinkel, Harold. 1964. Studies of the Routine Grounds of Everyday Activities. *Social Problems* 11:225–250.

Garfinkel, Harold. 1967. Studies in Ethnomethodology. Englewood Cliffs, NJ: Prentice Hall.

Garfinkel, Harold and Harvey Sacks. 1970. On Formal Structures of Practical Actions. Pp. 337–366 in John McKinney and Edward Tiryakian (eds.), Theoretical Sociology. New York: Appleton Century Crofts.

Halkowski, Timothy. 1990. Role as an Interactional Device. *Social Problems* 37:564–577.

Heritage, J. C. and D. R. Watson. 1979. Formulations as Conversational Objects. Pp. 123–162 in George Psathas (ed.), Everyday Language. New York: Wiley.

Kohler, Wolfgang. 1969. The Task of Gestalt Psychology. Princeton, NJ: Princeton University Press.

Mannheim, Karl. 1964. On the Interpretation of Weltanschauung. Pp. 33–83 Paul Kecskemeti (ed. and trans.), in Essays on the Sociology of Knowledge. London: Routledge and Kegan Paul.

Molotch, Harvey. 1973. Oil in Santa Barbara and Power in America. Pp. 297–322 in William Chambliss (ed.), Sociological Readings in the Conflict Perspective. Reading, MA: Addison Wesley.

Molotch, Harvey and Marilyn Lester. 1974. News as Purposive Behavior. *American Sociological Review* 39:101–112.

Sacks, Harvey and Emmanuel Schegloff. 1979. Two Preferences in the Organization of Reference to Persons in Conversation and Their Interactions. Pp. 15–22 in George Psathas (ed.), Everyday Language. New York: Wiley.

Sacks, Harvey, Emmanuel Schegloff, and Gail Jefferson. 1978. A Simplest Systematics for the Organization of Turn Taking for Conversation Pp. 7–56 in Jim Schenkein (ed.), Studies in the Organization of Conversational Interaction. New York: Academic Press.

Schegloff, Emmanuel. 1968. Sequencing in Conversational Openings. *American Anthropologist* 70:1075–1095.

Schegloff, Emmanuel. 1979. Identification and Recognition in Telephone Conversation Openings. Pp. 23–78 in George Psathas (ed.), Everyday Language. New York: Wiley.

Schegloff, Emmanuel and Harvey Sacks. 1974. Opening Up Closings. Pp. 233–264 in Roy Turner (ed.), Ethnomethodology. Baltimore, MD: Penguin.

Schutz, Alfred. 1967. Collected Papers I. The Hague: Martinus Nijhoff.

West, Candace. 1979. Against Our Will: Male Interruptions of Females in Cross-Sex Conversation. *Annals of the New York Academy of Science: Language Sex and Gender* 327:81–96.

West, Candace and Don Zimmerman. 1977. Women's Place in Everyday Talk. *Social Problems* 24:521–529.

Wilson, Thomas. 1970. Conceptions of Interaction and Forms of Sociological Explanation. *American Sociological Review* 35:697–710.

Wrong, Dennis. 1961. The Oversocialized Conception of Man in Modern Sociology. *American Sociological Review* 26:183–193.

Zimmerman, Don. 1970. The Practicalities of Rule Use. Pp. 221–238 in J. Douglas (ed.), Understanding Everyday Life. Chicago: Aldine.

Zimmerman, Don and D. Lawrence Wieder. 1977. You Can't Help But Get Stoned. *Social Problems* 25:198–207.

Zimmerman, Don and D. Lawrence Wieder. 1970. Ethnomethodology and the Problem of Order. Pp. 287–298 in J. Douglas (ed.), Understanding Everyday Life. Chicago: Aldine.

11

Conclusion

Although each of the several theoretical approaches in contemporary sociology and its development during the last 40 years have been summarized in its own terms, several intellectual commonalities among them have also been emphasized. First, they share a common point of critical reference in structural functional thought, especially the work of Talcott Parsons. Second, numerous overlapping substantive concerns and similar theoretical arguments have been apparent. Finally, each of the theories is specialized and must be supplemented by answers to questions that it does not address itself. Each of the theories answers such questions raised by the others.

Theoretical differences are not necessarily incompatibilities. The differences among the contemporary sociological theories have most often been differences of topic rather than substantive disagreements concerning a common topic. Disagreements among the schools of thought have primarily concerned philosophical and methodological assumptions—metatheoretical rather than theoretical issues. Dahrendorf stressed this distinction most clearly in his argument that a conflict theory of change and a structural functional theory of stability could be compatible even though the underlying imageries that guided the development of the two theories were contrary. Although one theory might focus on the conditions under which change will occur and the other on the conditions of stability, they can be compatible, and both can be accurate, unless one predicts change and the other stability under the same conditions.[1]

In reviewing the several contemporary schools of sociological theory, the theoretical ideas in each were linked not only to empirical findings but also to the specific intellectual context in which they developed. But now we are reminded that the integration of these theories depends to a great extent on the legitimacy of abstracting the theory itself from its original context. Thus, there are two distinct tasks involved in retrieving an overall sense of sociology from its component specialties. First, we require a brief overview of theoretical ideas in a substantively coherent order, free from the distractions of considering their conceptual origins and empirical support. Second, we consider the relationship between a theory and its intellectual context as an issue in its own right.

OVERVIEW

Humans are purposive. We are able to anticipate the outcomes of alternative courses of possible action and select the course with the best perceived outcome. Many of our purposes are linked, more or less directly, to biological needs and preferences. However, even in cases of relatively direct biological influence on purpose, social influences are important in the selection of specific ways to meet the purpose because our learning of both specific ends and means occurs in a social context. This is why, for example, many of us do not utilize the protein available in insects or in small backyard rodents and birds, even when they are presented to us alive and ready for slaughter by domesticated hunting cats.

The implication of learned culture and technology on even biologically driven conduct has two important implications for us. First, even when a human acts alone, and even when his or her action is in the service of a biological need, there is a social influence on the conduct. Usually, sociologists defer to psychologists and microeconomists in describing the processes involved in individual choices and consider them in the aggregate as statistical regularities (social facts as Durkheim calls them) or fate (C. Wright Mills). Second, when humans interact with one another, we have a more or less common understanding of our collective situation and that entire understanding influences our conduct. Even when the immediate situation imposes tasks on people in great detail, our conduct in the situation will also be influenced by the total social context, as well as the other concerns retained and organized in memory.

The purposes we pursue will not be limited to those defined by the immediate situation, nor necessarily consistent with them.

Sociologists organize social influence around two interrelated themes—systems and interests. For some purposes we can conceive of social life in terms of systems of organized activity. The system is divided into specialized sets of tasks with associated sanctions. Each person (or larger subsystem) participates in the system by performing a variety of discrete specialties or roles. If the roles are performed reasonably well, the system will produce and distribute what is needed for its own survival and for the motivation of its participants. For other purposes, societies are analyzed in terms of the interests of people and subgroups within them. Individuals and groups do not share equally in the goods produced by a society nor do they suffer equally from its problems. Identifiable groups, then, have different interests. Both ways of conceiving social life are crucial. Conflict over the meeting of interests greatly influences systemic output which, in turn, influences the degree to which interests are served.

Although purposive conduct is an attempt to serve one's own interests, interests and purposes do not typically coincide. Purposes are defined in terms of the individual's perceptions of his or her own needs and of the encompassing social situation in which satisfaction is pursued. In some versions of an ideal society, individuals would be informed of their situations and needs in such a way that they could understand their true interests. In such cases, purposes could coincide with interests. However, in existing societies social arrangements systematically influence perception so that identifiable groups of individuals are misinformed about their needs and about the social situation. Due to this misinformation, among other social arrangements, purposes are voluntarily sought that do not coincide with real interests. Better informed, and more powerful, groups need not expend as many resources to coerce action that serves their own interests if others in the society voluntarily comply out of ignorance.

At the societal level, the study of society in terms of groups with divergent interests and conflict among them is explicit and straightforward. The form of conflict among these groups and its outcomes are related to both the resources available to the groups and their ability to mobilize them, to utilize them effectively in their own interests. The ability to mobilize resources, whether conceived in terms of the differences between quasi- and conflict groups or the special characteristics of classes or elites, is dependent upon communication within the group, which makes possible the concerted adoption of real group interests as purposes.

At the level of interaction, individual action and interaction processes are understood by conceiving of the individual people observed as representatives of the groups in which they are members. The observed differences among people concerning the assignment of tasks and how each should treat the others are conceived as role conflicts built into the social structure rather than as interpersonal differences. Many of the resources employed by individuals and much of the ability to mobilize them are also characteristic of the position held by the person. The outcomes of interaction processes, and specifically the resolution of these conflicts, are not completely determined. However, they are sufficiently orderly to allow statistical relationships between the characteristics of situations and their outcomes. For structural reasons, similar conflicts arise in similar situations and similar resources are available to the participants. Consequently, the statistical distribution of outcomes can be stable, even though the outcomes are not fully determined in each instance.

Interaction processes bring initially divergent understandings of what should be done and by whom into enough agreement to sustain task performance. The primary concern of participants is usually not the conduct available for inspection during interaction. Rather, each wants assurances about conduct that occurs elsewhere and/or at other times and that cannot be observed directly but is necessary to the achievement of one's own goals. To a great extent, then, interaction is conducted through symbolic expressions or promises about one's own and others' unobservable task performance as well as direct exchange of goods. These promises define an identity for the person that includes his or her orientation to the tasks of the present situation and symbolic indications of other commitments and affiliations. The nature of symbolic communication and various social arrangements provide the opportunity and means for mutual deception. The strain of holding multiple conflicting roles and the possibility of achieving socially mediated rewards for tasks one has not done by deceiving others give all participants incentives to manipulate their own identities and to see through the manipulations of others.

At every level, systems are sustained, in part, by the ignorance of their participants concerning their own interests and the social situation, especially those parts of it beyond their immediate experience. Moore and Tumin (1949) argued that although ignorance is not universally necessary to social integration, it is not only commonly found but is also contingently necessary in systems with certain structural characteristics to preserve privileged positions, traditional values, stereotypes, and competition. Turner (1954) suggested that in learning abstract social values, we also learn a great many rules and qualifications concerning their application to specific settings. These rules, often implicit, dull the perception of the underlying value conflicts by discretely regulating the application of values to situations. Although the values implied by situationally discrete applications may contradict one another, the contradictions are not noticed because situational problems that might lead to the consideration of the underlying values in the abstract are prevented. The formal structures of everyday knowledge and the practices that sustain a sense of coherent reality lend themselves well to interpretation as the processes by which perception of conflicts in social life is dulled. Dullness can be expressed in contrast to the relative alertness of self-aware people and well-mobilized interest groups and classes as well as the attitude of scientific theorizing. Chua (1974, 1977) made this point in his observation that the attitude of everyday life can be conceived as a specification of the processes of ideological reproduction.

THEORIES AND THEIR INTELLECTUAL CONTEXTS

Within the scientific community, attention is primarily focused on theory as an explanation. With that focus, the content of the theory is considered primarily in interrelationship with the empirical data upon which it is based. However, theory is also a product of the historical epoch in which it develops and the position of theorists in society. It is easiest to illustrate this second way of considering theory with examples from earlier epochs, in which the peculiar assumptions and influences of social structure are made more visible by our freedom from them. Thus, the domination of medieval education by the Roman Catholic church and the political power wielded by it are easily recognizable as reasons why philosophy tended to be religious rather than secular during that period. We are no longer content with an explanation that philosophy was religious because religion was the true basis for all philosophy. It is more difficult to accurately assess the influence of cultural and social factors on ideas in our own era because our own thoughts are influenced by those same factors

Karl Mannheim's (1964) discussion of the documentary method of interpretation is an especially useful treatment of the long-recognized dual status of scientific ideas. Mannheim distinguished three kinds of knowledge—*objective, expressive,* and *documentary. Objective* knowledge is knowledge of something as an object in itself, without consideration of its symbolic importance. A scientific explanation of a phenomenon is the most thorough form of objective knowledge about it.

Natural objects can be known only in this way. Cultural objects, on the other hand, in addition to objective characteristics, have symbolic characteristics that indicate the realms of meaning for which they stand. First, the person who creates a cultural object (a bit of everyday behavior, a work of art, a scientific theory, etc.) will perceive some meaning in it when he or she attends to it. That is its *expressive* meaning. This meaning may be intended in advance or noticed in retrospect. The same cultural object can also be considered in concert with other products of the culture and a collective meaning perceived. Each object has meaning as an instance of the pattern or meaning perceived by considering the group of objects simultaneously. The pattern is not necessarily perceived by contributors to it. This is the *documentary* meaning.

Consider a common interaction ritual in these three ways. In the ritual, when a man and woman approach a door while walking together, the man steps ahead, opens the door, and holds it for the woman to pass through. Objectively, this description is simply a set of facts, considered in its own right. This ritual exists as an observable regularity of behavior in which various meanings may be perceived. It exists as an objective regularity somewhat independent of what participants or theorists make of it. Expressively, this sequence of events may indicate politeness, consideration, or affection to the man and woman who participate in it. Considered as a document, in the context of other events in our society, it is a ritual reminder that men and women have fundamentally different statuses in our society and that there is a relationship of domination, expressed here as *noblesse oblige*. The expressive and documentary meaning may not, but can, coincide. In this case, continued participation in the ritual as an *expression* of submission is unlikely even though an observer may perceive it as a *document* of submission.

A cultural object can only be understood fully when all three types of meaning are identified. But the three types of knowledge have different formal characteristics. Strict operational standards of measurement, insistence on well-defined terms and categories, and logical relations among statements only apply in the realm of objective knowledge. The selection and categorization of items to be interpreted and the perception of a pattern among the items are somewhat intuitive in the cases of expressive and documentary meaning. The pattern emerges from consideration of the items it organizes, while the organized pattern simultaneously informs the selection and interpretation of particular items. The meaning of Andrew Wyeth's famous painting "Christina's World" is an illustrative case. After many years, dozens of paintings of the same model were discovered and her personal relationship with Wyeth was acknowledge. These events transformed the expressive and documentary meaning of the painting by providing a personal context. The publicity was probably good for the business of selling the newly discovered paintings, too. These types of meaning are the results of different types of observation and analysis, and if the same items are considered in all three ways, the three types of meaning can vary independently of one another. Most important, the relationship of expressive and documentary meaning to the items in which they are perceived is not logical. The objective component of a theory is inspired and influenced by documentary and expressive influences, but it cannot be deduced from them and is not logically dependent on a particular formulation of them.

The perception of documentary meaning, of cultural patterns, in and through the examination of specific instances, is highly influenced by the selection of objects to be considered together. For example, if various artistic works of the same artist are examined, a documentary theme may be perceived in his work. If the artist's work is considered along with contemporaneous works of others, schools of artistic style (expressionism, realism, etc.) may be perceived. If the artist's work is considered along with contemporaneous literature, music, architecture, and so on, themes of the entire cultural era may be perceived. If the artist's work is considered in historical context, trends and events in the development of art and the transitions from one cultural era to another may be perceived. The same is true of theories.

Two very important issues in scientific theorizing are not fully explicit in the theory itself—the criteria for selecting questions worth studying and the criteria for recognizing an adequate explanation. These issues are partially implicit and part of the documentary meaning of scientific theory. Stephen Toulmin (1961) referred to this aspect of the documentary meaning of science as a cultural product as the ideal of the natural order. Scientists, he argued, have preconceptions about what things need to be explained, what things need no explanation, and the form of proper explanation. For example, Newton's first law of motion— objects in motion tend to continue in motion in a straight line unless acted upon by an outside force—calls for explanations of changes of speed, direction, starting, and stopping. The explanation must identify the force applied. But continuous motion in a straight line, the hypothetical ideal, never occurs in nature. We are not necessarily to look for explanations of actually observed events, but rather events, whether hypothetical or real, that are made interesting by comparison with an often implicit ideal.

Although the ideal of the natural order remains constant, theories are adjusted incrementally to accommodate new observations. However, a change in the ideal of the natural order requires not only substantive changes in the theory, but also changes in what questions are considered interesting and what sort of explanation will be considered acceptable. The transition from the domination of sociological thought by structural functional theorists to the current state of affairs can be seen as a change in the ideal of the natural order and not merely as a change in substantive theory. Initially, the profound differences between structural functional and conflict theories were considered to require separate theories of stability and change. Later, however, the structural functional theories were rejected completely in favor of developing conflict theoretic approaches to social integration and stability.

Sociologists became self-consciously concerned with their own underlying themes through Thomas Kuhn's (1962) discussion of scientific revolutions. Kuhn was concerned with the transition from one set of underlying themes to another in scientific communities. Kuhn called the implicit, underlying themes in a scientific community a *paradigm*. Although the concept of paradigm was very similar to that of an ideal of the natural order and to other conceptions of underlying themes in science, Kuhn's discussion was especially interesting to sociologists because it placed the paradigm not only in an intellectual context, but also in the context of the politics and history of scientific disciplines.

Ironically, self-conscious attention to the issue of unifying themes contributed to disunity among the sociological schools of thought. Kuhn's (1962) discussion of the transition from one paradigm to another helps explain how this could occur. In the presence of a paradigm, scientific investigation proceeds through what Kuhn calls *normal science.* Neither the significance of research questions nor the appropriate methodology is controversial. The research results make incremental additions to essentially unchallenged theory. This is approximately the situation that existed during the dominance of structural functional theory. However, as we have seen, many major lines of research produced anamolous results, and these results were increasingly organized by diverse non–structural functional theories. Kuhn refers to such periods in a discipline—periods characterized by important anamolous research results and diverse, competitive attempts to resolve them—as *crises.*

Crisis is resolved by the acceptance of a new paradigm to replace the one undermined by anamolous findings. This replacement is not immediate, however. In the historical examples cited by Kuhn, some crises lasted for several decades. It is possible to conceive of sociology as still in crisis or transition between paradigms. The evidence for this point of view is the continued division of the field into schools of theoretical thought, each addressing the substantive issues in the field in its distinctive way and the emergence of new schools of thought, such as feminism, that may soon be sufficiently developed to be considered schools in their own right, rather than specific applications of other schools. Whatever conclusions we draw about whether a paradigm has subsequently developed in sociology, it is clear that the several contemporary schools of sociological thought initially appeared during a period of intellectual crisis.

The simultaneous assertion of multiple, incompatible sociological paradigms reflected this crisis. As a kind of documentary meaning, the paradigm of a scientific community varies with the selection of items to be considered. As the schools of thought coalesced, each articulated a distinctive, coherent program for sociological research and theory. Each program was grounded in the particular history and commitments of its school of thought. The diversity of formulated paradigms reflects the specialized selection of items to be considered. Intellectual and practical difficulties do not arise from inadequacies of these formulations as paradigms or documentary interpretations of specific sociological approaches. Rather, they arise only from attempting to interpret a formulation grounded in the literature and practices of a specialty within the discipline as a paradigm or program for the discipline as a whole.

In principle, the philosophical and methodological principles and imagery underlying any of the specialized schools are flexible enough to form a basis for sociology. In practice, however, the unification of the discipline by conversion of the various schools of thought to a common underlying paradigm is unlikely. Historically, Kuhn observed, when a transition from one paradigm to another has occurred, the adherents to the initial paradigm seldom converted. Rather, new generations of scientists adopted the new paradigm and the old one disappeared primarily through the attrition of its adherents. Apparently, the underlying commitments formulated as a paradigm or philosophy of science are very profoundly held. A documentary meaning or paradigm for the discipline as a whole could be formulated, but it would have no adherent researchers and the problems of conversion would still apply.

The development of a single paradigm in sociology, then, is unlikely to occur soon. Historical evidence indicates that it will emerge by attrition after research compellingly answers crucial questions in the discipline. As a result, even if the process has already begun, we can expect it to last a generation. But incomplete unification at the paradigmatic or documentary level does not prevent theoretical convergence. Rather, the intellectual aspects of theoretical unification have historically preceded the emergence of metatheoretical consensus.

Shared Substantive Concerns

The objective meaning of our research, the explicit theoretical arguments and empirical findings, can be considered apart from the imagery and commitments that inspired them because they represent different realms of meaning. There is a remarkable convergence of interests among the specialized contemporary theories on diverse manifestations of conflict and on the implication of distributions of power (control of resources) and ignorance in processes of stability and change.

The convergence of diverse lines of argument on common substantive themes suggests significant implicit consensus, resulting perhaps from the strength of evidence and from as yet unarticulated documentary meanings of our period.

The convergence of interests is more detailed than a general interest in conflict as a fundamental condition of social life. In closing, I should like to indicate some more specific convergences and the important questions they raise. Conflict theories and exchange theories propose similar dual, seemingly contradictory influences of knowledge about exchange relationships in the society. Both argue that increased knowledge, especially consciousness of one's group interests and place in the overall system, is a crucial aspect of the formation of social classes. Both also argue that increased knowledge of inequities in the system can result in more equitable choices, and exchange theorists have demonstrated this empirically. These two schools have a common empirical interest in specifying the conditions under which increased knowledge results in each of these outcomes.

Role theory has been based on a conflict imagery for many years, but it developed separately from the large-scale conflict theories. Thus, although both approaches view interaction as an arena for conflict, and both view individuals as representatives of groups or structural positions, there is no integrated explanation of how conflicts on the societal scale come to be manifested as role conflicts. Both types of conflict theory have an empirical interest in how the structure of group interests comes to be reflected in the distribution of the opposing positions in role conflict.

Symbolic interaction has been empirically concerned with interpersonal bargaining or negotiating in various forms as the generic way in which anticipated lines of action are fit together. The underlying imagery of bargaining or negotiating has been role conflict. Observed interaction exhibits a great deal of creativity and mutual adjustment. The outcomes of interaction do not appear to be determined by antecedent conditions but emerge from interaction processes. However, the distribution of outcomes of structurally similar interactions is recognized to be stable in both role theories and interaction theories. These two types of theory have a common empirical interest in the conditions under which local creativity results in change on a larger scale rather than being negated by other local adjustments. The symbolic interactionists and large-scale conflict theorists also share an empirical interest in mediated symbolic conduct, especially when symbolism is directly involved in social control as it is in the news and politics.

Ethnomethodologists' methodological commitments reduce their interest in the relationships among interactions dispersed in time and space. However, as we have seen, an ethnomethodological analysis must begin with an understanding of the practical meaning achieved in the interaction. Only by reference to that meaning, can the consequences of different practices be identified. Thus, ethnomethodology has an interest in the sophisticated specification of the substantive meaning of conduct provided by the researchers in other schools. Specification of how the meaning is achieved is an interest shared with all the other theory groups, as a result of the importance of patterns of ignorance and knowledge to all of them.

Finally, all of the theories have internal tensions concerning consensus. On the one hand, all recognize the ubiquity of conflict in various forms. On the other hand, all seem to suggest that societal integration and stability result from consensus in some form. Unless a basis of consensus immune to the observed conflicts and complexities can be identified, a common interest in the articulation of a basis for stability without consensus is implied. One such basis, the convention, has been discussed.

NOTE

1. Emerson's view that symbolic interaction and exchange theory tap different processes occurring simultaneously in interaction is another instance. Both are specific applications of Merton's characterization of sociology as composed of theories of the middle range.

REFERENCES

Chua, Beng-Huat. 1974. On the commitments of Ethnomethodology. *Sociological Inquiry* 44:241–256.

Chua, Beng-Huat. 1977. Delineating a Marxist Interest in Ethnomethodology. *American Sociologist* 12:24–32.

Kuhn, Thomas. 1962. The Structure of Scientific Revolutions. Chicago: University of Chicago Press.

Mannheim, Karl. 1964. On the Interpretation of Weltanschauung. Pp. 33–83 in Paul Kecskemeti (ed.), Essays on the Sociology of Knowledge. London: Routledge and Kegan Paul.

Moore, Wilbert and Melvin Tumin. 1949. Some Social Functions of Ignorance. *American Sociological Review* 14:787–795.

Toulmin, Stephen. 1961. Foresight and Understanding. New York: Harper.

Turner, Ralph. 1954. Value Conflict in Social Disorganization. *Sociology and Social Research* 38:301–308.

Index